AF352532

The Indian Ocean and US Grand Strategy

The Indian Ocean and US Grand Strategy

Ensuring Access and Promoting Security

PETER DOMBROWSKI AND
ANDREW C. WINNER, EDITORS

Georgetown University Press
Washington, DC

Library of Congress Cataloging-in-Publication Data

The Indian Ocean and US grand strategy : ensuring access and promoting security / Andrew C. Winner and Peter Dombrowski, editors.
    pages   cm—(South Asia in world affairs series)
  Includes bibliographical references and index.
  ISBN 978-1-62616-140-5 (hardcover : alk. paper)—ISBN 978-1-62616-079-8 (pbk.: alk. paper) —
  ISBN 978-1-62616-150-4 (ebook)
  1. Indian Ocean Region—Foreign relations—United States.   2. United States—Foreign relations—Indian Ocean Region. 3. Indian Ocean Region—Strategic aspects.   I. Winner, Andrew C., editor of compilation.   II. Dombrowski, Peter J., 1963—editor of compilation.   III. Winner, Andrew C. American strategy in the Indian Ocean. Contains (work):   IV. Series: South Asia in world affairs series.
  DS341.3.U6I53 2014
  355'.033573091824—dc23
                                                                              2014011312

∞ This book is printed on acid-free paper meeting the requirements of the American National Standard for Permanence in Paper for Printed Library Materials.

15 14 13   9 8 7 6 5 4 3 2 First printing

Printed in the United States of America

Cover design by Auburn Associates, Inc. Cover photo courtesy of U.S. Navy / Mass Communication Specialist Seaman George M. Bell.

Contents

Acknowledgments

As is usual for a project like this one, the authors have incurred many debts. Scholars, policymakers, and officers both inside and outside the US government encouraged us and took the time to explain the nuances of policies and programs. First and foremost we would like to thank Lieutenant General (Retired) Chip Gregson, Kathleen Hicks, and Ambassador Sandy Vershbow, for asking the Naval War College to support an internal US government review of American strategy and policy in the Indian Ocean region. Their deputies and assistants—including, among others, Shawn Brimley, Janine Davidson, Amanda Dory, Lindsay Ford, and Robert Scher—all gave generously of their time and expertise. Our Naval War College colleagues Peter Dutton, Timothy Hoyt, and Gary McKenna worked long and hard. Finally, last but not least, we would like to thank Robert Art of Brandeis University for joining us for an early workshop as we considered turning policy-oriented research into scholarly chapters worthy of being read by a wider audience. Bob's insights into strategy proved invaluable in delineating the concepts underlying this entire volume. Three anonymous referees forced us to write more clearly. Don Jacobs, our acquisitions editor at Georgetown University Press, and T. V. Paul, the series editor, provided encouragement and valuable feedback. Naturally, we fully assume responsibility for all errors that remain.

CHAPTER 1

INTRODUCTION

American Strategy in the Indian Ocean

ANDREW C. WINNER AND
PETER DOMBROWSKI

The Indian Ocean is the third-largest ocean in the world. Its littoral consists of forty-seven countries, and several strategically important islands are contained within its boundaries. Access to the Indian Ocean is controlled by nine passages, of which five are key sea lines of communication (SLOCs) used to transport energy.[1] By some accounts nearly 40 percent of the world's energy supplies are either found in the Indian Ocean proper or pass through the region from the Persian Gulf to Europe and Asia. The Indian Ocean links the thriving economies of Asia as well as the mature economies of Europe with the carbon-rich fields of the Middle East and the raw materials of Africa. It also connects the vast manufacturing capability of China with the wealthy markets of Europe. The Middle East is China's largest source of oil, and Beijing's dependence on oil imports is only slated to grow—to 75 percent of its total oil requirements by 2035. Almost all of this oil will cross the Indian Ocean.[2] This increasing dependence of China on the importing of oil and other hydrocarbons is a central factor in the large and growing percentage of the world's energy, raw materials, and general merchandise trade flows that cross the Indian Ocean. In sum, the Indian Ocean has replaced the North Atlantic as the central artery of global commerce. Therefore, external security threats or internal disruptions in the Indian Ocean region could have serious implications for many countries and the global economy as a whole.

The Indian Ocean is also becoming, once again, a distinct and increasingly important geographic space as well as a potentially contentious political arena.[3] China's political and military interests have expanded apace with its economic growth and commercial reach. For the first time in the modern era Chinese naval vessels are patrolling the western reaches of the Indian Ocean. Chinese corporations, including some with close ties to the Beijing government and all with diplomatic support, are investing deep inside Africa, not to mention ports and other infrastructure in Pakistan, Sri Lanka, and beyond. India has watched each Chinese move with suspicion while remaining cautious of American overtures toward establishing greater bilateral political and military cooperation. Meanwhile, third parties from the Indian Ocean and beyond—from Australia to Japan to several European states—continue to maintain a presence in the region or are in the process of expanding previously limited roles.

The United States therefore needs to strongly consider whether to develop a strategy for how it is going to pursue and protect its interests in this distant maritime region. The rise of the Indian Ocean as an artery of global commerce and its potential as a venue for geopolitical conflict raise questions about whether, and how, American policymakers should adjust their previously limited approach to the region. The premise of this book is that a US strategy for the Indian Ocean is necessary, and the authors of the volume's chapters outline various potential strategic approaches. Before the United States decides whether to develop a distinctive regional strategy for the Indian Ocean, key questions must be answered:

- What exactly are the US interests in the Indian Ocean region?
- What are the key geopolitical characteristics of the region, and how are they evolving?
- How can the United States increase its leverage to protect and advance its national interests in the region?

Such questions are not new or unique to the United States and its regional strategies, much less to any potential approach to the Indian Ocean. But they are the basic questions that underlie the grand strategies of the great powers that are seeking influence around the globe.

This introduction first reviews the concept of the Indian Ocean as a region. It then summarizes US engagement in the region, including how American national interests may be placed at risk by current developments and/or benefit from policy, political, or organizational adjustments. It then considers how different grand strategic frameworks can help scholars and policymakers alike think through the pros and cons of differing approaches to the region. It then argues that by exploring the costs and benefits of the full range of strategic approaches in the context of the specific regional challenges and the constellation of political, economic, and security interests of both regional powers and extraregional powers, the United States can identify a strategic approach to the Indian Ocean region that provides influence within the bounds of fiscal, operational, and geopolitical constraints. The chapter concludes with short overviews of alternative American strategies toward the Indian Ocean, developed by the chapter authors and drawn from the community of scholars and policy professionals who are actively engaged in debates over the future of US strategy.

THE INDIAN OCEAN AS A REGION

For the purposes of this volume, the Indian Ocean is considered as having the following geographic scope: South Africa to Australia, including all subordinate bodies of water (e.g., Bay of Bengal, Arabian Sea, Red Sea), exclusive of the Southern Ocean. The question of whether the Indian Ocean should be understood as a tightly integrated whole or as a set of interlocked subregions is left to the analyses of the individual chapter authors within the context of their specific strategic foundations. At this point it is sufficient to recognize that the Bay of Bengal, the Arabian Sea, and so forth present unique maritime topographies and operational challenges with often quite distinct histories, traditions, and political structures.

The Indian Ocean is an unusual geographic space to discuss as a formal, or even emergent, region for a number of reasons:

- The notional Indian Ocean region differs from other geographic spaces commonly studied by many strategists in that its core is not a continent or even a closely linked set of territories and islands (e.g., Oceania) but rather a large body of water constrained on three sides by continents.
- Regional conflicts have not been rare; but even the most intense among them—the wars between India and Pakistan—have been contained. They have not, as yet, threatened global peace or spread widely, although with the emergence of openly declared nuclear weapons states and the increased activity levels of Chinese military forces in the ocean, escalation may be possible in the future.
- Superpower competition in the Indian Ocean was anticipated in the 1970s and 1980s, but it never materialized in any significant way before the collapse of the Soviet Union and the end of the Cold War.
- The security challenges most commonly associated with the Indian Ocean region are either sea based (piracy, proliferation, and trafficking) or land based, but with a significant maritime dimension (terrorism).

However, the Indian Ocean is an interesting and important, if not necessarily critical, theater for the United States for several reasons:

- As Robert Kaplan suggests in his recent book *Monsoon: The Indian Ocean and the Future of American Power*, there is a possibility that the Indian Ocean will

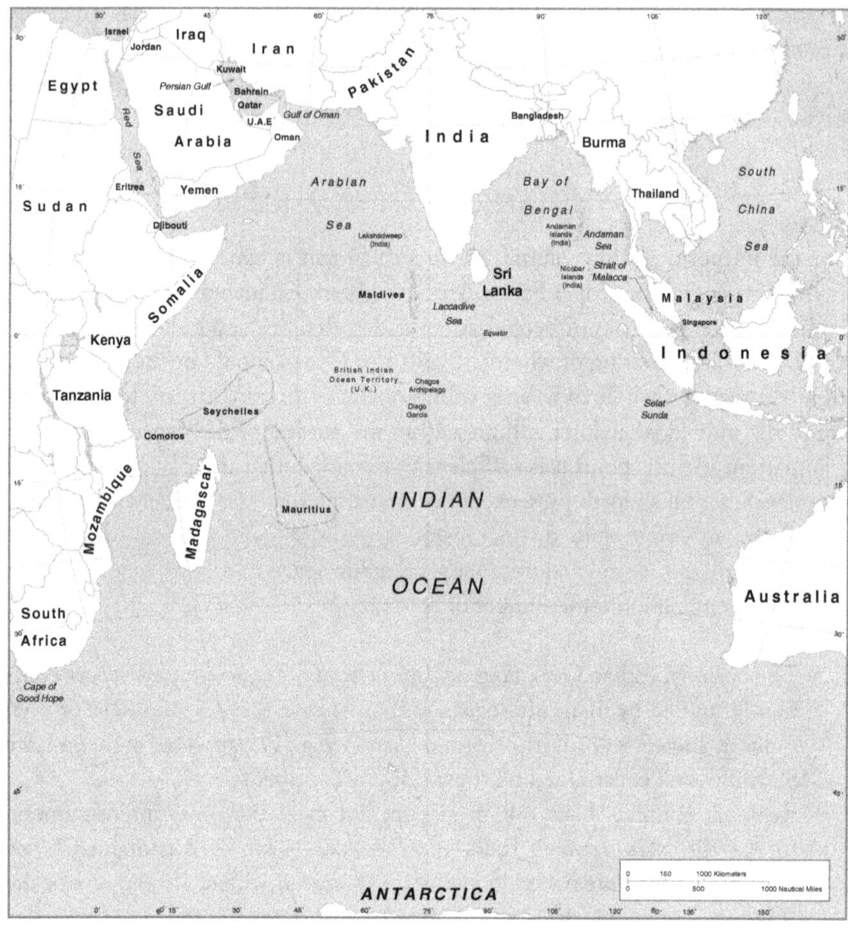

develop into a fully fledged region complete with self-identity and mature political, economic, and military institutions.[4]

- If the Indian Ocean does develop in ways that approximate the institutional dynamics and long-term evolutionary characteristics of other classically defined regions, such as Northeast Asia and Western Europe, it will in all likelihood do so because one or more outside powers, such as the United States and/or China, help by expending political capital, material resources, and diplomatic skills in ways that may or may not be welcomed by the countries in the Indian Ocean littoral.

- If the United States attempts to exercise regional leadership alone or in tandem with another power such as India, the primary instrument of American statecraft will, in all likelihood, be military and especially the so-called sea services—the US Navy, US Marines, and US Coast Guard.

- The Indian Ocean may soon emerge as a zone of conflict between the world's lone remaining superpower, the United States, and its emerging challenger, China.
- The interactions of four (and possibly more) nuclear powers in the Indian Ocean (India, Pakistan, China, and the United States) as well as several other states with modern, high-technology military forces (e.g., Australia) make the stakes for promoting regional peace and stability exceptionally high.

This section is organized into two subsections. The first considers whether the Indian Ocean can be considered a "region" and, if it is, examines the specific nature of the region. The second explores challenges to American interests in the Indian Ocean and whether meeting these challenges requires a comprehensive regional strategy. The subsections support arguments that are central for the rationale for undertaking this volume: (1) The Indian Ocean is an emerging region within the globalized economy and security architecture; and (2) the emergence of the Indian Ocean as a region for purposes of strategy development is largely dependent on external factors, specifically the posture of the United States military and associated diplomatic, political, and economic activities.

Defining the Indian Ocean Region

The recent past aside, historians and geographers remind us that the Indian Ocean has long been a region, at least if we focus on the organizing principles of governance by third parties entering into and controlling large swaths of the Indian Ocean littoral. Both Western and Asian empires have used the Indian Ocean to construct interconnected trade and migration networks with land-based enclaves, cities, and military installations.[5] From the West successive waves of Portuguese, Dutch, French, and British governments and commercial enterprises have used the seas to spread from the Middle East and Africa across the Indian subcontinent to Southeast Asia and eventually beyond. Various Arab empires and the Ottoman Empire also controlled swaths of the Indian littoral and commercial routes over the centuries. From the East, Chinese private traders searched far and wide for high-value commodities and, for a brief period at least, the Ming dynasty sent a "treasure fleet" under Admiral Zheng. He sailed across the Indian Ocean in search of diplomacy, trade, and exploration.[6] In each case, people, economic activities, languages, customs, and culture spread in ways that continue to tie peoples separated by thousands of miles.

Currently, with the exception of a small number of forward-thinking commentators and strategists in the United States and India, few think of the Indian Ocean as a single region.[7] In academic terms the Indian Ocean and its environs have witnessed very little of the regionalism or regionalization that has characterized South America, Africa, and East Asia, much less Europe—the case that has generated much of the theorizing and empirical research associated with the problems of "regions" in an increasingly globalized world.[8] Economic flows—from trade to investments—occur largely cross the Indian Ocean, that is, for example, from the Persian Gulf to China, or head out of the region, for example, from India to Europe—from one country or subregion to others: "Almost three-quarters of the trade traversing through the Indian Ocean, primarily in the form of oil and gas, belong to states external to the region."[9] In short, the bottom-up commercial connections said to drive regional economic integration are limited, despite the importance of the Indian Ocean to the functioning of the global economy.

As for regionalization, there are few regionally based economic, political, or military institutions active in the Indian Ocean that focus exclusively on the problems, and much less the potentialities, of the Indian Ocean's geography. Even one major counterexample—the Indian Ocean Naval Symposium—is of relatively recent vintage and has to date focused only on discussing a limited number of maritime security issues, what some strategists call "low-hanging fruit." The impetus for this symposium came largely from the Indian Navy, an institution whose worldview is somewhat different from, and perhaps ahead of, those of many Indian politicians and bureaucrats and, perhaps more tellingly, that of the dominant Indian strategic culture.[10]

Scholars have speculated that India's own distant maritime past, combined with the national growing and globalizing economy and the maritime exploits of China's People's Liberation Army Navy, might stimulate the emergence of a "seaward worldview" in India.[11] This in turn might eventually lead the Indian government to promote a more coherent and institutionalized "Indian Ocean" region. In the short to intermediate terms, however, this remains an aspirational vision of some maritime-minded Indian strategic and military thinkers. A careful assessment of Indian military thought and capabilities suggests that the Indian Navy, Air Force, and Army can and will continue to undertake power projection operations in the region, even given the Ghandian origins of Indian foreign and security policies; but it is less clear whether these activities will be in the service of broader regionalization or indeed provoke it in response.[12] Further, the United States, on its own or in careful and tentative partnership with India, might ultimately provide the impetus for regionalization.

India has the size and potential to emerge as a global economy player, but it is not yet there. The US Central Intelligence Agency estimates that in 2012, India possessed the world's fourth-largest economy measured in terms of purchasing power parity, and that it has been growing at roughly 7 percent a year for the past three years. But India has yet to emerge as a major trading partner—in 2012 it ranked twenty-first and ninth, respectively, for exports and imports. Much of that trade is not with other Indian Ocean littoral states (although India is becoming a larger petroleum refiner), but the refined products are often then exported to states outside the Indian Ocean region. In other words, the integration of the Indian Ocean region through regional trade does not seem like it will be a driving force supporting regional institutional growth.

With one notable and short-lived exception, third-party great powers have not been especially active or engaged in the region as a whole since World War II. The exception is a short period at the height of the Cold War, when Soviet naval deployments briefly preoccupied American policymakers, in large part because of fears that naval operations were a prelude to, or could support, overland moves on the oil-rich Persian Gulf.[13] As a result of this concern, coupled initially with the British withdrawal from Aden in 1967 and, in 1979, with the Iranian Revolution, the United States took steps to increase its military presence in the region as well as its ability to rapidly reinforce the Persian Gulf region.

The lack of strategic rivalry by the great powers could change as China begins to view the Indian Ocean as essential for its own security. One survey of China's maritime activities observes that although China's officials claim that its activities in the Indian Ocean are peaceful, "the development of military maritime infrastructure in the Indian Ocean would provide China access and a basing facility for conducting sustained operations and emerging as a stakeholder in Indian Ocean security architecture."[14] Some American national security analysts view China's activities, particularly as capabilities grow, as inevitably posing a strategic competition to the United States.[15] The increase in India's military capabilities that has accompanied its two-decade rise in economic growth will make it a resident great power that could then lead to a complicated three-way interaction with the United States and China. In strategic terms the implications of whether the Indian Ocean is a region depends in part on how "region" is defined and understood conceptually. From the perspective of US strategy we argue in large part from Peter Katzenstein's position on the relationship between globalization, regions, and the role of the United States: "Spurred by US policies that reflect its territorial and nonterritorial powers, complementary processes of globalization and internationalization are making this a world of porous regions. Its dynamics differ dramatically from the closed regions of the past. Finally, regional porousness is enhanced politically by vertical relations that link core regional states to America, region to subregions, and America to regions."[16]

US Engagement in the Indian Ocean Region

The Indian Ocean poses a special challenge for American policymakers. US military, diplomatic, and other governmental structures do not focus on the Indian Ocean as a single region. Up until 1976 the Defense Department literally divided military responsibility for the Indian Ocean in half between its two major regional commands—the Atlantic Command and the Pacific Command (PACOM).[17] Currently, the Department of Defense divides the region among three regional combatant commands—PACOM, Africa Command (AFRICOM), and Central Command (CENTCOM), each with responsibility for a portion of the Indian Ocean. Each of these three combatant commands has primary responsibility for US defense policy in approximately one-third of the littoral states of the Indian Ocean. (To be precise, a fourth regional command, the European Command, EUCOM, also has responsibility for a very small portion of a body of water that connects to the Indian Ocean—the Gulf of Aqaba, including Eilat, because Israel is in its area of responsibility.) The Department of State divides the region into geographic bureaus whose boundaries do not match up with those of the Department of Defense. These lead to so-called seams issues, where the coordination of priorities and the operations of the different elements of the US government result in less-than-optimal policies for US strategy writ large. It also makes even considering whether there should be a unified strategy for the region difficult, because bureaucratic entities generally abhor changes or even ideas that may lessen their prerogatives, responsibilities, and resources.

In terms of US defense planning processes and organizations, what constitutes a region is a choice made for reasons of politics and institutional design. Often, existing arrangements are the result of both tradition and history; occasionally, they are the result of changing threats and limited resources. New regions, complete with organizational innovation, emerge as geostrategic circumstances change. AFRICOM, for example, was officially established in 2008, in part because Africa is too big a geographic area with too many unique security challenges to continue leaving it under EUCOM, as had been the case throughout the Cold War. With the reduction of American forces in continental Europe, the rise of terrorism, and more civil wars in Africa, given CENTCOM's focus on Iraq, Afghanistan, and Pakistan, it made sense to establish a new regional command dedicated to Africa.[18] As the commercial importance of the Indian Ocean increases, war remains a possibility on the Indian subcontinent, and China's naval forces enter the Indian Ocean on a regular basis, the United States may eventually modify the organizational units of the Department of Defense, the Department of State, and other parts of the federal government.

US strategic planners are only just beginning to see any Indian Ocean–wide threats to US interests. This judgment does not mean that the United States will not react if it sees threats to those interests arising. Instead, it posits that existing US policies and defense activities in the region have, at least to date, protected those interests. It also assumes that the United States will be able to respond in a timely fashion to the development of longer-term threats that may require an augmentation of military forces. Transnational threats, such as violent extremist groups and the proliferation of weapons of mass destruction (WMD), are already being handled by either bilateral policies (e.g., US relations with Pakistan) or global institutions (e.g., United Nations Security Council Resolution 1540's implementation and the Proliferation Security Initiative).

Some American strategists believe that both the existing and emergent security challenges of the Indian Ocean region will continue to be adequately and efficiently handled within the existing global strategic framework adopted by the United States and embodied in the May 2010 *National Security Strategy*. Existing Department of Defense, combatant command, and interagency strategies, institutional arrangements, and military forces (including force deployments, structure, and posture) are sufficient to respond to the trends and drivers, not to mention the threats, identified for the Indian Ocean region over the next fifteen to twenty years. The status quo means that the United States deals with the Indian Ocean from a defensive point of view as a set of subregions demarcated by the boundaries of the regional combatant commands.

From the perspective of this book's authors, challenges to US interests in the Indian Ocean in recent years have not yet required a holistic regional strategy or set of policies. US deployments in the region, existing access and basing arrangements, and ongoing defense deployments have provided sufficient capabilities to both allow for a limited, but steady state, forward presence and to respond to any foreseeable contingencies. Even the famous use of an American aircraft carrier (modified to host Special Operations Forces, complete with specialized helicopters rather than its usual complement of strike aircraft) to stage the first American attacks on the Afghan Taliban after the September 11, 2001, terrorist attacks supports this claim. At the strategic level this judgment essentially endorses the general, global approach that has been articulated in the 2010 national security strategy and other planning documents, including the Nuclear Posture Review and the Quadrennial Defense Review, and has been pursued on a regional basis as implemented by the three regional Combatant Commands—PACOM, CENTCOM, and AFRICOM—that share responsibility for the region as whole. However, we believe it is time to rethink this judgment, in view of the Indian Ocean's growing commercial importance and the variety of challenges and opportunities it poses to long-standing American interests.

US OBJECTIVES IN THE INDIAN OCEAN According to the US national strategy documents, US military forces in the Indian Ocean region are primarily intended to serve as a stable forward presence sufficient to deter Iran and other states from undertaking aggressive actions in the Persian Gulf and the Northern Arabian Sea.[19] If deterrence were to fail, US forces would be available in theater and when necessary through augmentation to ensure sea control and project power inland. Power projection assets are also available to support counterterrorism activities in the region, especially in Afghanistan, Pakistan, Somalia, and Yemen. During peacetime, forward-deployed forces also support multinational coalitions and bilateral partners in the region in providing maritime security and, as required, humanitarian assistance and disaster relief. A regional presence is also required to support the orderly drawdowns of ground forces in Afghanistan, in accordance with existing policy.

Interagency activities in the Indian Ocean are largely subordinate to supporting ongoing conflicts in the region. Thus, economic statecraft involves supporting frontline states with aid and other economic benefits to ensure access for US forces and, to a lesser extent, promote the economic and political development necessary for more long-term and reliable partners to emerge. But the reality of how US policy attention is divided and resources are allocated means that the entire Indian Ocean region—other than the immediate region around the Persian Gulf—is largely an economy of force operation.

For the United States one major impediment to influencing individual countries in the Indian Ocean region is the relative paucity of economic connections (aside from petroleum and natural gas from the Persian Gulf) and a lack of long-standing formal treaty allies in the Indian Ocean littoral (except Australia and Thailand). There are few levers available for shaping the behavior of states, firms, and nonstate actors in the region. This may soon be exacerbated by the limits on American statecraft resulting from likely reductions in US foreign operations and defense budgets in the coming years. For important regional actors like India, the absence of meaningful intraregional connections or institutions also limits leverage. Other outside powers—including China, Japan, and several European states—may have more opportunities to practice economic statecraft, however, particularly as their economic stakes in the region increase.

Freed from the constraints imposed by diplomatic-speak and the cautious language of official US planning documents, Michael Green and Andrew Shearer have summarized key American interests in the Indian Ocean as related to "three geostrategic factors, maintaining an open Indian Ocean highway, defending chokepoints at either end of the Indian Ocean, and sanitizing the Indian Ocean as a secondary front in broader Asian regional competition . . . the same factors that have animated US policy toward the region for more than a century. That in itself is a useful test of the enduring nature of those particularly geostrategic definitions of US interests and a starting point for considering future strategy."[20]

IMPETUS FOR CHANGES IN THE US APPROACH TO THE INDIAN OCEAN
Maintaining the status quo approach to the Indian Ocean may hold long-term risks. One risk involves suboptimization in terms of security relations and operations. If the United States continues with defense relations and activities based primarily on divisions among the various regional combatant commands, it will

lose out on potential synergies that could bolster US interests in the Indian Ocean. For example, by leaving policy toward India's role in the Indian Ocean primarily to PACOM, Washington could lose opportunities to engage more fully with New Delhi on improving maritime security in East Africa or encouraging the Indian Navy to cooperate more closely with the US Navy in protecting the flow of oil through the Strait of Hormuz or fighting piracy off the coast of Somalia.

A second risk is that allies and partners in the region may perceive the status quo or a slight decline in US defense activities over time in the region due to the Afghanistan and Iraq drawdown as Washington pulling back more broadly. This may result in more aggressive behavior on the part of adversaries and potential adversaries; or it may lead to decisions by partners/allies that exacerbate tensions in the Indian Ocean. Although little such behavior has been observed so far, some scholars warn that bandwagoning, at least in Southeast Asia, may occur "in the sense that they want to trade with China and value maintaining good relations with China, recognizing the PRC's [People's Republic of China's] potential to become the most powerful state in Asia."[21] Although such behavior in the region overall could lead to a type of rough stability, the process of bandwagoning and balancing may create destabilizing situations as states sort out a new order in the region. The process of smaller states sorting out new security relationships could also bring the great powers into confrontation over local conflicts.

Many American strategists tend to focus most closely on the growing potential for great power conflict in a region. The potential threats to US national security in such an eventuality in the case of the India Ocean are (1) damage to the global economy; (2) local conflicts that provoke American involvement or even intervention in regional conflicts (Pakistan–India or India–China), where at least one of the parties to the conflict will seek US support; or (3) in the medium to long run induce, by accident or design, American military forces into a direct confrontation with China. Combined with serious transnational threats—largely confined to a "loose" nukes scenario or a serious case of proliferation that puts weapons-grade material in the hands of a terrorist group or a so-called rogue state—the Indian Ocean region, despite its relative quiet over the past decades, may eventually rise up the priority list for US strategists and policymakers.

With the publication of *Monsoon* by Robert Kaplan and several years of increasing press coverage of the Indian Ocean associated with the rise of piracy around the Horn of Africa and the potential rise of maritime terrorism, official Washington took notice of the Indian Ocean. The 2010 Department of Defense's Quadrennial Defense Review called for "a more integrated approach to the region across military and civilian organizations" and recommended that the national security community make an assessment of "US national interests, objectives and force posture implications" in the Indian Ocean as a way to provide a "useful guide for future defense planning."[22] The outcome of this assessment and potential changes to US government policies and organizations responsible for parts of the Indian Ocean is not known publicly, but some of the assessment may have influenced the Obama administration's January 2012 strategic review of priorities for defense.[23]

The January 2012 document "Sustaining US Global Leadership: Priorities for 21st Century Defense" was not a required review or requested by Congress. Instead, it was the Obama administration's updating of guidance to the Department of Defense in light of the withdrawal from Iraq, the successful raid that killed Osama bin Laden, the plan for a significant drawdown from Afghanistan, and the increased focus on fiscal constraints for defense and other government spending. A central element of the new guidance document was what became known as the "Asian pivot."[24] The document was very explicit in stating that "US economic and security interests are inextricably linked to developments in the arc extending from the Western Pacific and East Asia into the Indian Ocean region and South Asia, creating a mix of evolving challenges and opportunities. Accordingly, while the US military will continue to contribute to security globally, we will of necessity rebalance toward the Asia-Pacific region."[25] The strategic review clearly includes the Indian Ocean in this pivot, but the guidance did not explicitly state that a specific Indian Ocean strategy was either required or had been decided upon. Indeed, it is not clear whether the Indian Ocean was simply being subsumed as an element of a larger Asia-Pacific strategy. This is one of the issues with which the authors in this volume grapple—whether the Indian Ocean is indeed its own region, or whether it should be considered part of a broader "Indo-Pacific" region for the purposes of US strategy.

Taken individually, the publicly acknowledged specifics of the Asia pivot, over time rebranded as the Asia "rebalance" by the administration, are relatively modest—2,500 Marines on rotational deployment to Darwin, Australia; and four Littoral Combat Ships similarly deployed on a rotational basis in Singapore. Both those deployments are on the eastern edges of the Indian Ocean, again opening the question of whether a strategic approach to that region is being incorporated into something larger.

In the coming years the Asia rebalance may increase the importance of the Indian Ocean for American global strategies. Even more so than in earlier periods, the Indian Ocean will be a key transit point between the two poles of American global interests—the Persian Gulf and Greater Middle East on one hand, and East Asia and the Asian littoral on the other. With more limited forces following reductions in defense spending, it will be important for the US Navy and ground forces to be stationed in theater and transit between them. This is especially true during crises, when response time is often short. Further, as China develops a more capable military presence in the Indian Ocean to protect its SLOCs, access to the global commons, and secure natural resources and associated infrastructure, the United States may feel compelled to raise its visibility in the region. Of course, how the rebalancing is implemented in the Indian Ocean, not to mention Asia itself, depends on how American policymakers and military leaders interpret the intersection of the changing geostrategic dynamics in the region, American interests, and its own strategic options given the limits established by US domestic politics. These are the issues that the chapter authors address in varying degrees with regard to the Indian Ocean.

APPLIED GRAND STRATEGY

"Grand strategy" is an elusive but popular concept for understanding how nations, particularly great powers, pursue their national interests within the global system.[26] Grand strategy, properly conceived, is strategy writ large. It is the highest, broadest, most multifaceted and most multidimensional level of strategy.[27] It concerns the full range of international goals that states seek—diplomatic, political, economic, and military, for instance—how they attempt to ensure and enhance security, power, and prosperity (in all their forms); and how all the instruments of statecraft are employed. As Lawrence Freedman has argued, "Grand Strategy has traditionally been concerned with how and for what purposes states position themselves within the international system." The means they employ "might be social, economic, political, or military."[28]

To reason through the potential strategic approaches to the emerging Indian Ocean region available to the US national security community, this volume uses a technique we have called Applied Grand Strategy Analysis (AGSA). The AGSA process has been used and refined in a series of projects undertaken by the volume editors.[29] At its most basic, AGSA is a rationalist approach to developing competing strategic frameworks for the national or a subordinate level (e.g., for a specific region or military commands). Alternative strategies are developed from a common understanding of a specific geostrategic environment as bounded by time and place as well as a general acceptance of enduring national interests and goals. The authors of these alternative strategies build their individual options deductively from the well-understood precepts of classic grand strategies or inductively based on experience and the logical tracing of how the US government and its subunits actually work. The desired AGSA end state is a set of competing approaches that policymakers, scholars, and analysts can use to compare, contrast, and evaluate the various plans, policies, and government institutions that are involved in interacting with a particular region or substantive issue.

What follows is a brief discussion of the AGSA analytic process used to develop the analytic framework that organized the volume and provided guidelines to the authors for writing their individual chapters.[30] The first step in the AGSA process is to develop a better understanding of the current and likely future geostrategic environment, in this case in the Indian Ocean region. Because significant futures research is regularly conducted both inside and outside the US government, existing work was mined for insights relevant to the Indian Ocean region.[31] This mining and selection of key elements from a range of government- and academic/analytic-produced geostrategic environment documents provided a background against which the strategic analysis could take place. The review and culling of information helped identify key facts, trends, and uncertainties. The chapter authors were provided with this information as a starting point by the volume editors.

Most of the chapter authors were already experts on the Indian Ocean region, and for them this information was not necessarily new or needed. Other authors were more familiar with grand and military strategies rather than the Indian Ocean region, and therefore made more use of this material. In all cases authors were encouraged to seek out additional information, critically examine the geostrategic elements provided, and make their own judgments about the facts and particularly about the strength of the predictions about future trends and uncertainties.

The AGSA process also draws upon existing US government documents and outside analyses to develop a common set of US national interests as a starting point for developing alternative strategy options. Because strategy development and comparison projects such as this are meant to have lasting value, the attempt was made to go beyond the documents of any particular presidential administration. Past national security strategies and subordinate documents were examined to identify interests that were durable over time and across administrations of all political stripes.

At the same time, the volume authors were encouraged to make their contributions as current as possible. Although early draft chapters were completed before the January 2012 new defense guidance was issued, subsequent drafts incorporated shifts in the Obama administration's positions and grappled with how the Asia rebalance would affect American policies toward the Indian Ocean. The set of US national interests were provided to the chapter authors as a starting point for analysis and without prioritization. The authors were asked to either implicitly or explicitly rank the order of these interests as part of their development of a strategic option. They were also allowed to add or subtract from the list based on their own experience, training, and research.

The greatest uncertainty in the AGSA process is the future direction of US grand strategy as a whole. In this project there was uncertainty about both how to characterize the Obama administration's evolving grand strategy and what grand strategy or strategies future presidential administration might adopt. For the AGSA process to be useful, the intent is to develop a set of strategic options that will be lasting—that will have utility beyond the present and will be within the range of the possible in the future. Thus, we decided that at least some options would be derived from a well-developed set of grand strategy frameworks that were in use in the policy and academic communities.

The range of possible grand strategies was developed from the work of well-respected academic scholars.[32] Posen and Ross's four strategies—neo-isolationism, selective engagement, cooperative security, and primacy—were used as starting points in thinking about options for the Indian Ocean. Given the volume contributors' background work in developing an understanding of the Indian Ocean strategic environment and the US interests in the region, some changes and choices were made about which of these grand strategic frameworks to use in developing strategies for the Indian Ocean. At times, these categories were refined or updated to reflect more recent thinking, such as the discussion of offshore balancing in chapter 4, by Christopher Preble, and in chapter 5, by James Holmes and Toshi Yoshihara.

In addition to using Posen and Ross's four grand strategy frameworks as a top-down method of developing a more detailed strategic option for the Indian Ocean, the other chapter authors were allowed free rein to write their chapters without the constraint or guidance of a grand strategic framework. Those authors—Teresita Schaffer, in chapter 8; and Andrew Winner, in chapter 9—took the inputs of the geostrategic environment and the going-in set of US national interests and developed a bottom-up strategy based on their own knowledge and understanding of the region and of US capabilities.

The Indian Ocean strategy options developed in this volume's individual chapters address these categories in different ways, depending on the preferences of the authors. The chapters themselves are meant to stimulate debate within the US national security community. They are best used to illuminate the impact of current and short- to intermediate-term policy choices on long-range developments in the region. Moreover, when considered relative to each other, each has specific strengths and weakness, and each would require more or fewer changes to current US policies. From the perspective of the volume editors, no single approach is likely to prevail; nor would any single approach satisfy all national objectives within the regional or succeed within the limiting parameters of institutional arrangements.

PLAN OF THE BOOK

The body of this volume is divided into three parts. Part I covers strategy options, part II examines the evolving of recent US policies into the future, and part III offers conclusions.

Strategy Options

Part I of the volume includes chapters written in the spirit of AGSA. We asked a mixture of academics and policy professionals to develop future regional strategic options. In effect, this is a deductive approach vice the inductive drivers of the two chapters in the previous section. Each has a varying degree of expertise and background relevant to the Indian Ocean or one of its constituent parts.

Chapter 2, "Strengthening Partners to Keep the Peace: A Neo-Nixon Doctrine for the Indian Ocean Region," was written by Walter C. Ladwig III of the University of Oxford. Ladwig argues that in recent years the United States has been in a period of "imperial overstretch" analogous to that of the second Nixon term. He further argues that the military and political interests of the United States in the Indian Ocean are important but not vital. His chapter thus recommends strengthening American military capabilities and strategic ties with four key countries in the Indian Ocean region—India, South Africa, Indonesia, and Australia. Backed by the United States, these countries would take primary responsibility for security in the Indian Ocean. This strategy advocates a more engaged posture than pulling out or laissez-faire. Conversely, it is more narrowly regionally focused than chapter 9's Indo-Pacific security framework vision.

Chapter 3, "Reformulating Grand Strategy in the Indian Ocean Region: The Case of Containment," is by William C. Martel of the Fletcher School of Law and Diplomacy. Martel examines how and why the United States should consider a newly conceived grand strategy of containment for dealing with developments in the Indian Ocean region for the present era to 2025. This analysis focuses on the security and economic issues in the Indian Ocean region that pose the greatest threats to US interests. It critically evaluates the ability of a strategy of containment as traditionally constructed to support and advance US interests in the Indian Ocean region. It then explains the limits of even a limited form of containment in helping American policymakers deal with the challenges posed by the rise of China, the emergence of India as a critical regional power, the risks posed by extremism and the proliferation of WMD in the region, and the Indian Ocean region's growing contribution to global economic prosperity.

Christopher Preble of the Cato Institute contributed chapter 4, "Leaving Unipolarity Behind: A Strategic Framework for Advancing US Interests in the Indian Ocean Region." Much like Walter Ladwig, Preble begins with the premise that the United States is in a period of "imperial overstretch" and that it must abandon areas that are not central to its vital interests, trusting in the inherent balancing nature of the international system to ensure that less vital regions will police themselves. It concludes that the vital military and political interests of the United States do not require it to be the primary guarantor of the safety and security of the Indian Ocean. Instead, the United States should facilitate the emergence of a multipolar regional arrangement, with strong democratic states constituting the leading actors, to help achieve regional stability and security.

Naval War College professors James R. Holmes and Toshi Yoshihara wrote chapter 5: "Offshore Balancing in the Indian Ocean: Forward or Not at All." They claim that strict fidelity to an offshore-balancing strategy yields distinctive implications for the US posture in the Indian Ocean. Given the transcontinental distances and complex strategic geography involved, the Indian Ocean region will prove least susceptible among Eurasia's marginal seas to the effects of offshore balancing. Replicating Great Britain's balancing strategy appears far harder for Washington today than it was for London at the apex of its power. Indeed, they say that Nicholas John Spykman would blanch at the thought of trying to preserve the geopolitical balance in the Indian Ocean from Western Hemisphere home-ports. Offshore balancers assume that the United States has the luxury of just-in-time balancing. Such a strategy lies out of reach in the distant Indian Ocean.

Rodger Payne, chair of the Political Science Department of the University of Louisville, develops an argument at the polar opposite end of the grand strategic spectrum from the volume's other contributors. Payne applies ideas associated with cooperative security to the Indian Ocean region in chapter 6, "Cooperative Security in the Indian Ocean." In his understanding, cooperative security refers to the idea that nation-states, ordinarily working through intergovernmental institutions and often with nongovernmental organizations, should collaborate to seek consensual solutions on an array of common security problems. A cooperative security agenda extends beyond traditional geostrategic and military issues, such as international and intrastate war, terrorism, or the risks associated with the proliferation of WMD, to encompass other burgeoning threats to global peace and stability, including "inequality and economic instability, ... damage to our environment, food insecurity, and dangers to public health." Many proponents of cooperative security view security as indivisible, meaning that insecurity in one state or region should be viewed as a common security concern. By the same logic, reductions in security threats in one state or region should be viewed as desirable. This upends and transcends the logic of the security dilemma. Payne argues that the Indian Ocean is a region ripe for such a strategic approach based on cooperative security. The intrastate conflicts are relatively muted and manageable. The region's transnational threats are well recognized and enjoy a high degree of consensus on the need to address them. Finally, most of the Indian Ocean's transnational security issues are not being addressed by the way the United States currently manages its interests in the region.

In chapter 7, "From Hub to Hinge: A Strategic Framework to Promote US Security Interests in the Indian Ocean," Michael Auslin of the American Enterprise Institute suggests that the primary challenge for US policy in the next generation will be to integrate the Indian Ocean into the broader US security of the vast Indo-Pacific region. US strategy should have two major ordering approaches: first, an enhanced military presence that presents a credible force posture to deal with both steady state conditions and possible conflict contingencies; and second, a newly crafted set of overlapping and mutually reinforcing alliances, strategic partnerships, and access-granting relationships that will help share burdens, allow operational and planning flexibility for US forces, and create a community of interests underpinning a liberal security regime. This community should emphasize setting a "first order" pattern of security cooperation and the effective imposition of liberal norms in the Indian Ocean. The community should be explicitly linked to, and be bolstered by, the liberal, alliance-based structure that the United States has already established in the Western Pacific.

Evolving Recent US Policies Forward to the Future

The two chapters in part II, which represent our second set of strategic alternatives for the Indian Ocean, begin with the assumption that the present policies and programs in the region are the best predictor for the future. Adjustments can and should take place at the margin and within the overarching framework of current institutional arrangements and policy objectives. For these options, we asked for contributions from Teresita Schaffer, a policy professional with a long history of engagement and leadership responsibility in the region, and Andrew Winner, the director of the Naval War College's Indian Ocean Regional Studies Group.

According to Schaffer in chapter 8, "The Indian Ocean: Protecting Access to a Volatile Powerhouse," the principal objectives of a US Indian Ocean strategy are to manage China's growing presence by ensuring that its relationships in the Indian Ocean region are counterbalanced by a strong network of ties with the United States, and preventing China from becoming a clear threat to US interests. A second objective is to prevent Iran from creating threats to US interests, either by working with nonstate actors in the short term or by creating a hostile environment through its political relationships in the longer term. US coalition building and network building can serve both purposes. Schaffer's approach thus focuses on countering potentially destabilizing increases in access and influence on the parts of China (primarily) and Iran (secondarily). The United States thus needs to build coalitions for security that would directly counter the two likely threats to security in the region—China and Iran.

In chapter 9, "Combating Transnational Security Threats in the Indian Ocean: a Focused US Regional Strategy," Andrew Winner argues that the primary challenges to US interests in the Indian Ocean are transnational: terrorism, WMD proliferation, the intersection of those two issues, illegal trafficking of other types, piracy and maritime crime at sea, and natural disasters. Other US interests involving state-on-state security dilemmas or threats to freedom of navigation can be achieved by addressing these transnational security issues. Those US interests that involve discrete parts of the Indian Ocean, such as Iranian anti-access capabilities in and around the Strait of Hormuz, can be handled by existing, regionally based, or bilateral strategies and policies. These interests are relatively long-standing (post–Cold War) and bipartisan and have been reiterated in the Obama administration's January 2012 paper "Sustaining US Global Leadership: Priorities for 21st Century Defense." This strategic concept advocates building new and strengthening the existing web of bilateral and multilateral security enterprises in the Indian Ocean to address this set of threats because, by their nature, they cannot be countered unilaterally.

Conclusion

The book's final chapter, which constitutes part III, assesses the utility of thinking about the Indian Ocean as a coherent theater for practicing a regionally specific set of political, diplomatic, economic, security, and military policies. It puts the Indian Ocean in various policy contexts and frameworks—ranging from the Obama administration's recent focus on the Asia-Pacific region to earlier concerns about a single power dominating the Eurasian landmass. It offers the beginnings of an analytic framework for evaluating the contending strategic approaches offered by the individual chapter authors and concludes that regardless of the institutional arrangements internal to the US government, the United States would be well served to develop a coherent approach to US interests in the Indian Ocean and its littorals.

NOTES

The views expressed here are those of the authors and do not necessarily reflect the views of the US Naval War College, the US Navy, or the Department of Defense.

1. Integrated Headquarters, Ministry of Defence–Navy, *Freedom to Use the Seas: India's Maritime Military Strategy* (New Delhi: Ministry of Defense, 2007), 25–41.
2. US Energy Information Administration, "China: Analysis," April 22, 2013, revision, www.eia.gov/countries/cab.cfm?fips=CH.
3. Sugata Bose, *A Hundred Horizons: The Indian Ocean in the Age of Global Empire* (Cambridge, MA: Harvard University Press, 2006); John Garofano and Andrea J. Dew, eds., *Deep Currents and Rising Tides: The Indian Ocean and International Security* (Washington, DC: Georgetown University Press, 2013).
4. Robert D. Kaplan, *Monsoon: The Indian Ocean and the Future of American Power* (New York: Random House, 2011).

5. Bose, *Hundred Horizons*; K. N. Chaudhuri, *Trade and Civilisation in the Indian Ocean: An Economic History from the Rise of Islam to 1750* (Cambridge: Cambridge University Press, 1985); Thomas R. Metcalf, *Imperial Connections: India in the Indian Ocean Arena, 1860–1920* (Berkeley: University of California Press, 2008); Michael Pearson, *The Indian Ocean* (New York: Routledge, 2003).

6. James R. Holmes, Andrew C. Winner, and Toshi Yoshihara, *Indian Naval Strategy in the Twenty-First Century* (New York: Routledge, 2009), 1.

7. Robert D. Kaplan, *Monsoon: The Indian Ocean and the Future of American Power* (New York: Random House, Inc., 2011); Holmes, Winner, and Yoshihara, *Indian Naval Strategy*; Michael J. Green and Andrew Shearer, "Defining US Indian Ocean Strategy," *Washington Quarterly* 35, no. 2 (2012): 175–89.

8. Efforts to understand regions, regionalization, and regionalism have generated a vast literature. For an outstanding research guide to various perspectives see T. V. Paul, ed., *International Relations Theory and Regional Transformation* (New York: Cambridge University Press, 2012).

9. Harsh Pant, "India's Growing Naval Power: Indian Ocean in Focus," in *Seapower and the Asia-Pacific: The Triumph of Neptune*, ed. Geoffrey Till and Patrick C. Bratton (London: Routledge, 2012), 112.

10. Other regional organizations are detailed by Ambassador Teresita Schaffer in chapter 8 of the present volume.

11. Holmes, Winner, and Yoshihara, *Indian Naval Strategy*, 6–26.

12. Walter C. Ladwig III, "India and Power Projection: Will the Land of Gandhi Become a Conventional Great Power?" *Asian Survey* 50, no. 6 (November–December 2010): 1162–83.

13. Selig S. Harrison and K. Subrahmanyam, eds., *Superpower Rivalry in the Indian Ocean: Indian and American Perspectives* (New York: Oxford University Press, 1989).

14. Vijay Sakhuja, "Maritime Multilateralism: China's Strategy for the Indian Ocean," *China Brief* (Jamestown Foundation) 9, no. 22 (November 4, 2009), www.jamestown.org/single/?no_cache=1&tx_ttnews percent5Btt_news percent 5D=35692.

15. Ashley J. Tellis, "Indian Ocean and US Grand Strategy," lecture at India International Centre organized by National Maritime Foundation, January 17, 2012.

16. Peter J. Katzenstein, *A World of Regions: Asia and Europe in the American Imperium* (Ithaca, NY: Cornell University Press, 2005).

17. Donald Rumsfeld, Secretary of Defense, "Memorandum for the Joint Chiefs of Staff, Subject: Unified Command Plan," March 23, 1976, http://library.rumsfeld .com/doclib/sp/489/Re%20President%20Approved%20Movement%20of %20Boundary%20Between%20Atlantic%20and%20Pacific%20Command% 20Dated%2003-19-1976%20and%2003-23-1976.pdf#search=%22Indian%20 Ocean%22. In this memorandum, the Pacific Command was given responsibility for the entire Indian Ocean and the eastern and southern coasts of Africa up to 17 degrees east.

18. Isaac Kfir, "The Challenge That Is USAFRICOM," *Joint Forces Quarterly*, no. 49 (2008): 110–13; James J. F. Forest and Rebecca Crispin, "AFRICOM: Troubled Infancy, Promising Future," *Contemporary Security Policy* 30, no 1 (2009): 5–27.
19. A significant official rendering of this policy is: "Credible combat power will be continuously postured in the Western Pacific and the Arabian Gulf/Indian Ocean to protect our vital interests, assure our friends and allies of our continuing commitment to regional security, and deter and dissuade potential adversaries and peer competitors." This can be found in the tri-service maritime strategy document: US Coast Guard, US Marine Corps, and US Navy, *A Cooperative Strategy for 21st Century Seapower*, October 2007, www.navy.mil/maritime /Maritimestrategy.pdf.
20. Michael J. Green and Andrew Shearer, "Defining US Indian Ocean Strategy," *Washington Quarterly* 35, no. 2 (2012): 178.
21. Denny Roy, "Southeast Asia and China: Balancing or Bandwagoning?" *Contemporary Southeast Asia* 27, no. 2 (2005): 319.
22. US Department of Defense, "Quadrennial Defense Review Report," February 2010, 60–61, www.defense.gov/qdr/images/QDR_as_of_12Feb10_1000.pdf.
23. US Department of Defense, "Sustaining US Global Leadership: Priorities for 21st Century Defense," January 2012, www.defense.gov/news/defense_ strategic_guidance.pdf.
24. Hillary Clinton, "America's Pacific Century," *Foreign Policy*, November 2011, www.foreignpolicy.com/articles/2011/10/11/americas_pacific_century.
25. US Department of Defense, "Sustaining US Global Leadership," 2.
26. The approach described in the following paragraphs and used to structure this volume should not be confused with the interesting analysis using the same term by Clark Murdock and Kevin Kallmyer. Clark Murdock and Kevin Kallmyer, "Applied Grand Strategy: Making Tough Choices in an Era of Limits and Constraint," *Orbis*, Fall 2011, 541–57.
27. For a discussion of "The Scope of Grand Strategy," see Edward N. Luttwak, *Strategy: The Logic of War and Peace* (Cambridge: Belknap Press of Harvard University Press, 1987), 179–89. In this volume Luttwak also distinguishes among the various levels of strategy. A discussion of "The Dimensions of Strategy" is provided by Colin Gray, *Modern Strategy* (Oxford: Oxford University Press, 1999), 16–47.
28. Lawrence Freedman, "Grand Strategy in the Twenty-First Century," *Defence Studies* 1, no. 1 (Spring 2001): 11. For alternative formulations, see Michael Howard, "Grand Strategy in the Twentieth Century," *Defence Studies* 1, No. 1 (Spring 2001): 10; Murray and Grimsley, "Introduction: On Strategy," in *The Making of Strategy: Rulers, States, and War* (Cambridge: Cambridge University Press, 1994), 1–23; Thomas J. Christensen, *Useful Adversaries: Grand Strategy, Domestic Mobilization, and Sino-American Conflict, 1947–1958* (Princeton, NJ: Princeton University Press, 1996), 7
29. AGSA is a post hoc term for a process by analysts at the Naval War College's Center for Naval Warfare Studies while supporting the development of

A Cooperative Strategy for 21st Century Seapower (known as CS 21), the US Navy's top-end strategic vision announced in 2007. US Navy, US Marine Corps, and US Coast Guard, *Cooperative Strategy for 21st Century Seapower.*

30. Peter Dombrowski and Andrew C. Winner, "The United States Maritime Strategy and Implications for the Indo-Pacific Region," in *Australia and Its Maritime Interests: At Home and in the Region*, ed. Andrew Forbes (Canberra: Sea Power Centre–Australia, 2008), 67–93.

31. See, e.g., National Intelligence Council, *Global Trends 2030: Alternative Worlds* (Washington, DC: National Intelligence Council, 2012), www.dni.gov/index. php/about/organization/global-trends-2030; US Joint Forces Command, "Joint Operating Environment, 2010."

32. Barry R. Posen and Andrew L. Ross, "Competing Visions for Grand Strategy," *International Security* 21, no. 3 (Winter 1996–97): 5–53.

PART I

STRATEGY OPTIONS

≈

STRENGTHENING PARTNERS TO KEEP THE PEACE

A Neo-Nixon Doctrine for the Indian Ocean Region

WALTER C. LADWIG III

It has been suggested by some American foreign policy thinkers that the United States is approaching a watershed moment, comparable to the end of World War II or the Cold War in terms of the degree to which it will need to reorient its foreign and defense policies. Indeed, domestic economic weakness, the debilitating effects of two protracted counterinsurgency campaigns, and the rise of new powers in Asia are challenging its ability to maintain the unrivaled primacy it has possessed since the collapse of the Soviet Union.[1] Echoing fears of "imperial overstretch," where historically the economic unsustainability of extensive military commitments abroad has led great powers into decline, the chairman of the US Joint Chiefs of Staff has identified America's growing debt burden as the most significant threat to the country's national security.[2] As the Pentagon adapts to what some are calling a new age of austerity, over the next decade US defense spending is set to decline by at least $450 billion and potentially by as much as $1 trillion.[3] Normally, such budgetary weakness would be expected to herald a period of strategic restraint in American foreign policy, but US global commitments are not shrinking; indeed, they may expand further as the Obama administration reorients its attention toward Asia.[4]

Although arguments about American decline in the popular press are frequently overstated, in an environment of geopolitical uncertainty and fiscal austerity, attempting to do more with less requires a national security strategy to clearly distinguish the nation's vital interests from issues of secondary concern. Even a country that continues to think of itself as being the indispensable nation must recognize that not every development abroad affects an important US security interest. Excessive activity in a region of marginal national interest can stimulate resentment, squander scarce resources, and contribute to overextension. Conversely, making new commitments that are underresourced will contribute to perceptions of American impotence. The Obama administration has already committed the latter blunder with the announcement of the "pivot" to Asia, which has proved to be long on rhetoric and short on resources. Although only marginally increasing US military presence in the Asia-Pacific region, the move has simultaneously alienated Beijing while raising false expectations about American support among allies and potential partners in Southeast Asia. Sensible regional strategies solve diplomatic problems; they do not create them.

In the light of the conventional wisdom that the Indian Ocean is growing in economic and strategic importance, this chapter seeks to avoid the errors of the pivot by proposing a modest American regional strategy that calibrates the level of American effort in the region with the core security interests at stake. Rather than struggle against the emergence of new powers, the "Neo-Nixon Doctrine" proposed here embraces this trend by incorporating the Indian Ocean's emerging powers into a multipolar regional security architecture that promotes an open economic order and liberal-democratic values while minimizing the fiscal and military burden on the United States for ensuring regional stability. In doing so, this strategy prioritizes core US interests by not diverting scarce defense resources to a peripheral concern, while furthering the regional ambitions of local partners with the goal of forming a stable and enduring order in the Indian Ocean.

Unsurprisingly, the strategic approach outlined in this chapter shares elements with several of the other concepts contained in this volume; however, none recognizes the peripheral nature of the region for US interests and cultivates a regional order based on strengthening the capabilities of the region's leading democratic states in the manner described here. In chapter 4 of this volume, Christopher Preble shares many of the Neo-Nixon Doctrine's assumptions about the limited nature of US interests in the Indian Ocean region and echoes its call for local powers to take the lead role in providing regional security. The primary difference occurs in implementation; whereas Preble would largely devolve responsibility to India, this approach envisions a more proactive diplomatic role for the United States in shaping a regional architecture based on the region's four leading liberal democracies: Australia, India, Indonesia, and South Africa. Likewise, there are several superficial similarities between the approach described here and that proposed by Michael Auslin in chapter 7, particularly with respect to the focus on the Indian Ocean's leading liberal democratic states and the need to bolster local capacity to provide security. However, the differences outweigh the similarities.

Auslin implicitly assumes that the Indian Ocean is important to US strategic interests, whereas the Neo-Nixon Doctrine recognizes the region is peripheral to America. In contrast to the call for an enhanced and visible American military presence in the region, this approach favors a much more restrained role. Finally, given the vast size of the Indian Ocean region as well as the marked diversity of the states in the region in terms of their interests and power, this approach recognizes that it is difficult enough to craft a strategy for a single region without attempting to introduce the challenges of the Asia-Pacific region by linking them in the manner that Auslin does. Finally, in chapter 8 Schaffer's focus on coalition building for security in a manner that reinforces an open and inclusive regional architecture parallels the approach outlined here. However, though China is seen as an extraregional actor of potential concern, the Neo-Nixon Doctrine is not as China-centric as Schaffer's strategy. As a result, the focus of this approach is on cultivating the Indian Ocean's major democratic powers rather than wooing smaller states from Beijing's side.

THE INDIAN OCEAN: CENTER STAGE OR REGIONAL SIDESHOW?

As was noted in chapter 1, a host of scholars and analysts have joined Robert Kaplan in dubbing the Indian Ocean as the "center stage" of global politics in the twenty-first century.[5] Yet it is important to ask to what extent are US national security interests actually affected by developments in this potentially volatile region? The Indian Ocean has not traditionally held pride of place in US strategic thinking. Throughout the 1960s, American planners largely considered the Indian Ocean to be a backwater. Britain's dominance at sea, combined with its imperial role in South Asia, led the United States to regard the region as a British preserve.[6] In the early years of the Cold War, American strategy concentrated on the Atlantic and the Pacific Basin, because Western Europe and Japan were viewed as essential territory in the struggle against global communism, whereas American involvement in the Indian Ocean littoral consisted primarily of economic and military aid, rather than the deployment of military forces.[7] America's direct involvement only increased in the wake of British withdrawal from East of Suez in the late 1960s, which appeared to coincide with increased Soviet presence in East Africa and South Asia. The overthrow of the shah—which eliminated a key security buffer between the Soviet Union and the Persian Gulf—and the 1979 Soviet invasion of Afghanistan justified the heightened American concerns about the security of the region in the 1980s.

In the absence of the threat to the region posed by a hostile rival superpower such as the Soviet Union, the restrained approach toward the Indian Ocean pursued during the early Cold War period has much to commend it, because regional developments are unlikely to have a direct impact on the United States. Despite the above-mentioned importance of the Indian Ocean as an energy corridor, the United States itself is not significantly reliant on the region for access to hydrocarbons. Including marginal oil producers such as India, Australia, Malaysia, and Indonesia, the Indian Ocean region barely accounted for 15 percent of US oil imports in 2010.[8] In contrast, many of America's allies and key trading partners are highly dependent on the Indian Ocean for energy. To the east, Japan receives 90 percent of its oil imports via the Indian Ocean, while 75 percent of China's imports and 85 percent of India's oil imports transit the region.[9] Similarly, the economies of important American allies and partners in the Asia-Pacific region—such as Thailand, Singapore, the Philippines, Taiwan, and South Korea—all receive more than two-thirds of their hydrocarbon imports from the Gulf. To the west, roughly one-third of Europe's oil imports pass through the Indian Ocean.[10] Although the Indian Ocean region directly accounts for only a fraction of US oil imports, it can be argued that the region retains critical importance for American energy security because oil is a globally integrated commodity, and therefore a supply disruption anywhere would raise prices around the world, which would have an impact on US economic growth. Sensible though this argument may seem, it is based more on hyperbole than hard fact. Although generations of policymakers in the West have undoubtedly been scarred by the oil shocks of the 1970s, as Eugene Gholz and Daryl Press have demonstrated in great detail, the industrial world actually has sufficient oil reserves, in both government-controlled stocks and commercial inventories, to weather an oil supply disruption on par with the worst in history.[11] Moreover, there is evidence to suggest that the American economy is significantly less vulnerable to oil price shocks today than it was in the 1970s.[12] The energy security of the United States simply does not turn on developments in the Indian Ocean.

With respect to the goods trade, the Indian Ocean is also a far more important conduit for the nations of East Asia and Europe than it is for the United States. The Asia–Europe shipping route, via the Indian Ocean, is the world's largest containerized trading lane. Moreover, security scholars have noted that the European economy is "heavily reliant upon the timely unhindered movement of vessels in the waters between the Indian Ocean and the Suez Canal."[13] Despite the lack of direct exposure to the commerce of the Indian Ocean, analysts have suggested that, as the world's largest economy, the United States has a strong economic interest in the security of regional shipping because the globalized nature of commodity markets means that the American economy would feel the effects of any major tremors in the Indian Ocean.[14] Despite the purported effects of globalization in linking economies around the world, the actual vulnerability of the United States to this kind of threat is frequently overstated, in large part because true threats to international trade are quite small. Even in the case of a major regional war, the economic impact on a nonparticipating, large, open economy, such as the United States, is typically small in terms of capital flows, trade, and direct investment.[15] Thus, economic imperatives cannot justify a major American commitment to the Indian Ocean.

The strategic importance of the Indian Ocean region to the United States is not based on its direct impact on America but on its importance for key US allies and partners. As outlined by Christopher Layne, the United States' strategic priorities since the end of World War II have been to prevent a hostile peer competitor from dominating Western Europe and industrialized East Asia.[16] Insofar as developments in the Indian Ocean affect key US allies and partners in Europe and East Asia—which are dependent on the region's energy and trade flows—they are of importance to the United States. Therefore, the United States does have an interest and a role to play in promoting regional stability and security. However, given that regional developments have a far greater direct impact on the nations of Asia and Europe, the cost and effort to promote regional security must be in line with the actual scale of the economic and political costs the United States would have to bear in the event of significant instability. How can the United States best secure its interests in the Indian Ocean while promoting the well-being of its key allies and partners? By helping regional powers to help themselves.

A NEO-NIXON DOCTRINE FOR THE INDIAN OCEAN

Because the vital military and political interests of the United States do not require it to play a leading role in guaranteeing the security of the Indian Ocean littoral, the best means for achieving regional stability is to facilitate the emergence of a multipolar regional arrangement led by strong democratic states. Inspiration for this approach comes from a previous period of perceived "imperial overstretch" in the 1960s, when the Nixon administration grappled with America's deteriorating global position resulting from its protracted involvement in Vietnam. Popularly understood, the so-called Nixon Doctrine limited unconditional American security guarantees to smaller allies. Instead, these local partners were charged with the primary responsibility for providing for their own defense, which would be facilitated by American aid and advice.[17] Although in many ways a pragmatic response to global developments, a key shortcoming of the original Nixon Doctrine was its reliance on pro-Western autocrats, such as the shah of Iran, whose unstable political systems proved to be a poor foundation for an enduring regional security structure. In fact, the failure of the shah's regime actually set the stage for increased US regional involvement in the Persian Gulf, which is precisely what the Nixon Doctrine was seeking to avoid. In contrast, this proposed "Neo-Nixon Doctrine" would focus on cultivating the major Indian Ocean littoral nations that are free, democratic, and financially capable of being net providers of security in their region.[18] Consequently, this regional security architecture will be built on a significantly more solid foundation.

The four principal states on which to anchor the strategy are Australia, Indonesia, India, and South Africa. These countries increasingly possess the economic means and military capabilities necessary to provide for regional security, and each of these nations is also a presumptive hegemon in its respective subregion of the Indian Ocean littoral (Oceania, Southeast Asia, South Asia, and Southern Africa), which makes it natural for them to assume a leading role in regional security. In explicitly seeking to foster the emergence of a robust multipolar security structure that can contain most security threats without direct US involvement, this strategy of self-interested altruism leverages the primary geopolitical trend in the region—namely, the emergence of second-tier powers. By putting liberal democracies—who have a shared interest in maintaining an open economic order and minimizing great power conflict—at the center of this arrangement, US regional goals can be advanced by encouraging local powers to pursue their own national interests. This core of major littoral powers can also provide a foundation for multilateral efforts that bring both regional and extraregional actors together to address issues of collective concern, such as energy security and the free transit of goods.

As with the original Nixon Doctrine, capacity building of regional partners is the primary means by which the United States can facilitate security in the Indian Ocean region. Developing these countries' military strength in a manner that would allow them to emerge as independent regional actors would be the primary focus of American efforts. In particular, arms sales and technology transfers would seek to enhance their capability to secure their own territory, police their immediate region, and deter intervention by hostile powers. This requires the deployment of defensive weapons systems for safeguarding territory such as maritime surveillance aircraft and unmanned aerial vehicles; antisubmarine warfare platforms; advanced air defense systems; diesel-electric submarines; long-range antiship missiles; and smart naval mines. Patrolling and policing further from home would be facilitated by an expanded expeditionary capability, which requires both airborne and naval tankers. Given the notable effectiveness of amphibious platforms in responding to regional humanitarian crises, expanding the number of amphibious ships in partner navies should be a priority.[19]

It is significantly easier to convince a foreign partner to acquire a system or technology that America feels is most appropriate to its needs if such items are given as grants, rather than attempting to persuade the partner to purchase the particular item through arms sales. The reality of a strategy designed to facilitate regional security by local powers is that they know it is in the US interest to help build their capacity. As a result, they may be less likely to purchase the types of systems the United States advises them to acquire with their own funds if they believe that the United States will gift these to them anyway. Although this kind of free riding is not optimal, subsidizing the military capacity of local partners can be more cost-effective than taking the lead in providing regional security, particularly because the manpower, operations, and maintenance costs of the additional military capability would be borne by the local country.

A key advantage of this strategy is that it furthers the interests of local powers while also securing American aims. US aid would enhance their power and facilitate their order-producing role in their respective subregion, both of which would boost their claim to major power status. In many respects, the United States would simply be encouraging an extension of existing behavior. For example, of its own initiative, the South African navy has undertaken antipiracy patrols in the Mozambique gap, while the Indian Navy has patrolled off the coast of Madagascar and Mozambique as well as in the Gulf of Oman, and worked to enhance the coast guard capacity of several small island nations in the Indian Ocean, such as the Maldives and the Seychelles.

Although American partners in the Indian Ocean focus on providing local security, the United States could concentrate on maintaining control over the global commons.[20] This would help ensure that the local partners retain unfettered access to the global trading system, beyond the reach of their individual militaries. Rather than undertake a large-scale forward deployment of forces in the Indian Ocean, the United States would carefully husband its own military power, intervening only if the leading local powers proved incapable of managing regional security on their own. This does not mean that the United States would completely withdraw its military presence from the region; however, maritime forces and air power based offshore, rather than forward deployed ground forces, would constitute the bulk of American military presence in the region. Joint training and bilateral/multilateral military exercises would also be an important focus of American efforts both to strengthen local military capability as well as to deepen interoperability with regional forces in case US intervention should ever be necessary. Continued political and military engagement will also be necessary to preserve access to a network of forward operating bases that would facilitate US power projection into the region in case of a major contingency.

With respect to irregular security challenges in the region, American nuclear nonproliferation efforts would continue unabated. Ideally, regional security cooperation would extend to nuclear matters in a manner that addresses the concerns of countries such as South Africa, India, and Indonesia, who have previously resisted joining multilateral efforts like the Proliferation Security Initiative. At the same time, insofar as nuclear proliferation by states in the Indian Ocean region is driven by security concerns vis-à-vis the United States, a restrained US posture could reduce some of that anxiety. With respect to terrorism, the capacity-building focus of this strategic approach could extend to the counterterrorism realm, and to states beyond the democratic major powers, wherever the contacts, local knowledge, and language skills of foreign police and intelligence services are best positioned and willing to uncover and disrupt terrorist groups. The United States can bolster such agencies through training, equipment, and technical support—the latter of which is America's comparative advantage—and can act as a key force multiplier without an overtly visible presence. Ideally, counterterrorism efforts would be handled by local governments, but should they prove unable to act, the United States would be prepared to assist with air strikes or small-scale raids carried out by special operations forces stationed at low-profile remote bases in the region. To the extent that anti-American terrorism is fostered by the visible presence of US forces in key countries in the region, an Indian Ocean strategy that minimizes the "footprint" of US forces would reduce that source of antagonism.[21]

Diplomatic Measures

In addition to strengthening the capability of individual states, the United States must facilitate the deepening and broadening of existing political and security relationships among India, South Africa, Indonesia, and Australia in a manner that would enable them to manage regional crises in partnership. Rather than starting from scratch, however, this effort capitalizes on the existing ties that these countries have already forged with each other. For example, India currently has strategic partnerships with Australia and Indonesia and has sought to deepen its defense cooperation with South Africa through joint military training, whereas Australia and Indonesia are each other's most important foreign policy partners in the region.

Although the United States can leverage its own bilateral relationships with these states to promote regional cooperation, the goal is not to recreate the East Asian hub-and-spokes alliance system. Instead, the objective is to foster regional linkages that can enhance political coordination and contingency planning to the point where joint or multilateral operations could be readily undertaken in the absence of direct US leadership. The first step in the process would be a series of bilateral and multilateral discussions among Canberra, Delhi, Jakarta, and Pretoria on issues of common concern. Some dyads of countries will have far more in common than others. For example, though direct cooperation between Indonesia and South Africa may be too distant a prospect to contemplate at present, both Australia and Indonesia cooperate closely on regional challenges including counterterrorism, people smuggling, and transnational crime, and India and South Africa have both taken steps to enhance the maritime security of the smaller island nations of the Indian Ocean off the coast of Africa. Growing out of this bilateral cooperation, regular multilateral exercises can promote interoperability, intelligence cooperation, and shared threat perception. Modeled on the Milan series of naval exercises organized by India, these should include other littoral nations (Malaysia, Thailand, and Singapore) and like-minded extraregional actors (Japan and South Korea), with the ultimate aim of converting these regular maneuvers into a full-fledged joint task force for the Indian Ocean. Military-to-military exchanges of officers from these target countries should be significantly increased, with specific attention given to developing bilateral ties not only between the United States and the next generation of military leaders in the target country, but also among the future military leaders of the major regional democracies.

Although there is a strong normative element to basing a regional security strategy around a core of liberal democracies, the goal is not to form an ideological bloc in the Indian Ocean, nor is the success of this approach predicated on changing the domestic political arrangements of key Indian Ocean states. Instead, it attempts to forge a lasting regional security architecture that blends realist and idealist considerations by putting at its core the leading economic and military powers in the various subregions of the Indian Ocean who also share a common commitment to upholding international norms and common interests with respect to regional security, which are important for both maintaining stability in the region and ensuring long-term cooperation. Other nations or extraregional powers, who are concerned with the security and stability of the Indian Ocean, would be welcome to contribute to these efforts provided they embrace these established norms for managing the sea-lanes and airspace of the littoral region. Thus the preference for liberal democratic regimes in this approach is a pragmatic choice based on their stability and preferences for an open regional order.

Multilateral Security Initiatives

Dissimilar capabilities and divergent priorities have generally prevented pan-Indian Ocean multilateral forums from developing into strong institutions. However, both India and Australia have historically been enthusiastic proponents of regional organizations.[22] The United States should attempt to channel both countries' efforts into the leadership of a regional collective security effort, by working through an existing organization which has the legitimacy of indigenous origins that a more blatantly American-fostered effort would lack.

One institution with particular promise is the recently established Indian Ocean Naval Symposium (IONS). This Indian initiative, open to naval chiefs from each country in the region, provides a forum for the heads of regional navies to discuss maritime security concerns. At the regional level, IONS can assist in promoting collective action among member states and can serve as a model for similar groupings of chiefs of the army, air force, and even police. The United States should support IONS by encouraging Australia, Indonesia, and South

Africa to host future symposia to give the nascent institution staying power and a broader endorsement from the leading navies of the region. It should also encourage leading nations to give IONS institutional roots by establishing a permanent secretariat to both channel and sustain organizational initiatives.

The United States should also encourage IONS members to create a second broader forum, which includes extra-regional actors as dialogue partners, to foster real discussion among key stakeholders in the Indian Ocean. An "IONS +" that included the United States, Russia, China, Japan, South Korea, Singapore, France, and the United Kingdom would provide an opportunity for interested nations to focus on common concerns such as energy security and piracy in the Indian Ocean. Meaningful engagement on these "small" security issues could facilitate the kind of diplomatic intercourse and information sharing that can reduce the mistrust and doubt which presently exists among some regional and extraregional powers. Moreover, active membership of a regional cooperative security organization would be a key way for major regional and extra-regional powers to demonstrate their benign intentions and support for the regional status quo.

The focus on IONS does not mean that other regional institutions are irrelevant. The Indian Ocean Rim Association for Regional Cooperation (IOR-ARC) is sometimes discussed as a candidate for a pan–Indian Ocean forum. However, the IOR-ARC is limited by its inadequate budget, weak institutional capacity, and a lack of regional leadership. Moreover, the organization traditionally focuses on trade liberalization, investment facilitation, and promoting technical cooperation among member states, rather than security issues. Although cooperation in these areas is undoubtedly important for promoting regional integration over the long term, for the purposes of this strategy the IOR-ARC and similar subregional organizations will play a supporting role at best.

ENGAGING MAJOR REGIONAL POWERS

Implementing the Neo-Nixon Doctrine in the Indian Ocean will require American policymakers to adopt a new mindset, because unlike in East Asia, the majority of the proposed partner states are not treaty allies of the United States. Washington will have to become comfortable with the notion that these counties will follow foreign policies based on their own self-interest, which will converge with the United States in some areas and possibly diverge in others. Moreover, it should be recognized ahead of time that as the United States succeeds in strengthening these states, their foreign policy autonomy may grow. However, on balance, strong democratic states in the Indian Ocean with the military means to defend themselves and provide for security will foster a regional order that is in keeping with US interests.

India

Within the Indian Ocean, India emerges as the fulcrum of the Neo-Nixon Doctrine because it can play a role in key subregions such as South Asia, Southeast Asia, East Africa, and, to an extent, the Persian Gulf. With the largest indigenous navy in the region, as India's economy continues to achieve record economic growth, its interest in maintaining good order at sea and protecting the region's sea lines is converging with that of other trading nations.[23] New Delhi has already demonstrated a desire to play a leading role in Indian Ocean security, and cooperation on regional security could be the "next big thing" to drive forward Indo–US relations. In bolstering India's naval capacity—beyond the systems discussed above—the United States should consider sharing naval nuclear technology. Because India has already managed to construct an indigenous test-bed nuclear submarine, assistance from the United States should be actively extended to help jump start India's naval nuclear propulsion program, either by loaning a nuclear submarine for experimentation as the Russians have done or engaging in direct technology collaboration. This would facilitate the emergence of a true blue-water Indian Navy which could undertake sea lane security missions far from home. The Neo-Nixon Doctrine will have a high degree of synergy with India's regional ambitions by supporting New Delhi's clear emergence as the legitimate hegemon in South Asia and the leading power in the Indian Ocean region.

Indonesia

Given its size, economic strength, and natural role as the leading state in the Southeast Asia subregion, Indonesia is an obvious focal point of American attention. This is particularly true in light of the democratic consolidation that has taken place there since 2004, while traditional American partners in the region such as the Philippines and Thailand have struggled with democracy and human rights. Although not comparable to the Indian and Australian navies, the Indonesian navy is more than capable of defending its exclusive economic zone.[24] Moreover, it shares the interests of the United States and other major regional powers in both ensuring the free trade of goods and suppressing piracy. In terms of bilateral ties with other leading Indian Ocean nations, Australia and Indonesia each recognize the other as being one of their most important bilateral partners, while India and Indonesia have forged a strategic relationship. The Neo-Nixon Doctrine would facilitate two key goals for Indonesia: achieving closer security cooperation with the United States and playing a greater role in international affairs. Although the United States and Indonesia have a common interest in arresting the spread of violent extremism and managing geopolitical change in the Indo-Pacific, which can provide an impetus for closer cooperation, it will take time to strengthen the bilateral partnership. Focusing on broad areas of common interest, as the Neo-Nixon Doctrine does, is the best way to take the relationship forward.

Australia

Australia is a treaty ally of the United States and possesses a navy with a powerful regional force projection capability, perhaps only exceeded in the Indian Ocean by that of India.[25] Moreover, it has strengthened its security ties with Indonesia and India has emerged as its second most important bilateral link in the entire littoral region. Because it is not viewed as a security threat, Canberra also has a significant ability to forge partnerships with many key Indian Ocean littoral nations.[26] This puts Australia in a position to expand the breadth and scope of its maritime surveillance and patrolling into the eastern Indian Ocean. However, inducing Australia to assume a more robust role in the Indian Ocean may pose some diplomatic challenges. Although Australia possesses one of the largest exclusive economic zones in the Indian Ocean, it has traditionally neglected this region in favor of the Asia-Pacific region as the focus of its foreign policy. Moreover, though Australia has a strong interest in not seeing the Indian Ocean become an arena of great power competition, the country's dependence on China as a market for its raw materials has made some of its leadership wary of actions that could be construed as contributing to the containment of China. Nevertheless, the United States' plans to increase its military presence in Australia and in the broader Asia-Pacific region has bipartisan support in Australia, which suggests that Australia will be willing to share more of the burden in maintaining an open regional order.[27]

South Africa

Alongside India and Australia, South Africa has traditionally been a regional leader in its corner of the Indian Ocean. However, in recent years its attention has increasingly been focused on internal issues and on continental Africa. Strategically located along the Cape of Good Hope—the favorite route for oil tankers too large to transit the Suez Canal—South Africa is the only Sub-Saharan African country with the ability to carry out meaningful antipiracy operations in its subregion. Although the South African navy has been undertaking antipiracy efforts in the southeastern Indian Ocean, these operations are severely constrained by current budgetary limitations. It may be worthwhile for the United States to consider partially financing South Africa's efforts to combat piracy and patrol its adjacent sea lanes. Although US–South African ties are notionally cordial, Pretoria tends to support nations with views that are not in sync with the West. Nevertheless, this foreign policy orientation poses less of a problem for the Neo-Nixon Doctrine because the strategic approach does not attempt to cajole South Africa to follow a

Western agenda, but rather empower it to contribute to Indian Ocean security by doing what it is already doing.

REGIONAL CONSIDERATIONS

Although a strategy for the entire Indian Ocean region is the focus of this chapter, it needs to be recognized that there will necessarily be some subregional differences in strategy application across this widely varied and geographically expansive area. At the very least, consideration needs to be given to differences between the eastern and western portions of the Indian Ocean.

The Eastern Indian Ocean

Coordination and cooperation among the respective navies of Australia, India, and Indonesia will help ensure the free transit of shipping through the vital choke points of the Malacca and Lombok Straits. The United States can encourage and support these efforts by sharing intelligence, surveillance, and reconnaissance data with the three countries to create full-spectrum maritime domain awareness in the eastern reaches of the Indian Ocean. India has already undertaken coordinated patrolling of the northern approaches of the Strait of Malacca with Indonesia. Expanding that effort to include more regular Indian–Indonesian combined patrols, Indonesian–Australian patrolling in the vicinity of Lombok, as well as intelligence sharing and combined exercises, can help ensure that the sea lanes in the eastern stretches of the Indian Ocean are secure.

The Western Indian Ocean

Although the India–Indonesia–Australia triad brings together the most capable nations in the region to focus on the eastern Indian Ocean, there is no similar configuration of leading states to the west of the ocean. Because Europe directly benefits from oil transiting the Cape, the EU or individual member states might become a source of financial support for the South African navy. The French in particular could emerge as a security partner for South Africa. France maintains a permanent military presence in the region—including more than a dozen naval vessels—through its overseas territories in the southern Indian Ocean and bases in Djibouti and Abu Dhabi. Moreover, it has been conducting antipiracy operations off the coast of East Africa since 2005. Paris and Pretoria already undertake joint military exercises, including antipiracy training, and are looking to deepen bilateral cooperation in the southern Indian Ocean. France also has good relations with India—to whom it has supplied advanced conventional submarines— and has bilateral agreements with Australia which facilitate surveillance and law enforcement operations in their adjoining territorial waters in the southern Indian Ocean.[28]

Between India and South Africa, there is a notable gap in the Persian Gulf region. In the short term the United States must still play an active role in providing security in this zone. Achieving American security goals in the Persian Gulf—which center on preventing major hydrocarbon reserves coming under the control of a hostile power—does not require the maintenance of forward ground forces. With the three contenders for regional leadership—Saudi Arabia, Iran, and Iraq—all strong enough to defend themselves but too weak to mount a bid for regional hegemony, the status quo is relatively safe. If necessary, the United States can provide security assistance to enable local states to balance each other and to block the rise of a single region-dominating power. However, the primary security function carried out by the United States in the region should be to oppose any violation of the territorial integrity of any major oil-producing state, which can be accomplished with a naval presence and intervention forces that are not stationed in theater.

AMERICA'S ENABLING CAPABILITIES

The Neo-Nixon Doctrine does not require the United States to maintain a significant peacetime military presence in the Indian Ocean littoral region. Those assets which are forward deployed, mainly from the Air Force and the Navy, will be key capability enablers for the local powers America is assisting. Given the United States military's comparative advantage in intelligence, surveillance, and reconnaissance, the deployment, for example, of long-range high-endurance unmanned aerial vehicles such as the RQ-4 Global Hawk and the MQ-4C Triton maritime surveillance platform can facilitate common domain awareness. At sea, the US Navy would maintain a carrier equivalent in the northwestern Indian Ocean, combined with a robust deployment of guided-missile submarines which can prolong time on station by leveraging the submarine tender and crew swap facilities at Diego Garcia. In terms of the air force, the main focus would be on strategic air lift, long-range bombers, and tankers that stage through forward bases. In the event a direct American intervention is required, attack submarines would be valuable tools for seizing and maintaining command of the sea so that the United States could use major sea lines to surge forces from out of theater to assist partner nations.

Preserving the capability to surge forces into the region in a contingency puts a premium on the prepositioning of equipment stocks as well as ensuring access to forward operating sites that can facilitate power projection. The United States already has access to facilities on the rim of the Indian Ocean, such as the headquarters of the Fifth Fleet in Bahrain, the air force's facility at Al Udeid in Qatar, a military presence in Djibouti on the African continent, and Changi Naval Base in Singapore on the far side of the Strait of Malacca. The Neo-Nixon Doctrine does not require an extensive network of permanent US bases in the region. However, the ability to surge forces would be enhanced by contingency access to air and naval bases or cooperative security locations in Indonesia, Sri Lanka, India's Andaman and Nicobar islands, Australia's Cocos (Keeling) Islands, HMAS Stirling on the west coast of Australia, and the Seychelles.

Diego Garcia emerges as an important hub in this regard. The island facilitates US power projection through the prepositioning of US Army and US Marine Corps brigade sets, long-range bomber operations that stage through the facility's runway, the replenishment of naval surface combatants, and the strike and special operations capabilities of guided-missile submarines that can call at the atoll's wharf. The US government must take proactive steps to ensure continued access to this facility after the present lease agreement with the British government expires in 2016.

RISKS AND UNCERTAINTIES

There are several risks inherent in a regional strategy that empowers local actors to maintain regional security. However, upon close examination, none appears so serious as to render the proposed Neo-Nixon Doctrine unworkable.

First, it might be the case that the leading countries of the region are uninterested in assuming a regional leadership role or providing regional public goods in the manner described. This issue is most salient with respect to India, where the government has historically resisted proposals for multilateral security dialogues that are not initiated by the United Nations or a broad based regional grouping. However, all four of the leading democratic states in the region have previously undertaken efforts to provide security in their respective subregions as well as to forge strategic ties with each other. The Neo-Nixon Doctrine simply requires more of the same. Moreover, for states concerned about preserving their strategic autonomy, this proposal does not necessarily require a formal multilateral structure. At a minimum, it would be sufficient to expand existing cooperation so that a joint crisis response—such as the unprecedented cooperation between the Indian and Australian navies in the wake of the 2004 Boxing Day tsunami—can be conducted efficiently.

A second related concern is that the state of bilateral relations between the major democratic powers in the region, or between those countries and the United States, precludes the kind of cooperation required. Indonesian–Australian ties, for example, have peaked and troughed over the past decade. Yet that has not prevented the two governments from deepening their security ties in the interim. Indeed, the opportunity to cooperate on regional security matters provides a new forum for the pursuit of common interests, which may give an impetus to bilateral relationships, such as the one between Jakarta and Canberra.[29] Similarly, America's ability to cooperate with and assist India over the past decade has been constrained by Washington's dependence on Pakistan for logistical support of its military operations in Afghanistan. However, as the United States moves to draw down its role in Afghanistan, the divergence of strategic interests between Washington and Islamabad has become clear.[30] Although the United States will continue to require cooperation from Pakistan, regional policy will undoubtedly focus on the convergence of its interests with India.

Third, critics may argue that a restrained regional role could embolden a local revisionist state or an extraregional power to challenge the status quo. Doubts about America's willingness to intervene in a major crisis could lead local powers to bandwagon with, rather than balance against, such challengers. These concerns are valid. However, because the Indian Ocean has never been a theater of primary importance for the United States, American restraint would not be considered as significant a sign of decline or disinterest as it would be in East Asia or Western Europe. Moreover, concerns that local powers might bandwagon with challengers in the absence of a major US presence overlook these states' own interests and capabilities. Uncertainty about American intentions actually provides an incentive for them to develop their own military capabilities, which would further US goals.

A fourth possible concern is that the "self-reliance" expected of major regional powers may lead to the development of nuclear weapons, which runs contrary to US nonproliferation policy. This is indeed a possibility, but it must be recognized that a major US regional presence also has the potential to encourage other littoral countries to seek nuclear weapons. Moreover, as the United States tacitly acknowledged in its nuclear deal with India, the development of nuclear weapons by a democratic state for self-defense is not the same as proliferation by a revisionist state.

Fifth, it could be argued that the bolstering of the military capabilities of certain states in the region might alarm some of their smaller neighbors. It should be noted, however, that the majority of the weapons systems to be transferred to local partners are defensive in nature. Moreover, the counties being assisted are democratic states, which have already demonstrated the ability to be responsible stakeholders through their own efforts to contribute to regional security. Although enhancing the military capability of leading states may cause some anxiety, it is certainly balanced by the reduced tensions associated with a more subdued American presence.

A sixth potential criticism is that the United States is so far removed from the region that unless American forces were forward deployed, they would be unable to respond to a major crisis in a timely manner. However, because the first-responder role under this strategy is devolved to local states—with the United States intervening only if they fail—the likelihood of a crisis requiring an immediate American response is very remote. Moreover, prepositioned stocks of equipment in theater, such as the US Army and US Marine Corps brigade sets at Diego Garcia, can accelerate the response. Historically the United States has been able to deter further military action by revisionist states in the region with only symbolic "tripwire" forces, such as the elements of the Eighty-Second Airborne that were deployed to Saudi Arabia in the immediate aftermath of Saddam Hussein's 1990 invasion of Kuwait.

Finally, there is a concern that when the United States relies on other countries to advance its interests, they often end up advancing their own instead. The key fact to emphasize is that America's regional interests are well aligned with those of the major states of the Indian Ocean region. At its core, this strategic approach is based on the belief that on aggregate, the preferences of the region's leading democratic states will intersect with America's foreign policy goals. Moreover, it is assumed that these states are more likely to cooperate with each other to maintain stability and provide regional public goods (such as sea-lane security) in a manner that enhances collective security in a mutually beneficial manner. Although disagreements may occur over tactics or the relative priority given to a particular issue, the desired end state is largely similar.

CONCLUSION

The security and stability of the Indian Ocean not only benefits the nations of the immediate littoral region, but also America's European and Asian allies, and therefore the United States itself. In approaching this region of extrinsic importance, the resources and effort that Washington dedicates must align with the real security interests at stake. Rather than take the lead in guaranteeing regional security, the United States should help the leading democratic states of the region to help themselves.

Strengthening the capacities of Australia, India, Indonesia, and South Africa to more effectively police their immediate regions advances America's regional goals while limiting its involvement in conflicts and crises that are peripheral to core American interests. Moreover, by supporting and strengthening the natural hegemons in the various subregions of the Indian Ocean littoral in their efforts to secure their own interests, American power is more likely to be viewed as a force for good. If properly bolstered by the United States, this core of democratic powers can deter any revisionist state that may seek to overturn the regional status quo. Cooperative security efforts channeled through an indigenous regional security organization—incorporating regional and extra-regional stakeholders—can both assist the collective efforts to respond to low-level regional instability, such as piracy, and provide a platform for the major powers active in the Indian Ocean region to discuss their interests and concerns in a manner that can ameliorate tensions. The sum total of these efforts would lay a solid foundation for an enduring regional order that enhances stability and prosperity for all nations in the region.

NOTES

An earlier version of this chapter appeared in *Strategic Analysis* 36, no. 3 (May 2012): 384–99. E.g., see the comments of the cochairman of the President's Intelligence Advisory Board, David Boren, in "Panetta's Pentagon, without the Blank Check," by Peter Baker, *New York Times*, October 23, 2011.

1. For a discussion of the significance of this, see Samuel P. Huntington, "Why International Primacy Matters," *International Security* 17, no. 4 (Spring 1993).
2. "Mullen: Debt Is Top National Security Threat," CNN, August 27, 2010, http:// articles.cnn.com/2010-08-27/us/debt.security.mullen_1_pentagon-budget-national-debt-michael-mullen?_s=PM:US. For the classic treatment of imperial overstretch, see Paul Kennedy, *The Rise and Fall of Great Powers* (New York: Vintage, 1980), 514–15.
3. Baker, "Panetta's Pentagon"; Charles Keyes, "Dire Warnings from Pentagon Over Potential Defence Cuts," CNN.com, November 14, 2011.
4. Mike Mullen, testimony before the Committee on Armed Services, US Senate, February 17, 2011, http://armed-services.senate.gov/Transcripts/2011/02%20 February/11-04%20-%202-17-11.pdf; Elisabeth Bumiller, "US Pivots Eastward to Address Uneasy Allies," *New York Times*, October 24, 2011.
5. Robert Kaplan, "Center Stage for the 21st Century: Power Plays in the Indian Ocean," *Foreign Affairs* 88, no. 2 (March–April 2009).
6. Gary Sick, "The Evolution of US Strategy towards the Indian Ocean and Persian Gulf Regions," in *The Great Game: Rivalry in the Persian Gulf and South Asia*, ed. Alvin Z. Rubinstein (New York: Praeger, 1983), 49–50.
7. Rasul Rais, *The Indian Ocean and the Superpowers* (Totowa, NJ: Barnes & Noble, 1987), 37.
8. "US Imports by Country of Origin," US Energy Information Administration, www.eia.gov/petroleum/data.cfm.
9. Kaplan, "Center Stage for the 21st Century," 20; "China's Crude Oil Import Data," March 2010, http://data.chinaoilweb.com/crude-oil-import-data/latest .htm; "India," US Energy Information Administration, November 21, 2011, www.eia.gov/countries.
10. Neena Rai, "Somali Pirates Threaten European Oil Supply," *The Source* (*Wall Street Journal*), July 22, 2011, http://blogs.wsj.com/source/2011/07/22/ somali-pirates-threaten-european-oil-security.
11. Eugene Gholz and Daryl G. Press, "Protecting 'The Prize': Oil and the National Interest," paper presented at the annual meeting of the International Studies

Association, Le Centre Sheraton Hotel, Montreal, March 17, 2004; Eugene Gholz and Daryl G. Press, *Energy Alarmism: The Myths That Make Americans Worry about Oil*, Cato Institute Policy Analysis 589, April 5, 2007.

12. Olivier J. Blanchard and Jordi Gali, *The Macroeconomic Effects of Oil Price Shocks: Why Are the 2000s So Different from the 1970s?* MIT Department of Economics Working Paper 07-21, August 2007, www.crei.cat/people/gali/pdf_files/bgoil07wp.pdf; Paul Edelstein and Lutz Kilian, *Retail Energy Prices and Consumer Expenditures*, CEPR Discussion Paper DP6255, April 2007, http://ideas.repec.org/p/cpr/ceprdp/6255.html.

13. Christopher Spearin, quoted by Rai, "Somali Pirates Threaten European Oil Supply;" United Nations Conference on Trade and Development, *Review of Maritime Transport 2008* (New York: United Nations, 2008), 23.

14. James R. Holmes, Andrew C. Winner, and Toshi Yoshihara, *Indian Naval Strategy in the Twenty-First Century* (London: Routledge, 2009), 108.

15. Eugene Gholz and Daryl G. Press, "The Effects of Wars on Neutral Countries: Why It Doesn't Pay to Preserve the Peace," *Security Studies* 10, no. 4 (Summer 2001): 1–57.

16. Christopher Layne, *The Peace of Illusions: American Grand Strategy from 1940 to the Present* (Ithaca, NY: Cornell University Press, 2006), 27, 45.

17. For a detailed examination of the Nixon Doctrine, see Jeffrey Kimball, "The Nixon Doctrine: A Saga of Misunderstanding," *Presidential Studies Quarterly* 36, no. 1 (March 2006).

18. This is as measured by Freedom House, the Polity IV database, and membership in the Group of Twenty.

19. Walter C. Ladwig III, "Drivers of Indian Naval Expansion," in *The Rise of the Indian Navy: Internal Vulnerabilities, External Challenges*, ed. Harsh V. Pant (Farnham, UK: Ashgate, 2012), 32.

20. On the importance of this, see Barry R. Posen, "Command of the Commons: The Military Foundation of US Hegemony," *International Security* 28, no. 1 (Summer 2003).

21. For an argument to this effect, see Robert A. Pape and James K. Feldman, *Cutting the Fuse: The Explosion of Global Suicide Terrorism and How to Stop It* (Chicago: University of Chicago Press, 2010).

22. Regarding multilateral institutions in the Indian Ocean region, one Australian think tank judges that "there's nothing in the [Indian Ocean region] even remotely comparable with forums such as APEC, the Pacific Economic Cooperation Council, or the Pacific Islands Forum with its strong associated bodies, such as the Forum Fisheries Agency." Sam Bateman and Anthony Bergin, eds., *Our Western Front: Australia and the Indian Ocean* (Canberra: Australian Strategic Policy Institute, 2010), 33.

23. Nirupama Rao, "Future Directions in India–US Relations," speech given at Yale University, October 2, 2011; Integrated Headquarters, Ministry of Defence–Navy, *Freedom to Use the Seas: India's Maritime Military Strategy* (New Delhi: Ministry of Defence, 2007), 54, 96; Integrated Headquarters, Ministry of Defence–Navy,

Indian Maritime Doctrine (New Delhi: Ministry of Defence, 2004), 63–64. For a discussion of Indian naval capabilities, see Walter C. Ladwig III, "India and Military Power Projection: Will the Land of Gandhi Become a Conventional Great Power?" *Asian Survey* 50, no. 6 (November–December 2010): 1173–76.

24. James Goldrick and Jack McCaffrie, *Navies of South-East Asia: A Comparative Study* (Abingdon: Routledge, 2012), 12.

25. Eric Grove, *The Future of Sea Power* (London: Routledge, 1990), 238.

26. Bateman and Bergin, *Our Western Front*, 47.

27. Jackie Calmes, "A Marine Base for Australia Irritates China," *New York Times*, November 17, 2011.

28. A cluster of archipelagos and volcanic islands located southeast and east of Africa, known collectively as the "French Southern and Antarctic Lands," provides France with territorial claims in the southern Indian Ocean and Antarctica.

29. For the claim that the Indonesian-Australian relationship has "plateaued," see Fergus Hanson, *Indonesia and Australia: Time for a Step Change* (Sydney: Lowy Institute, 2010), 13.

30. Leon E. Panetta and Mike Mullen, Testimony before the Committee on Armed Services, US Senate, September 22, 2011, www.jcs.mil/speech.aspx?ID=1651.

CHAPTER 3

Reformulating a Grand Strategy in the Indian Ocean Region

The Case of Containment

WILLIAM C. MARTEL

This chapter examines whether the United States should formulate a grand strategy of containment for dealing with developments in the Indian Ocean region (IOR) for the present and future. This analysis focuses primarily on security and economic issues in the IOR that pose the greatest threats to US interests—notably how the forces of extremism, the risks of proliferation, the rise of great powers such as China, and the prospect of confrontation threaten peace, security, and prosperity in the region. Although various policymakers and scholars have advanced other grand strategy formulas, this chapter critically evaluates the ability of a strategy of containment to support and advance US interests in the IOR. The critical element here is whether such a strategy will help American policymakers deal with the political, military, economic, and alliance challenges posed by the rise of China; the emergence of India as a critical regional power; the risks posed by extremism and the proliferation of weapons of mass destruction in the region; and threats that could put at risk the IOR's growing contribution to global economic prosperity.

In theory, a strategy of containment should help contain the risks to US interests and values posed by various states, groups, movements, and developments in the IOR while simultaneously limiting or moderating those forces that threaten the US strategic interest in peace, security, and prosperity. Furthermore, containment should use political, economic, and military instruments of power and persuasion to help the IOR evolve in a positive and peaceful direction while minimizing the risks to US interests and values. Although it derives from the US grand strategy of containment that emerged during the Cold War, an updated strategy of containment will not be effective when it must handle several different categories of problems, as explained below.

With this as background, this chapter examines five central questions about the IOR from the perspective of a grand strategy of containment. First, what are the origins of containment strategy? Second, what is containment designed to handle, what precisely do we seek to contain, and why is a grand strategy of containment appropriate on some levels for dealing with the threats and opportunities the United States faces in the IOR? Third, why is the current US strategy for the IOR inadequate, and in what ways does it insufficiently inform US policy? Fourth, what risks and uncertainties, and also strengths and weaknesses, affect a grand strategy of containment for the IOR? Fifth, and finally, what overall conclusions should policymakers and scholars derive from containment as a framework for guiding US policy in the region? A central argument of this chapter is that many weaknesses of containment would make it inappropriate for addressing the myriad challenges that the United States faces in the region.

This chapter first explores why it is imperative for policymakers and scholars to reexamine the nature of the United States' grand strategy in the IOR.[1] In January 2012 the Obama administration declared that the United States would engage in a "pivot" in its strategy toward Asia. Although some might argue that the United States does not have a coherent grand strategy for the region at present, the emerging importance of the IOR and the US pivot to Asia suggest that US policymakers are reformulating the country's grand strategy to ensure that it is capable of dealing more effectively with the challenges to the vital US security and economic interests that face this region. This research raises two broader questions about US grand strategy. First, does the United States need to reformulate and articulate its *overall* grand strategy; and second, does the United States need to formulate a grand strategy *for the IOR*? The purpose of this chapter is to focus on the latter question, of how to formulate a grand strategy for dealing with the IOR.

The increasingly central role that the IOR plays in the global economy reinforces the reason why great powers and regional powers alike should pay much closer attention to the region and be heavily involved in formulating policies for the future. Policymakers should keep in mind that the highly divergent political, economic, and security interests among the states in the IOR can be a source of crises and confrontations that affect security. To avoid an IOR that is plagued with such confrontation and conflict, American policymakers must instead strive to develop a regional system of competition and cooperation.

CURRENT GRAND STRATEGY INSUFFICIENTLY INFORMS US POLICY IN THE IOR

The central problem is that the current US strategy does not adequately inform the policymakers who are responsible for dealing with the challenges in the IOR. Because this is an area of increasing importance for the United States, this chapter examines how some elements of containment, as formulated at the outset of the Cold War in the late 1940s, can provide useful guidance for US policymakers as they manage a complex array of political, economic, and military challenges to US interests. Thus, it is useful to examine the ways in which containment both helps and hinders how the United States manages challenges and opportunities in the IOR.

At present, the current US grand strategy does not sufficiently inform US policy in the IOR. One reason is the large number of conceptual shifts in American foreign policy that have occurred across four presidential administrations since the late 1980s.[2] The George H. W. Bush administration emphasized the search for new concepts to guide policy—including "status quo plus," "beyond containment," and "postcontainment," among others—and thus to describe the nature of US strategy as the Soviet Union collapsed in the midst of broad hopes for "a new era of international stability."[3] The Bill Clinton administration focused on political engagement and the enlargement of the number of democratic, free market states as the basis for efforts to formulate a successor grand strategy.[4] After the terrorist attacks of September 11, 2001, the George W. Bush administration embraced the policies of unilateralism and preemption to prevent terrorist attacks.[5] Most recently, the Barack Obama administration has embraced a policy of engagement while rejecting some aspects of the leadership role that defined the previous administration's foreign policy.[6] During these two decades, American foreign policy has swung between the extremes of a cooperative defense of the status quo and a unilateral effort to revise the system. To explain why there have been such dramatic shifts in policy, one must look for the answer in the failure of the United States to develop a new grand strategy that helps policymakers formulate policies for dealing with fundamental changes in international politics.

These arguments apply with particular force to the geopolitical and strategic conditions that are shaping the IOR. Without a coherent grand strategy, the United States will rely on a more narrowly delimited set of policies—from democracy promotion to threats of military preemption—to guide how it responds to current problems and challenges. The problem is that, in comparison with the formal strategy of containment that operated during the Cold War, this grand strategy does not provide useful principles for guiding the choices of American policymakers. In effect, the grand strategy of containment is inadequate for meeting the challenges that America faces in the IOR. Therefore, to understand the grand strategy of containment in the context of US policy, we must start with the origins of containment.

THE ORIGINS OF CONTAINMENT

In this chapter on containment and its application to American challenges in the IOR, the best place to begin is to discuss the foundational principles and origins of containment and then to examine whether a modified version of containment might help guide US policies toward the region. In practice, containment rested on several principles. With the decades-long ideological and strategic competition between the United States and the Soviet Union, containment called for the United States to organize its allies into a coherent group to oppose Soviet policies. It was based on the argument that in order to be successful, containment needed to rely on the efforts of many states, and needed to rest on a broad consensus about the serious nature of the adversaries that posed a threat to the United States and the West.

Ultimately, the concept of containment rested on the principle that the United States would work with its partners to "contain," or hold back, the ideological, political, and military power and influence of the Soviet Union and its allies. First, the idea was to hold ("contain") the Soviet Union within its geographic sphere of influence, while preventing that sphere from expanding throughout Eurasia. Second, the concept rested on a set of ideological principles, notably the value of promoting democracy and free markets, which stood in direct opposition to communism and totalitarianism. Third, it rested on the strategy of assembling significant military power to deter the Soviet Union from engaging in adventurous or expansionist policies. Fourth, it envisioned policies that were designed to prevent the spread of economic and technological means of power in order to prevent Moscow from using the West's resources to strengthen its own power and influence. For instance, this policy sought to prevent the leakage of sensitive commercial and military technologies that would have increased Moscow's overall military and economic capabilities.

Formulated in the wake of the post–World War II devastation of Europe and the Soviet Union's significant military and ideological power, the elements of containment were first outlined in George F. Kennan's 1947 article in *Foreign Affairs*, "The Sources of Soviet Conduct." Its purpose, as expressed by Kennan, was to contain the spread of Soviet power and influence.[7] As its initial architect, Kennan defined the strategy of containment on the basis of the following principle: "The main element of any United States policy toward the Soviet Union must be that of a long-term, patient but firm and vigilant containment of Russian expansionist tendencies."[8] To translate this grand strategy into practical policies, containment would call for the United States to practice "a policy of firm containment, at every point where they [the Soviets] show signs of encroaching upon the interests of a peaceful and stable world."[9]

In the early years of the Cold War, the practical expression of containment was to prevent the spread of Soviet influence and to deter the threat of confrontation between Washington and Moscow. Containment also was defined by the threat of nuclear weapons and the massive military establishments that were central to the strategic calculations of the United States and Soviet Union. Later, with the emergence of Mao Zedong's government in China, the Korean War, and the Vietnam War, the concept of containment evolved into a strategy in which the United States engaged in a half-century-long global struggle to prevent the expansion of Soviet power and the USSR's ideology of communism.

In policy terms, containment relied on the credibility of American pledges to resist the Soviet Union's policies and actions and those of its client states. For more than forty years, the United States and the Soviet Union and their respective clients were divided by a deep ideological and geographic chasm as to the nature of political and economic power. These two states, in occupying center stage in international politics, were the architects of a global bipolar order whose hallmarks were ideological hostility and geopolitical confrontation. During the second half of the twentieth century, Washington and Moscow built a relatively peaceful international order and avoided direct confrontation by establishing a modicum of trust and predictable relationships through both deterrence and effective diplomacy over a wide range of issues.

The grand strategy of containment, as formulated by Kennan, emerged directly from the prevailing conditions at the end of World War II and represented an evolutionary, and perhaps radical, departure for the United States. In response to geopolitical competition, ideological hostility, and the division of Europe after World War II, the United States was transformed from a historically detached state into its current position as the most powerful actor on the world stage. One corollary of the global responsibilities inherent in containment, which persists to this day, is the lasting and almost reflexive expectation held by US policymakers and the public that the United States is obligated to play a central role in resolving the world's fundamental problems. But as America and the world today face far more complex, potentially dangerous, and largely unfamiliar problems, the logic inherent in this expectation seems less compelling. In effect, the grand strategy of containment symbolized the Americans' view of their post–World War II role and responsibility in world affairs.[10]

In particular, as the United States confronts complex security challenges in the IOR, policymakers face the central question: Does the US grand strategy of containment provide effective guidance for the United States in view of the threats it faces in the IOR? To answer this and subsidiary questions, this chapter asks: What precisely does the United States seek to contain in the IOR? Although containment worked during the Cold War, it provides insufficient guidance for the specific policies that the United States should put into practice in the IOR. In effect, containment provides some useful principles and helpful guidance for contemporary policymakers who are contemplating the right strategy for dealing with the IOR. Containment has strengths that may be applicable in some senses, notably in the case of military measures, but not in others, such as in the economic and political domains.

WHAT CONTAINMENT IS DESIGNED TO HANDLE

The first step for the United States is to consider the specific problems for which the grand strategy of containment might provide useful conceptual and policy guidance. Put differently, the question is what precise problems does the United States seek to contain, and how well does containment deal with these problems? This chapter considers several emerging challenges that US policymakers must consider as they formulate a grand strategy and specific policies for dealing with the IOR.

First, the rise of extremism in the IOR, and broadly throughout the Middle East and Southwest Asia, represents a significant challenge to US interests. It also threatens the American desire to build political and economic stability in the IOR. The risk is that extremist movements—as seen, for example, in Pakistan—could threaten the region's governments by raising the dangers of societal unrest and the emergence of governments that are hostile to the West. Such extremist ideologies are hostile to the democratic institutions (or self-rule) and free markets on which modern societies and the global economy depend. One could envision movements with anti-Western leanings—for example, the Muslim Brotherhood and its affiliates throughout the region—that have historically opposed the flow of oil and gas to the advanced economies precisely because they have sought to harm these economies. The risk is that extremist movements could assert control in societies facing violent and nonviolent political struggles, of which the popular movements in Egypt, Libya, Yemen, Bahrain, Kuwait, and Saudi Arabia are contemporary examples.[11] For US strategy, the challenge is to develop approaches that can help policymakers manage relations with both nonstate actors and fragile states whose ability to resist extremist movements is relatively weak.

Facing these powerful anti-Western forces in the Middle East and Southwest Asia, US policymakers need a grand strategy that is relevant to thwarting the emergence of extremist organizations and preventing them from undermining these societies. Policymakers rightly fear that extremism will come to dominate certain societies, weaken the already-fragile status quo in these countries, and ultimately threaten US interests. As seen in the context for the military raid that killed Osama bin Laden, who had been living near Islamabad for several years, extremist groups such as al-Qaeda and the Taliban remain a strategic challenge to the United States. Containment historically involved a distinct ideological dimension, in which the United States helped societies resist the overtures of extremist movements and sought to help states resist radical political and economic agendas by providing political and economic aid. A prominent example is the US support during the Truman administration in the Greek civil war in the late 1940s.

The second and related problem is to effectively prevent the proliferation of weapons of mass destruction in this very nuclear neighborhood. Concerns about proliferation relate to two specific problems in the IOR. One is Pakistan, which possesses a growing nuclear arsenal with 90 to 110 nuclear weapons and a variety of ballistic and cruise missile delivery systems.[12] India also possesses nuclear weapons and ballistic missiles, which fuels concerns about a crisis that could lead to a nuclear confrontation between New Delhi and Islamabad. Because India and Pakistan are strategic rivals and both possess nuclear arsenals, the United States needs a strategy to minimize tensions between these regional powers. A related challenge is to strengthen the foundations of deterrence, particularly in view of the proliferation of nuclear weapons, ballistic missiles, and other advanced conventional military technologies among various states in the IOR, including Pakistan and India.

A fundamental concern is persistent reports of close ties between extremist organizations, such as al-Qaeda, and Pakistan's Inter-Services Intelligence Directorate. Such relationships raise concerns for the United States and other states that a political upheaval could result in nuclear weapons falling into the hands of extremists.[13] By implication, a strategy of containment in the IOR involves dealing with the nuclear dimension.

The third problem is the threat posed by states or groups to the economic activities on which the regional and global economies depend. Facing the economic importance of commerce in the IOR, a central objective of US strategy is to maintain global access to markets, strategic resources, and sea lines of communication. For example, in 2012 more than 60,000 vessels transited the Strait of Malacca. If the strait were blocked, nearly half the world's fleet would require rerouting. The US strategy is to encourage states to engage in the economic discourse on which the global economy depends, and one element is the region's critical role in the global production and distribution of energy. There also is the role of raw materials and natural resources in the region. For example, it was reported in 2010 that Afghanistan may contain enormous reserves of critical natural resources, including "iron, copper, cobalt, gold and critical industrial metals like lithium."[14]

The challenge for a US grand strategy is to ensure that states in the IOR can engage freely in the global economy. Consequently, US strategy must promote building political relations that contribute to maintaining significant maritime forces and capabilities in the region. In the case of energy, states in the IOR play a critical role in the production and transit of energy resources that are critical to the global economy. This reality alone demonstrates that maritime forces will play a necessary role in the strategy of promoting free commerce in the region. It also suggests that a cardinal principle of the strategy must be helping states to develop the robust economies and security forces that will contribute to developing and protecting both their prosperity and also that of their region.

The fourth aspect of a grand strategy of containment is to develop policies that prevent conflicts among the great powers in the IOR. One aspect of American grand strategy toward the IOR is its emphasis on China's military developments—in particular, whether US military capabilities are sufficient to deter and if necessary prevail in a military confrontation, which is often classically defined as centering on the Taiwan Strait. The broader point is that an effective US grand strategy will force policymakers to consider deliberately how China's rise in political, economic, and military terms affects US interests and policies in the IOR. Furthermore, thinking along these lines will encourage US policymakers to reexamine how to build a strategy that relies on deterrence and crisis management, in order to help avoid the miscalculations and errors that can lead to wars between great powers and regional states.

A critical objective of a grand strategy is to ensure that US policymakers are aware of the need, and take specific steps, to help Washington prevent conflicts between the great powers. It is easy to imagine how such conflicts could emerge between the United States and China, or between regional powers such as India and Pakistan. For this reason, the IOR will play an increasingly important role in US strategy and in the overall conduct of international politics. The US strategy in the IOR must build the basis for long-term peace and prosperity by encouraging the region's states to develop stable governance and relations. Thus, the strategy for the IOR needs to build directly on working by, with, and through transparent democratic governments. In practice, a strategy of containment should help US policymakers develop approaches that moderate tensions and hostilities among the states in the region and among the great powers in the event that their vital interests clash.

In strategic terms the global balance of power and the question of whether the international system is stable are influenced by developments in the IOR. In practice conditions in the IOR have significant consequences for US security and prosperity for its regional and global friends and partners. The IOR is critical to US interests, and its overall significance is likely to increase during the next several decades. This is not to argue, however, that current developments will continue unabated. To cite one example, a reasonable assumption is that states in the IOR will experience dramatic increases in population. Recent research suggests, however, that China's period of population growth has declined to half that of the previous decade, whereas states such as India are expected to maintain significant rates of population growth.[15]

Thinking systematically about grand strategy forces policymakers to understand how important regional cooperation is to balancing the United States' interests and power with those of the other states in the IOR. Improving the capabilities of the US military so that it can conduct effective conventional strikes against military and infrastructure targets, as well as maintaining supremacy at sea, will remain core principles. In view of the world's dependence on the free flow of goods in the IOR, this military strategy depends on defending sea lines of communication and ensuring the unimpeded transit of goods and resources. A final consideration in developing strategy is to consider the balance between the proportion of the defense budget dedicated to ground forces (i.e., the US Army and US Marine Corps) and that to the US Navy and US Air Force. The capabilities of these latter services are much more suitable to countering threats in the IOR. US force planning will also depend on whether the United States finds itself involved in a ground-force-intensive counterinsurgency operation(s) and postconflict stabilization effort(s) in the near to medium terms.

For reasons explored in this chapter, American policymakers cannot escape one simple reality: The IOR's increasing economic, political, and military importance strengthens US strategic interests in the region. This relationship between US strategic interests and the IOR can be expressed in terms of both the United States' broad national interests and its specific interests in the region. In effect, US grand strategy must defend and promote US national and regional interests, which rest on the fundamental principles of promoting security, prosperity, values, and international order. The problem is that containment does not effectively support this strategy.

THE RISKS AND UNCERTAINTIES OF CONTAINMENT

Because developments in the IOR call for a broad reexamination of US grand strategy in the Asia-Pacific region, the first step is to examine the value of containment as an overall strategy for addressing the various problems that the United States confronts in the IOR.[16] Some observers argue that the strategy of containment no longer fits the modern world.[17] In line with this argument, several risks and uncertainties call into question the value of relying on containment to guide US policy in the IOR.

First, the United States does not have the desire to physically contain the power and influence of the states in the region, such as China—nor would it want to, in most cases. The fundamental reason is that a principal instrument of the power and influence of the states in the IOR is more economic than military or political. In the midst of a deep recession with trillion-dollar deficits from 2009 to

2012, and with deficits of roughly half a trillion dollars projected for the next five years, the United States does not have the will to use its term economic power to contain China. To the contrary, China and other states, by funding American deficits by purchasing US Treasury notes, are effectively containing the United States. The director of the International Monetary Fund, Christine Lagarde, has raised precisely this point, warning that the "fiscal cliff" threatens "the supremacy of the United States and its leadership role in the world."[18] The states of Asia sit at the strategic crossroads of the global economy—as seen, for example, by the scale of energy resources moving through the region. Both India and China have rapidly growing economies, as measured by their exports and consumption of energy.

For the purposes of strategy, it is of no practical significance for policymakers to argue that the United States can contain the IOR in economic terms when the economies in the region are so large, dynamic, and expanding. Because these states are powerful contributors to global economic prosperity (in contrast to the command economies in many of the countries of the former Soviet Union and its allies), containment might not be the best strategy for managing the economic power of states in the IOR, including China.

Just as the economic weakness of the Soviet Union made containment feasible, today the economic power of such states as China makes containment difficult. A core principle of US foreign policy is to encourage states to develop strong, market-based economies so that they can become politically free and economically prosperous. Thus, it is directly contrary to US interests to take steps—such as those described by containment policy—that inhibit economic growth and technological progress when states are committed to free market principles. This, however, is precisely the condition that describes the nature of economic and commercial activity in the IOR. A central element of the US grand strategy is to build strong trade relationships in the IOR to increase the ability of these states to become integral parts of the global economy and diminish or prevent the rise of competitive forces that lead to conflicts. Unlike the grand strategy of containment, which held that it was essential to build interlocking directorates of states designed to prevent the Soviet Union from strengthening its economy, the problem today is that US policy seeks to encourage trade as an instrument for building regional and global stability. This economic reality stands in sharp contrast to the classic strategy of containment, when the objective was to limit the adversary's economic power. It effectively undermines containment, while noting that containment has other strengths.

Second, the strategy of containment remains more relevant only in the realm of military power. Although there is no single state that the United States seeks to contain militarily, US policy has been to prevent such states as China from becoming the predominant military power in the region. This is precisely the reason for the Asia pivot by the United States. The fact that China remains of great concern to the United States is likely the principal motivation behind the call for a strategy of containment, which seeks to contain or manage the rise of China's military power. US secretary of defense Leon Panetta affirmed this point when he said that the United States "is not trying to contain China," which suggests that American policymakers do not want to be seen as overtly working to contain China's military power—just as they did against the Soviet Union. It is prudent, however, for Washington to demonstrate that US military power is a counterweight to that of Beijing, which is a close approximation of containment in the modern era.[19] One also must consider China's military power in the Pacific and its growing political influence in the IOR. With China's expanding economy and growing political power, it already *is* a critical actor in the IOR, against which some are hoping that containment will provide a viable strategy. Whether containment will work remains in some doubt.

An axiom in international politics for scholars and policymakers is to deliberately avoid calling overtly to contain China's military power along the same lines as the United States dealt with Soviet military power. Despite this hesitation, there are signs Washington seeks to build a network of like-minded, free-market-oriented states in the region, which are united by their desire to limit China's growing military power and political influence. As examples, one can cite US cooperation with Japan on ballistic missile defense, Washington's provision of ballistic missiles to South Korea to counterbalance North Korean and hence Chinese influence, and the United States' effort to establish a permanent presence of 2,500 US Marines in Australia.[20] But the response is worrying, given that diplomats in Asia have declared that they will resist American efforts to contain China.[21] The difference, however, is that Washington policymakers do not seriously contemplate a military confrontation with Beijing on the same scale or with the same degree of probability as did their Cold War predecessors, who actively worried about the risk of confrontation with Moscow. Such forces serve to weaken the relevance of containment.

The central problem for the United States in pursuing a strategy of containment is that the initial construct of containment that existed during the Cold War, which rested on establishing policies for containing the power of one state, is not relevant for dealing with the IOR. What was important about containment was the principle of building policies and alliances that were designed to hold back Moscow's military influence and prevent its political expansion. The problem today is that using the strategy of containment for the IOR does not apply well to the idea of holding back the power and influence of states in the region whose economic power is often dramatically greater than their military power. In practical terms, the United States cannot contain the economic power and influence of such states as China, which is deeply connected to the global economy—and dramatically more so than the Soviet Union ever was.

Another risk is that the concept of containment is much less relevant to building alliances and relationships with such states as India and Pakistan as a way to exert pressure on China—to "contain" China's influence. It does not seem that Islamabad or New Delhi is pushing other capitals in the region to align with Washington.[22] It is difficult to imagine why states would align with Washington for the purpose of containing Beijing in view of its growing economic power and increasing role in the IOR. Nor would states run the risk of being hurt by economic containment policies if the political will or economic commitment of the United States were to falter, given its economic slowdown and trillion-dollar deficits for the foreseeable future.[23] Finally, containment would not succeed in view of how integral China's economy is to global commerce.

Third, containment simply does not fit as precisely as policymakers would like for dealing with the specific challenges posed in the IOR. One can, however, develop an alternative strategy that rests on several related but distinctly different policies. In the modern context of implementing a strategy for the IOR, a more useful approach would develop policies that seek to limit, moderate, or restrain—but not contain—the policies and actions of states that contribute in worrisome ways to the geostrategic trends outlined above. This alternative strategy needs to deal with the fact that today Washington is less engaged and more comfortable with "leading from behind," while Beijing is increasing its military power, growing economically, and becoming more engaged in Asia and elsewhere. As quoted in *The Economist*, when senior aides said that President Obama aims to be "present but not deeply involved" around the globe, it reaffirms the fact that China's strategic imprimatur is growing while that of the United States is shrinking.

Building on an argument raised by George Kennan in the late 1980s in an essay titled "Containment Then and Now," the United States needs an alternative concept to containment that fits today's conditions in the IOR. To quote Kennan, Washington is "going to have to develop a wider concept of what containment means—a concept more closely linked to the totality of the problems of Western civilization at this juncture in world history—a concept, in other words, more responsive to the problems of our own time."[24]

Several guidelines or principles should help shape an alternative now that containment no longer fits our world—and thus show how to move beyond containment. Though once quite useful, containment does not align with how the modern world is organized politically and economically. Simply put, containment is less practical in a highly interconnected global economy where states do not face a singular ideological threat.

When states and individuals have unparalleled access to social media and technology, they possess total, absolute, and practically instantaneous connectedness. This connectedness contributes to levels of transparency that are historically without parallel. As states in Asia continue to develop modern infrastructures, including cell phone networks, various groups and movements will be able to out-maneuver governments and evade efforts to contain their activities.

A central problem with containment is that because economic forces are vastly more powerful than political ideologies, it is difficult to contain states in the modern, globalized culture. It is not clear what containment means when modern states and individuals freely exchange the political ideas, economic goods, and services that generate wealth and power.

In practical terms, the US strategy for the IOR must be defined in broader terms than simply containing China's military power. The risk is that US policymakers might think about grand strategy in ways that are limited to the ideas that, though highly relevant when they emerged in the 1940s and 1950s, are largely useless for managing today's challenges in the IOR. Another way of saying this is to suggest that containment is a surrogate for strategic thinking because it is familiar. But this is not the same as saying that it provides coherent guidance.

Ultimately, the fundamental challenge is how to practice a strategy that is useful for dealing with the rise of extremism in the IOR. As a force of great concern to policymakers, extremism builds on forces that exist across societies, notably the globalization of information and communication in the modern world. It is unclear how to contain such forces because modern societies thrive on the free flow of information, finance, culture, and politics that helps unify disaffected individuals into coherent groups whose members adopt extremism as an antidote to modernity. Containment is less relevant, if not meaningless, for dealing with extremism—for the same reason that containment is ill suited to dealing with states that engage in free market forms of economic discourse.

EVALUATING CONTAINMENT

It is essential for policymakers to evaluate the strategy of containment for meeting the challenges of the IOR. The first and principal strength is immediately obvious. American policymakers, many of whom are intimately familiar with containment, are intuitively comfortable with the notion of a grand strategy that seeks to hold back the military power and political influence of China as a threat to the interests and values of the United States. Containment is a highly relevant concept because it calls for the development of policies that are designed explicitly to limit or moderate the actions and policies of states that threaten American interests. It has the virtue of simplicity because it rests on holding back or limiting the actions and policies that put American interests at risk. Although this framework guided US policy from the 1940s until the 1990s, the predictable and familiar concept of containment does not translate into practical policies that help Washington deal with challenges to US interests in the IOR.

Second, containment coincides with emerging military and economic trends that derive from the actions of individual states, most prominently that of China. However, the actions of states in the IOR do not translate into policies that work well against individual states. How, for instance, do policymakers contain the forces that contribute to extremism or to free market economies? Containment is a convenient leitmotif when what we need are policies that focus on military threats, which call for increasing military capabilities and building alliances, as a way to contain growing military power. But this logic does not work when dealing with the forces of extremism and nuclear proliferation.

Third, one strength of containment was its ability to communicate unambiguously that the United States views certain developments as problems worthy of serious attention. As a doctrine, it signals that specific states and forces bear close scrutiny and that Washington is committed to dealing with these problems. One might even say that containment provides a useful instrument when policymakers want to signal a consensus that the United States and its partners face challenges to peace, security, and prosperity in a region of great strategic and economic importance. In this sense containment effectively communicates that the United States needs a coordinated policy for dealing with dangerous movements and forces in the IOR. As discussed above, it does not, however, provide useful guidance when dealing with the resurgence of al-Qaeda or other extremist groups in India and Pakistan that pose threats to the region's security.

Let us turn to the weaknesses with a strategy of containment, which are significant. The first and most critical difficulty with containment is that the United States does not face one singular or dominant threat in the IOR. Although China remains of strategic concern to the United States, there is no one state, issue, or development that the United States and its partners must contain as an existential threat. Second, it is unclear precisely how the United States should contain problems in the IOR when these problems derive not from the policies of one state but are effectively transnational in nature (e.g., extremism) or reflect the emerging consensus on how states ought to interact economically in international politics (e.g., free markets and global trade). Containment is transparent in conceptual terms, but as an operational principle it lacks the coherence that policymakers need to deal with such problems as extremism and nuclear proliferation.

Third, to be successful containment requires the coordinated efforts of many states in the IOR that are pursued consistently on a global scale.[25] But what remains unanswered is what, precisely, do these states seek to contain? If China's growing military and economic power is the reason for containment, policymakers should be cautious, because they will learn that many states will hesitate to sign up for policies that seek to "contain" China. But no consensus exists in the IOR that China is the main force to be contained, that it should be the focus of a general strategy pursued by many states, or that it is worth running the risk of polarizing the international system into states that support containment and those that oppose it. Fourth, the language of containment provides a much more effective instrument of rhetoric than a coherent set of policies. Its weakness lies precisely in the fact that it does not translate into concepts or policies that provide clear guidance for implementation as a coherent national strategy. However, this weakness may be counterbalanced by the fact that it can provide a basis for developing a consensus on critical problems facing the IOR.

CAN WE REDEFINE CONTAINMENT FOR THE IOR?

What is required is to redefine a strategy that reflects a consensus for dealing with the challenges posed by the IOR. Such a consensus will build on several principles. The foremost requirement is an explicit statement in political and strategic terms of what precisely is the central problem posed by the IOR. During the Cold War the guiding principles of containment were defined by George Kennan and outlined in greater detail by the Truman administration, both of which unambiguously outlined the core political principles that defined the nature of ideological and military competition between the United States and the Soviet Union. However, to be effective now, a strategy must articulate how to use political, economic, military, and technological instruments of power and suasion to help the IOR evolve in a positive and peaceful direction while minimizing the risks to US interests and values. A strategy for dealing with the IOR requires a consensus about the nature of the problems that the United States and other states face and the specific objectives that animate the strategy. This strategy is unlikely to require containment, as we knew it.

The second requirement is a statement and subsequent analysis of the principles that explain why containment provides useful guidance to states. To be successful, a grand strategy of containment must articulate the political and ideological differences between the United States and its partners and its ideological or strategic adversaries. Such a political statement or strategy will contribute to building a consensus in the United States and throughout the IOR on what risks and dangers they must manage. For now, I would argue that though dangerous, such developments as extremism, the proliferation of weapons of mass destruction, economic pressures, and the rise of China provide only a loose framework on which to formulate a central strategy for guiding the policy of the United States and its partners. Unless policymakers are clear about the nature of the threats, they will find it difficult to articulate principles on the basis of which other states are willing to organize themselves. In this strategic environment, containment is not terribly useful as an organizing principle.

The third point is to outline core strategic principles on which to organize states into coherent, perhaps formal, political and military partnerships or alliances, of which there are numerous examples from the Cold War, and many of which still exist (e.g., NATO). A strategy, to be successful, must articulate the threats that all states face and organize those into a compelling reason for states to band together for a common purpose. The political and economic dimensions of the strategy of containment were highly relevant during the Cold War because the core differences between the United States and the Soviet Union rested on a profound philosophical difference over the nature of politics and economics in societies. Because the states in the IOR today are pursuing largely free market economic philosophies, much as the United States and its principal partners are doing, any strategy must involve an economic component that unifies the actions of like-minded states. In a sense, a unified economic strategy already exists; whereas during the Cold War, the United States and its allies in Europe and Asia built their power and policies on the primacy of free market economies, today containment is less relevant precisely because we live in a world where states are pursuing markets and economic freedom.

The fourth point is that the strategy must reflect the efforts of many states, and cannot be a grand strategy pursued by one state. In this sense, containment during the Cold War was instructive. It was organized by the United States to deal with the challenge posed by one state (the Soviet Union), involved the coordinated actions of multiple states within various alliances, endured for decades, and was in the end highly successful. To succeed, a strategy for the IOR must reflect the common interests of many states and unify those interests into a common strategy. Beyond the military power of China, it is unclear on what basis that consensus could be built. And without such a consensus, containment is not relevant as an organizing principle for strategy.

For containment to operate successfully today, it must derive from a broad consensus on the nature of a common foe or enemy that is sufficiently dangerous to compel common action, a unifying ideology or strategy that describes that danger, compels states to form alliances or partnerships based on shared ideas about common military and economic threats, and a political and economic strategy to guide the implementation of that strategy. The next step is to organize the actions and policies of like-minded states that are united by these principles into a coherent strategy. Because this strategic consensus does not yet exist, the central task for American policymakers is to build it, and a grand strategy can be an immensely powerful instrument for building it. For these reasons, containment is unlikely to provide the basis on which to form a strategic consensus.

WHAT IS MISSING FROM THE STRATEGY OF CONTAINMENT IN THE IOR

From this review of the principles of containment, it can be seen as inadequate in three strategic dimensions. The first is that no common principle defines in ideological or political terms the dangers against which states need to organize themselves. In the past the principles of promoting freedom and free markets provided coherent organizing principles; but one of these—free markets—has emerged as practically a universal principle for organizing like-minded states. Second, there is no consensus on the threat. Although China's military power, extremism, nuclear weapons, and economic challenges are significant, this mix of threats involves so many states, forces, and conditions that it diffuses any sense of strategic urgency. Nor is there any consensus on what is to be contained, whether those forces can be contained, and much less how to do so.

Third, there is no consensus on what challenges—whether arising from an ideology or a state—are sufficiently distinct and compelling to persuade states to act in common. It is difficult to argue that China poses a military threat that is so sufficiently compelling that states need to organize themselves into a system of alliances to counterbalance China. Nor is it likely that many states could be persuaded that China is an existential threat against which they should be willing to run the risks of forming an overt alliance with the United States. Finally, what would be the outcome of that alliance? Would it be to change China's political system, recalling China's record of success in free market economic terms? Or would it be to contain China's military power? But again, is difficult to establish containment as the organizing principle on which to form a unified strategy.[26] Or would it be to use the strategy of containment, loosely defined, as an instrument for organizing states around a coherent policy? But for this strategy to succeed, it must derive from a singular threat, which we clearly lack today.

CONCLUSIONS ABOUT CONTAINMENT IN THE IOR

There are several criticisms about the ability of a strategy of containment and its ability to manage challenges and opportunities in the IOR that policymakers should ponder with great care. First, the United States has the economic and technological ability to physically contain the power and influence of the states in the region, notably China, if wants to do so—but the political consensus in the United States is focused on domestic economic challenges. Furthermore, a weaker and disabled China would be a detriment to US national interests. Unlike during the Cold War, when the objective was to weaken and harm Russian interests, China and the United States are inextricably linked in this globalized age. As discussed above, a principal instrument of the power and influence of states in the IOR lies in the economic realm. These states sit at the strategic crossroads of the global economy, as seen by the scale of energy resources and goods that transit the region. Containment offers no practical guidance. It is largely irrelevant to say that the United States can contain the IOR in economic terms when the economies in the region contribute in profound ways to global economic prosperity, though many of the states in the IOR are symbols of successful free market economies.

Second, it is directly contrary to US interests to take any actions or implement policies that seek to inhibit economic growth and technological progress in the IOR. And containment, however it is practiced, will be interpreted in precisely this fashion. A core principle of US foreign policy is to encourage states to develop strong, market-based economies so that they can become politically free and economically prosperous. Indeed, a central element of US strategy is to help states build strong economic relationships as a way to prevent or diminish the rise of military competition among them. Unlike dealing with the Soviet Union during the Cold War, when it was essential to build interlocking directorates of states whose objective was to prevent Moscow from building its own economic and military power, US policy has been and remains to encourage precisely the scale of economic development we are seeing today as an instrument for building peace and stability in the IOR. Containment is directly at odds with this objective.

Third, in the realm of military power the concept of containment is somewhat relevant, yet putting this into practice remains elusive. If there is one state that the United States seeks to contain in military terms, it has been and remains China, to prevent it from becoming the dominant military power in the region. One strategy for the United States is to demonstrate that its military power serves as a counterweight to China. US strategy, therefore, operates less to contain than to balance or restrain China's military power. Although Washington could contain Beijing's military power, just as it contained Moscow's military power, the United States is better able to form a consensus by subtly building a network of like-minded states that share the view that any failure to limit China's military power and political influence will pose risks for Asia and the world. Because the United States does not seriously contemplate a military confrontation with China, as it did with the Soviet Union during the Cold War, the urgency and relevance of containment are entirely absent from contemporary strategic calculations.

Fourth, this logic leads to the conclusion that the United States must move beyond containment if it is to implement a strategy that deals effectively with China's growing military power. What was important about containment was how the United States built policies and alliances that held back Moscow's influence and prevented its expansion. Today, we lack a consensus on an enemy or the actions necessary to contain it—or even whether it would be possible to contain such an adversary, which renders the strategy of containment problematic.

Fifth, a grand strategy of containment for the IOR does not apply well to the idea of holding back the growing political and economic power and influence of states in the region or dealing with other transnational problems. The United States does not seek and cannot in practice contain the power and influence of China, which is so deeply connected to the global economy. The other problem is that containment could be helpful for building alliances and relationships with India and Pakistan, if they support the need for a strategy based on exerting pressure on China—principally, limiting China's influence and seeking more moderation in China's policies. For example, New Delhi may agree with Washington on the desire to limit Beijing's influence and power by increasing the military and strategic cooperation and coordination between the two states. But with the United States–Pakistan relationship, the dynamic is quite different. Pakistan sees China as its perpetual ally, whereas Washington's objective is to convince Islamabad that it, too, is a reliable ally, so that it turns less frequently and fully to China. It is on this basis that the United States can strengthen its influence in the IOR.

For these purposes, any US grand strategy must be defined in broader terms than simply containment. Furthermore, without a coherent grand strategy, the United States relies on a diverse array of policies—ranging from democracy promotion to threats of military preemption—for responding to problems and challenges in the IOR. Yet there is no consensus that would allow the United States to formulate and implement a strategy of containment that provides useful guidance to policymakers.

The conclusion fundamentally is that containment is not strongly relevant to managing problems in the IOR—or elsewhere, for that matter. In one sense containment remains a broad concept, which rests on policies that seek to limit or moderate the actions and policies of states that contribute to dangerous and destabilizing trends. The inexorable problem, however, is that the United States does not face a singular or dominant threat in the IOR that is comparable to what containment was designed to handle.

In conclusion, the salient question is whether containment is a practical strategy for the United States. Although containment has several useful components (as outlined above), the inescapable question remains: Until there is something to be contained in the IOR and the problems in the IOR are seen to be containable, the applicability of containment in practice is in doubt. The reason is that it is the product of an earlier era, when policymakers had great clarity about the dangers of the world we faced. We lack such clarity today because the strategic conditions in the IOR do not align with what containment was designed to do. A better argument is to reformulate containment by putting the emphasis on "managing" problems rather than containing them—and this logic puts strategy into an entirely different realm than how scholars and policymakers defined containment several generations ago.

For the reasons outlined in this chapter, containment is not the right strategy for the IOR. Although containment has strengths that may be applicable in some areas, such as military measures, it will not work in other areas, notably in economics and politics. In the end, policymakers must understand that moving toward a strategy of "containment," with all that this term conjures, is emblematic of the onset of a more dangerous, confrontational, and hostile world that many societies will oppose. When containment is framed in these terms, it will not generate significant domestic political support in the United States or among its partners. The enduring question for policymakers is whether the United States has the political will at this time to develop a consensus and then implement a strategy of containment in view of the significant limitations on containment itself. The answer, at this point in time, is no.

NOTES

1. See "Toward a New Grand Strategy," in *Looming Discontinuities in US Military Strategy and Defense Planning: Colliding RMAs Necessitate a New Strategy*, by Paul K. Davis and Peter A. Wilson (Santa Monica, CA: RAND Corporation, 2011), xvi.

2. See William C. Martel, "Grand Strategy of 'Restrainment,'" *Orbis*, Summer 2010, 358–59.

3. On grand strategy during the Bush administration, see Walter Russell Mead, "The Bush Administration and the New World Order," *World Policy Journal* 8, no. 3 (Summer 1991): 375–420; Raymond Taras and Marshal Zeringue, "Grand Strategy in a Post-Bipolar World: Interpreting the Final Soviet Response," *Review of International Studies* 18, no. 4 (October 1992): 355–75; and Walter Russell Mead, "An American Grand Strategy: The Quest for Order in a Disordered World," *World Policy Journal* 10, no. 1 (Spring 1993): 9, who described the "false dawn of a new world order." Also see Jeremi Suri, "American Grand Strategy from the Cold War's End to 9/11," *Orbis*, Fall 2009, 616–21.

4. On principles governing Clinton's foreign policy, see Charles William Maynes, "A Workable Clinton Doctrine," *Foreign Policy*, no. 93 (Winter 1993–94): 3–21; Joseph S. Nye Jr., "The Case for Deep Engagement," *Foreign Affairs* 74, no. 4 (July–August 1995): 90–102; Michael Mandelbaum, "Foreign Policy as Social Work," *Foreign Affairs* 75, no. 1 (January–February 1996): 16–32; Richard N. Haass, "What to Do with American Primacy," *Foreign Affairs* 78, no. 5 (September–October 1999): 37–49; Stephen M. Walt, "Two Cheers for Clinton's Foreign Policy," *Foreign Affairs* 79, no. 2 (March–April 2000): 63–79; Samuel R. Berger, "A Foreign Policy for the Global Age," *Foreign Affairs* 79, no. 6 (November–December 2000): 22–39; Samuel R. Berger, "Clinton's Foreign Policy," *Foreign Policy*, no. 121 (November–December 2000): 18–20, 22, 24, 26, 28–29; President William Clinton, *A National Strategy of Engagement and Enlargement* (Washington: US Government Printing Office, 1994); and President William Clinton,

A National Security Strategy for a Global Age, White House, December 2000. On formulating grand strategy, see Suri, "American Grand Strategy."

5. On principles governing the Bush administration's policies, see Condoleezza Rice, "Promoting the National Interest," *Foreign Affairs* 79, no. 1 (January–February 2000): 45–62; and George W. Bush, *The National Security Strategy of the United States of America*, White House, March 2006.

6. See, e.g., Robert Kagan, "Bipartisan Spring: Washington May Be Deeply Polarized on Domestic Matters, but When It Comes to Foreign Affairs, a Remarkable Consensus Is Taking Shape," *Foreign Policy*, March 3, 2010, www. foreignpolicy.com/articles/2010/03/03/bipartisan_spring: "The Obama administration took office guided by the philosophy that whatever Bush did, it should do the opposite, and this policy of 'un-Bush' dominated the first months." See also Ryan Lizza, "The Consequentialist: How the Arab Spring Remade Obama's Foreign Policy," *The New Yorker*, May 2, 2011 www.newyorker.com/reporting/2011/05/02/110502fa_fact_lizza.

7. See X (George F. Kennan), "The Sources of Soviet Conduct," *Foreign Affairs* 25, no. 4 (July 1947): 566–82. Also see George F. Kennan, "Containment Then and Now," *Foreign Affairs* 65, no. 4 (Spring 1987): 885–90; George F. Kennan, "On American Principles," *Foreign Affairs* 74, no. 2 (March–April 1995): 116–26; and David Mayers, "Containment and the Primacy of Diplomacy: George Kennan's Views, 1947–1948," *International Security* 11, no. 1 (Summer 1986): 124.

8. X, "Sources of Soviet Conduct," 575.

9. Ibid., 581.

10. On the evolution of the US grand strategy of containment, see John Lewis Gaddis, "Containment: A Reassessment," *Foreign Affairs* 55, no. 4 (July 1977): 873–87; John Lewis Gaddis, *Strategies of Containment* (New York: Oxford University Press, 1982); John Lewis Gaddis, "Containment and the Logic of Strategy," *The National Interest*, no. 10 (Winter 1987–88): 27–38; and Stephen M. Walt, "The Case for Finite Containment: Analyzing US Grand Strategy," *International Security* 14, no. 1 (Summer 1989): 5–49.

11. See, e.g., Michael Scott Doran, "The Heirs of Nasser," *Foreign Affairs* 90, no. 3 (May–June 2011): 17–25.

12. See Hans M. Kristensen and Robert S. Norris, "Pakistan's Nuclear Forces, 2011," *Nuclear Notebook Bulletin of the Atomic Scientists*, July 1, 2011, http://bos.sagepub .com/content/67/4/91.full.pdf.

13. "Backgrounder: The ISI and Terrorism: Behind the Accusations," Council on Foreign Relations, May 4, 2011, www.cfr.org/pakistan/isi-terrorism-behind-accusations/p11644.

14. See James Risen, "US Identifies Vast Mineral Riches in Afghanistan," *New York Times*, June 13, 2010, www.nytimes.com/2010/06/14/world/asia/14minerals .html.

15. See Michael Wines and Sharon LaFraniere, "New Census Finds China's Population Growth Has Slowed," *New York Times*, April 29, 2011, which reflects "the slowest rate of growth in nearly half a century."

16. See Davis and Wilson, *Looming Discontinuities in US Military Strategy and Defense Planning*.
17. William C. Martel, "Containment RIP," *The Diplomat*, September 24, 2012, http://thediplomat.com/2012/09/24/r-i-p-containment/?all=true. Cf. William C. Martel, "Why America Needs a Grand Strategy," *The Diplomat*, June 18, 2012, http://thediplomat.com/2012/06/18/why-america-needs-a-grand-strategy/.
18. "Lagarde Says 'Fiscal Cliff' Threatens US Supremacy," *France 24*, December 7, 2012, www.france24.com/en/20121207-lagarde-says-fiscal-cliff-threatens-us-supremacy.
19. "Panetta: US Not Trying to Contain China," *Voice of America*, September 19, 2012, www.voanews.com/content/panetta-us-not-trying-to-contain-china/1510768.html.
20. See Jake Tapper, "Seeking to Contain China, US to Establish Permanent Military Presence Down Under," ABC News, November 16, 2011, http://abcnews.go.com/blogs/politics/2011/11/us-to-establish-permanent-military-presence-down-under/.
21. See "Asia Will Resist US Efforts to Contain China, Says Singapore Diplomat," *Washington Times*, October 14, 2012, www.washingtontimes.com/news/2012/oct/14/asia-will-resist-us-efforts-to-contain-china-says-/.
22. See Alissa J. Rubin, "Pakistan Urged Afghanistan to Distance Itself from the West, Officials Say," *New York Times*, April 27, 2011, www.nytimes.com/2011/04/28/world/asia/28kabul.html: "The Pakistani government has urged Afghanistan to distance itself from the West and tie its future more tightly to that of China and Pakistan."
23. See "CBO Projects Slightly Smaller Deficits under Current Law," Committee for a Responsible Federal Budget, March 21, 2011, http://crfb.org/blogs/cbo-projects-slightly-smaller-deficits-under-current-law.
24. See Kennan, "Containment Then and Now."
25. Because how we define success remains a challenge for scholars and policymakers, see William C. Martel, *Victory in War: Foundations of Modern Strategy* (New York: Cambridge University Press, 2011).
26. The United States, after all, has large and highly capable military forces; but that fact alone does not provide sufficient justification for a strategy of containment against Washington. Some, however, in Russia and China have made that argument.

CHAPTER 4

LEAVING UNIPOLARITY BEHIND

A Strategic Framework for Advancing US Interests in the Indian Ocean Region

CHRISTOPHER A. PREBLE

Included within the introduction to the National Intelligence Council's report *Global Trends 2030: Alternative Worlds* was the stark prediction that "by 2030, no country—whether the United States, China, or any other large country—will be a hegemonic power." The report continued: "The empowerment of individuals and diffusion of power among states and from states to informal networks [will usher] in a new era of 'democratization' at the international and domestic levels."

This change will be momentous for the United States, as well as for the world. For even as the United States "will remain the 'first among equals' alongside the other great powers in 2030; . . . the 'unipolar moment' is over and Pax Americana—the era of unrivalled American ascendancy in international politics that began in 1945—is fast winding down."[1] The implications are clear. Strategists and policymakers—not just in Washington, but everywhere in the world—must move aggressively to adapt to a new multipolar order in which responsibility for maintaining peace and security is shared among the many beneficiaries of this order.

To date, US policymakers have been reluctant to embrace a new, post-unipolar order. They have not focused particular attention on the Indian Ocean region (IOR). The strategic framework presented here aims to fill this gap. It proceeds from the assumption that the *Global Trends 2030* report accurately predicted the likely balance of power within the next quarter century. The United States should anticipate this looming shift, and should prioritize its roles and missions in order to advance its strategic interests. The IOR is and should be low on the list of priorities. The United States has relatively few core security interests in the region, and certainly far fewer than in most other parts of the world.

Furthermore, US interests in the IOR are likely to decline in relative importance between now and 2030. The United States can monitor developments in distant regions without a large or intrusive military presence there, it can surge forces to the region in the rare cases when they will be required, and it should otherwise expect countries with far more tangible and urgent interests in the region to take responsibility for securing these interests. This would begin with the countries within the Indian Ocean littoral region, but should also include those countries most dependent upon the transshipment of goods through the region, including countries in East Asia, the Middle East, and Europe.

THE STATUS QUO CONFRONTS FISCAL REALITY: DOWNSIZING THE US MILITARY AND US GRAND STRATEGY

The strategic framework presented here diverges in some important respects from other accounts, both in its interpretation of what missions are vital to US national security, and of how to accomplish them.[2] It differs from other strategy documents in its assessment of who should bear the costs of policing the globe, and for how long. The US national and regional objectives as laid out in the 2010 National Security Strategy, and in the 2010 Quadrennial Defense Review (QDR), are too broad and often conflict. These documents outline what amount to laundry lists of policy preferences, without any sense of which ones are essential for US security; the implication is that all of them are. These exercises also generally avoid consideration of the costs. They fail to address whether the resources required to achieve the various goals are available, or can be made available.

It is appropriate for US policymakers to prioritize role and missions, and to differentiate vital regions from peripheral ones. The revised strategic guidance issued in January 2012 professes to do this. It notes that the nation faces "an inflection point." It plans for a transition from recent land wars to "preparing for future challenges." And it recognizes "the national security imperative of deficit reduction through a lower level of defense spending."[3]

The list of objectives is as long as in previous strategy documents. For example, it stipulates ten primary missions for the US military, including "provide a stabilizing presence" around the world. But the document concedes, with emphasis, that *"with reduced resources, thoughtful choices will need to be made regarding the location and frequency of these operations."* And equally important, it stipulates a major goal of "building partnership capacity." "Whenever possible," the document explains, again with emphasis, *"we will develop innovative, low-cost, and small-footprint approaches to achieve our security objectives."*[4]

US policymakers may simply be making a virtue of necessity, but it is a change that is long overdue. The US military cannot be everywhere, and it cannot do everything. The salient constraint is political will. If the public is unwilling to provide the additional resources that will be required to sustain the United States' current foreign policies through higher taxes, or to make other sacrifices, including cuts in popular domestic programs, then the strategist must either rethink the means or reconsider the ends.

The latter is the wiser course, in most instances. For decades the American people have borne a disproportionate share of the costs of global governance. Even the advocates of America's current grand strategy admit that there is little public support for this strategy, and that it would evaporate if scrutinized too closely.[5] It is highly unlikely that the public would support the sorts of trade-offs that would be required to sustain global hegemony beyond the next fifteen to twenty years, especially given the current fiscal crisis and the long-term imbalance between promised benefits and anticipated revenues.

But this is not simply a question of political will and popular support. National security is a function of a nation's fiscal health. Echoing the former chairman of the Joint Chiefs of Staff, Admiral Mike Mullen, the national debt is the single greatest challenge to US national security.[6] In December 2012 Mullen predicted that Pentagon spending cuts are probably inevitable, and he urged military planners "to be ready." The drawdown, however difficult, will be manageable. "The Pentagon can work its way through that," he said, but not without rethinking its strategy.[7]

Mullen is right. Balancing means and ends is an all-hands-on-deck enterprise; the military should be expected to help put the country on a sound financial footing. But the uniformed services cannot do it alone; they need civilian policymakers to reconsider the purpose of American military power. If the Pentagon's budget declines significantly, they will need to downsize the strategy.

Although several studies have identified a number of savings that could be obtained though still retaining US current strategy, significant cuts—for example, on the order of those considered under the sequestration provisions of the Budget Control Act of 2011—would be unwise without a commensurate change in the nation's grand strategy. A number of prominent think tanks and outside experts have put forward proposals to do just that.[8] As of this writing, however, Washington politicians, with very few exceptions, are not prepared to reconsider the strategic status quo. They should be. All prior assumptions about what military commitments are necessary, or about the types of risk that the nation is willing to tolerate, should be subjected to serious scrutiny and debate.

This chapter assumes that, by 2030, the United States will remain the dominant military power in the Western Hemisphere, in the Pacific, and in the Atlantic Ocean region. Because of its prodigious technological edge over any potential peer competitor in nearly every significant domain, the US military will retain the ability to intervene outside its core security zones in the rare instances when its immediate security interests are threatened. In the case of the IOR, US facilities at Diego Garcia, and a possible expansion of current facilities in Australia, will likely prove sufficient for most small-scale contingencies in the region, including humanitarian assistance and postdisaster recovery. These can be quickly augmented by US naval assets periodically deployed to the region on a rotational basis, and could be reinforced by additional forces from Guam, Hawaii, or the continental United States, if the crisis calls for longer-term operations.

In chapter 5 below James Holmes and Toshi Yoshihara assert that "former friends and allies would prove less amenable to US entreaties" if "forced to rearm and assume greater regional responsibilities." But Americans can be confident that many of the countries in the region will cooperate with the United States, if and when circumstances arise that would call for intervention to protect vital US interests. It is, of course, "conceivable," as Holmes and Yoshihara explain, "that . . . governments would refuse a US expeditionary force access to their soil." But it is at least equally conceivable that they will do so under the current grand strategy; consider the case of Pakistan, which continues to thwart US actions in the region despite having received tens of billions of dollars from US taxpayers over the past decade.

In short, Holmes and Yoshihara misconstrue the reason why countries currently cooperate with America, and therefore they misdiagnose their propensity to cooperate with America in the future if they were no longer locked in a patron–client relationship—their interests generally do, and will, align with those of the United States. They do not wish to see the IOR become a hotbed of piracy and lawlessness. They place a very high value on trade and the free movement of goods. And they will not take kindly to a regional hegemon attempting to assert itself at their expense. As such, US vital interests do not necessitate a large and obtrusive military presence in the IOR. On the contrary, adding new permanent US bases or extending new security guarantees is likely to have the perverse effect of discouraging the countries in the region from assuming responsibility for their own security. Holmes and Yoshihara seem particularly distressed by the prospect that countries in the region "would likely seek other forms of insurance," but most Americans would welcome such expressions of responsibility and self-defense. The competing strategy presented here is consistent with the public mood.

The geostrategic environment in the IOR in the near term to the midterm, and in the midterm to the long term, is likely to proceed along the trajectory of the recent past, and US interests in the region are likely to decline relative to other regions, especially including the Western Hemisphere. Accordingly, countries in the IOR will be expected to play a larger role in their own backyards. India will continue to expand its military capabilities, possibly well beyond its general focus to the north and west. Its traditional rival, Pakistan, will continue to contest India's claims in Jammu-Kashmir, but is not, and will not be, in a position to challenge India's naval superiority. China, India's other main rival, has expanded its ties with Pakistan, and has developed seaports there, as well as in Sri Lanka and Burma. China hawks stoke fears of Beijing's supposed involvement in the Coco Islands at the northern end of the Andaman Islands archipelago, but others are skeptical.[9] Conflict between the two rising powers in Asia is neither inevitable nor desirable for either party. Beijing's primary focus will be on its domestic challenges; it will struggle to maintain robust economic growth, stifle internal dissent (including possible unrest in Tibet), and fend off challenges to one-party rule. Its foreign policy, meanwhile, will likely remain focused to the east—on recovering Taiwan; on adjudicating territorial disputes with Japan and South Korea; and on contesting US power and influence in East and Southeast Asia. There are powerful incentives for China to peacefully resolve its disagreements over various issues with all these countries.

The most important of these issues is trade, upon which China heavily depends. With respect to trade and economics in the IOR, and the likely impact on US security, the Indian Ocean itself will remain an important transshipment point for trade to and from Asia and Europe. Globalization will affect the fishing economies of most Indian Ocean states. Some individuals may be able to capitalize on the growth of consumer economies in the region, and beyond. Others, pressured by greater competition within international waters, or by illegal fishing within the territorial waters of states unable to secure their rights, may turn to other means of support, including piracy, as we have seen off the coast of Somalia, and in the Gulf of Aden and the Arabian Sea. Piracy will especially pose a problem for shippers, who will be expected to bear the costs of mitigating the threat. But unregulated fisheries and transnational crime (including piracy) do demand greater attention from the countries in the region, and from those nations that are most dependent upon the flow of goods through these contested waterways.

The US military should continue to plan to operate in the IOR, as it has done in the recent past. As a practical matter, it is limited by the paucity of suitable locations for stationing large numbers of troops. More to the point, such a large-scale presence is not necessary for advancing US interests in the region. Therefore, the US military should maintain a small footprint, and periodically deploy naval assets to the region. It should negotiate additional basing arrangements, secure overflight rights, and explore possible logistical staging areas and storage depots, in the unlikely event that a regional contingency requires the introduction of large numbers of US troops. Beyond these prudent but modest steps, Washington should resist the temptation to expand into a far distant area of operations that holds little strategic value.

THE IOR AND US GRAND STRATEGY: ANTICIPATING THE END OF THE UNIPOLAR MOMENT

For several decades the United States has maintained a dominant military posture in most major regions of the world. This power was initially intended to deter Soviet (and, occasionally, Chinese) aggression during the Cold War, but the United States retained much of it even after the collapse of the Soviet Union. Notable scholars and pundits articulated the rationale for this post–Cold War posture in the early 1990s, and many have reaffirmed their arguments in recent years.[10] Their justifications vary, but the conventional wisdom can be boiled down to interests, efficiency, and values.

Interests

As the world's largest economy, the United States benefits disproportionately from the global trading system, and it should therefore bear the costs of providing security for that system. Command of the commons especially safeguards the free flow of goods and allows the United States to affirm—and, when challenged, enforce—international norms that allow for the equally fluid movement of capital, and increasingly of services.[11] Furthermore, the US military posture in Europe, the Middle East, and Asia prevents conflict by reassuring countries in those regions, thus discouraging them from taking steps to defend themselves that might be interpreted as hostile intent by their neighbors. Reducing the incentive for states to maintain a substantial military capability purportedly serves US interests by preventing the outbreak of wars, which would inevitably, so it is claimed, draw in the United States.

Efficiency

Americans have invested hundreds of billions of dollars in the past several decades in military technologies, and they have spent many billions more recruiting and training personnel. The United States maintains this force posture primarily for its own defense; the benefits that flow to other countries and regions are a useful by-product of US efforts. Americans are able to bear the burdens of global hegemony with minimal effort. Political and economic constraints limit the desire of other countries to achieve a comparable level of security independent of the United States, and efforts to fill the void left behind would likely fail if attempted.[12]

Values

The United States is a unique country with unique responsibilities for securing world order. Unlike other countries that can and must focus on preserving their own physical security, the United States—protected by vast oceans to the east and west, and by peaceful, friendly neighbors to the north and south—has often used its military power to advance a broader set of objectives, including individual liberty, free trade, and respect for human rights. Such efforts are consistent with the nation's founding principles, and enjoy broad public support. Indeed, both of the major political parties are essentially in agreement that advancing universal values is a core obligation for the US military, although they disagree on how to fulfill this mandate.

Each of the above-noted rationales is flawed. The advocates of unipolarity (aka primacy) believe that that strategy makes sense for the United States because of their particular theories about how the world works. These theories shape assessments about what is likely to occur if the United States were to use its military less often than it does today. Some of these theories are untested; others are simply wrong. On balance, global hegemony is not "worth the candle," and it will become even more difficult to sustain as the United States' share of global economic output declines in the next ten to twenty years.[13]

GLOBAL PEACE AND FREE TRADE ARE A GLOBAL RESPONSIBILITY Contrary to claims, the United States is remarkably secure and prosperous, and its geostrategic good fortune does not impose any special obligation on American troops or taxpayers to serve an amorphous global good. Insecurity in a far distant corner of the world does not inevitably threaten US interests, in part because there are other countries in the world that can and should deal with those local challenges before they become regional or global ones. Meanwhile, although the United States does benefit from global trade, many other countries also benefit, even more than Americans do. Therefore, it is neither fair nor politically realistic to expect Americans to bear the burdens of global governance indefinitely. On the contrary, all who benefit should be expected to bear some share of the costs associated with keeping the world free and at peace. With respect to the IOR, therefore, the countries in that region should have primary responsibility for peace and security there.

SELF-DEFENSE IS MORE EFFECTIVE THAN EXTENDED DETERRENCE Providing global public goods of relative peace and security, and facilitating a free and open global trading system, was the wise course for the United States in the wake of World War II, when Europe and Asia were shattered by war and threatened by a common enemy: the Soviet Union, and soon thereafter Maoist China. But America has entered a new era, when its formal allies and other trading partners are in a position to do more for their own defense, and should be encouraged to do so. The credibility of a given country's determination to defend itself from attack is a much stronger deterrent than the promise of a third party to treat an attack on an ally as though it were synonymous with an attack on it. Threatening retaliation for an attack on one's own territory, forces, or population is more credible than threatening similar action in response to an attack on an ally—particularly when doing so could mean a nuclear strike in return.[14] This explains why extended deterrence is difficult. As Thomas Schelling notes in his classic work *Arms and Influence*, extended deterrence "requires projecting intentions. It requires having those intentions . . . and communicating them persuasively to make other countries behave."[15]

AMERICA'S VALUES DEMAND THAT IT ALIGN ITS ENDS WITH ITS MEANS
Americans value prudence and restraint; they disdain profligacy and recklessness. There is nothing honorable about making promises that cannot or will not be kept. This applies to promises made to allies that have come to depend on the United States for their own security but rightly worry about Washington's ability to follow through on those commitments if challenged. It also applies to the promises that the US government has made to its own citizens, and to succeeding generations. The federal government has been issuing IOUs that the nation's children and grandchildren will need to honor. Eventually, the books must be brought into balance.

Advocates of primacy do not dispute that it is costly, but they claim that the alternatives would be even costlier.[16] Indeed, many see only one alternative: "chaos."[17] In 1996 William Kristol and Robert Kagan claimed that "American hegemony is the only reliable defense against a breakdown of peace and international order."[18] Harvard's Niall Ferguson worries that a reduction in US military power would result in a world characterized by "waning empires. Religious revivals. Incipient anarchy. A coming retreat into fortified cities."[19] The world order today, writes Robert Kagan, "is as fragile as it is unique," and "preserving [it] requires constant American leadership and constant American commitment."[20]

But such dire claims confuse what causes peace and prosperity, and they misconstrue what would likely occur if the United States were to focus primarily on its own defense, and to expect other countries to do the same. The current strategy is costly and counterproductive. It requires a vastly larger standing military than would a strategy that expects other countries to take primary responsibility for their own defense. And the US forward posture and security guarantees explicitly discourage them from doing so.

The relative peace that the world has enjoyed since the end of World War II, and the dramatic expansion of global trade during that time, generally coincide with a long period of US military dominance. But correlation does not prove causation. Although it is true that the human race enjoys a measure of security and economic opportunity that our ancestors would envy, it is not axiomatic that this is a function solely, or even primarily, of the US global military posture.

The defenders of the status quo do not wish to test that proposition. According to Johns Hopkins University's Michael Mandelbaum, "The abdication by the United States of some or all of the responsibilities for international security would deprive the international system of one of its principal safety features, which keeps countries from smashing into each other." "For better or for worse," he concludes, "the world has, in the first decade of the twenty-first century, no substitute for the United States as the provider of governmental defense services to the international system."[21]

The alternative strategic concept spelled out in this chapter aims to solve this problem. Shifting and shedding the burdens of global governance should be a top priority for US policymakers, just behind ensuring the physical security of the United States. A number of US government documents and strategy statements address the need to close the vast and growing gap between US military capacity and that of other states. They do not, however, offer a credible plan for making this happen, in part because they do not appreciate how US military dominance discourages other countries from doing more.

For example, the 2010 QDR and the revised strategic guidance issued in January 2012 both refer on a number of occasions to building partner capacity, and working with other countries to address common challenges. The QDR includes vague language about evolving US strategic posture in different regions, but the bottom line is the same as it has been for decades: a de facto permanent presence for US forces in Europe and Asia, and continued attention to security in "key regions"—a phrase that appears seven times but is never actually defined, and therefore could be construed as everywhere in the world. Meanwhile, the Pentagon continues to maintain a forward-deployed posture in most regions. It assumes that the US security umbrella will remain open over Europe for the indefinite future, though with fewer US ground troops permanently stationed there. The US security commitment in East Asia, meanwhile, is expected to grow. And the Pentagon continues to plan for contingency operations around the globe on the presumption that the United States will remain the de facto first responder for international crises.

Some in Washington might wish for other countries to share the costs of global security, but most senior officials behave as though they expect the United States to remain the dominant player in most regions of the world. The governing assumption, as the QDR explains, is that "the United States remains the only nation able to project and sustain large-scale operations over extended distances."[22] Former secretary of defense Robert Gates echoed those sentiments when he told reporters that the US military had a special obligation to serve as "the underwriter of security for most of the free world."[23] In his cover letter to the revised strategic guidance, President Obama explained that "in a changing world that demands our leadership, the United States will remain the greatest force for freedom and security that the world has ever known."[24] Although these claims can be explained as understandable expressions of pride in the country and its military, they send mixed messages about Washington's desire to see other countries do more.

This is not new. Since the dawn of the Cold War, successive US administrations have been complaining about inadequate burden sharing. Capacity building—which presumes that security responsibilities will someday be handed over to the locals—is easier said than done. It is also true, however, that the longer the US military operates as the protector of a particular country, or of a particular region, the harder it becomes to extricate itself.

The best way to ensure that the liberal democracies in the IOR will eventually become self-sufficient is to take off the training wheels. When that occurs, there will be some skinned knees and bruised egos, but at least US military personnel will not be the only ones doing the pedaling. This has long been a problem in Europe and East Asia, where longtime allies have been sheltered under the American security umbrella for at least two generations. Tens of millions of British, Germans, Japanese, and South Koreans have no firsthand memory of a life without the United States. Transitioning security responsibilities in those countries will be difficult, and will take time.

By contrast, US policymakers have generally resisted the impulse to extend the American security umbrella over countries in the IOR. They should not change course, particularly at a time when America should be looking to reduce its overseas obligations, not add new ones.

Beyond general promises to safeguard the global commons, or to extend security guarantees to individual nation-states, US policymakers should differentiate between those threats that the nation must address and those that are best left to others. Geographic proximity should factor into those considerations. It is inconceivable that Americans would treat a security threat in the Bay of Bengal as synonymous with a threat in the Gulf of Mexico. By the same token, India, Bangladesh, Singapore, and Australia have shown no particular enthusiasm for assisting the United States and Mexico with halting cross-border drug violence. Conversely, the Australians were not shy about sending troops to the Solomon Islands in 2003, and into East Timor in 2006. Meanwhile, although the Indians were humbled and chagrined by their decision to assist Sri Lanka's bid to quell the Tamil insurgency, the fact remains that they did choose to intervene. US policy should do nothing that might discourage countries in the IOR from continuing to tackle the security challenges in their strategic neighborhood.

For decades, the United States has been the leading provider of many global public goods, the most important of these being security; the US military has performed admirably as the policeman for the world. But these forces have never been omnipotent; there are limits to US power, including an increasing unwillingness on the part of many Americans to shoulder the burdens of global governance in perpetuity.

Thus, the United States' leaders should transition away from the nation's current unipolar posture by speaking honestly with the American people about the true costs of this power, and with the rest of the world about the need to share in the burdens of keeping the world relatively prosperous and at peace.

APPLYING THE STRATEGIC CONCEPT TO THE IOR: HOW US POLICY THERE CAN SHAPE THE NEW MULTIPOLAR ORDER

It will take time to transition the global system from a dependence on US global hegemony to a multipolar order, where other countries are expected to be responsible for their own defense and to play a constructive role in their respective regions. The world has grown accustomed to having the United States acting as its de facto government. Change is difficult.

Applying this strategic concept to the IOR, however, can and should begin immediately. The dire fiscal situation compels the US government to prioritize global commitments. The IOR's strategic importance to the United States is limited, in part due to its sheer distance—more than 10,000 miles from Washington, and nearly 9,000 miles from Los Angeles. Even if geography and physical distance are less relevant than in the past, and the purported leading threats in the first half of the twenty-first century are likely to be transnational, the IOR is no more likely than other regions of the world to be the locus of these threats. Terrorism is not unique to the IOR. Infectious diseases can just as easily arise in Sub-Saharan Africa or Central and East Asia as in the Indian Ocean littorals. Cybercrime is nearly ubiquitous. Natural disasters can strike anywhere on the planet. More to the point, these sorts of threats pale in comparison to the global wars that claimed over 60 million lives and destroyed entire cities in the first half of the twentieth century; and they do not lend themselves to military solutions. There has never been an urgent need for a large-scale, permanent US military presence in the IOR. And there is not a need for one now.

Thus, a global grand strategy not predicated on US hegemony, and applied to the IOR, entails continuing the US government's past practices in the region. The Department of Defense (DOD) will continue to bear primary responsibility for advancing US strategic objectives in the IOR, as it does in all other regions; but these objectives are modest, and they can be achieved with a modest force posture. Efforts to dramatically expand the capacity of US nondefense agencies, and to improve interagency coordination, will continue to be impeded by a profound, and nearly insurmountable, obstacle: the enormous resource disparity between DOD and all other federal agencies. This resource gap is likely to remain very wide, and it may grow even wider, even if the military budget declines slightly during this period.

Other government agencies do have a role to play, however. Specifically, Washington should implement four key diplomatic initiatives that reflect a determination to prioritize among a set of important national objectives:

1. Make no new security guarantees to defend the countries in the IOR, or the countries on its periphery. This would include any countries whose shorelines include the Indian Ocean, in South Asia, Southwest Asia, or East Africa. The US government should adopt this policy immediately.

2. Forge a new strategic relationship with India. Lingering hostility toward India, a holdover from the Cold War, is easing in Washington, though relations with Pakistan have strained to the breaking point. US dependence upon Pakistan will decline in the coming decade as US military operations in Afghanistan are brought to a close (thus obviating the need for logistical support through Pakistan), and as the focus of US counter-terrorism efforts shift from Central Asia to the Arabian Peninsula, the Horn of Africa, and the Maghreb. A strategic shift that aligns the United States with what is likely to be the dominant power (both militarily and economically) in the IOR is also more consistent with US values than current US ties to the only nominally democratic Pakistan. Given that much of the US taxpayer money that has been steered to Islamabad over the years has been diverted toward Pakistan's strategic competition with India, reducing or terminating US financial and military aid to Pakistan would improve India's already-strong relative standing. Fears that China will exploit a rift in US–Pakistani relations to expand its influence in South Asia / Central Asia, and ultimately to the IOR, are overblown. A formal alliance between the United States and Pakistan has not prevented Beijing from expanding trade and other ties with Islamabad. Cultural differences render even short-term cooperation between China and Pakistan difficult, and make a long-term alliance unlikely.

3. Clarify the terms of US basing and overflight rights, and of the US Navy's access to port facilities. Codifying these agreements in peacetime will help to prevent misunderstandings during periods of tension or conflict. These agreements will generally be durable enough to ensure US access to the region, as the countries in the IOR broadly share US interests, and thus they will be inclined to cooperate with America in the highly unlikely event that US military intervention is warranted.

4. Have a serious conversation with the countries in the IOR, and on its periphery, about their responsibilities for maintaining peace and order in the region. Those countries in East Asia with which America has bilateral

security treaties, including South Korea and Japan, and the member states of the North Atlantic Treaty Organization (NATO), should bear a greater share of the burdens associated with keeping the IOR open to trade. Although these countries are not part of the IOR, expanding their military capacity for self-defense and for protecting their interests outside the immediate neighborhood will serve US, and global, interests there.

These diplomatic initiatives should be undertaken in tandem with an approach to US military power in the region that reflects Washington's determination to balance means and ends, and to reduce the burdens of global governance on US troops and taxpayers. This strategic concept prioritizes the six key military mission areas identified in the 2010 QDR:

1. Defend the United States and support civil authorities at home. This is the primary obligation of the US government to its citizens, and therefore is, and should be, the first order of business for the US military and other national security agencies. There are few urgent security threats emanating from the IOR, and those that do (e.g., transnational crime and terrorism) are generally not best addressed by military means.

2. Build the security capacity of partner states. This must be a top policy priority of the US government, just behind defending the United States, and it is the underlying rationale behind this strategic framework. But the focus should be less on attempting to build for others and more toward inducing others to build up themselves. Past efforts by the United States to build partner capacity have failed, in part because of the perverse incentives created by US primacy. States have a strong interest in free-riding on US power, and little incentive to increase their national security spending while sheltered under the US security umbrella. That would change under this strategic framework.

3. Prevent nuclear proliferation, and counter weapons of mass destruction. As long as the United States professes a desire to prevent the further spread of nuclear and other mass-casualty weapons, it should focus its efforts elsewhere; the IOR is unlikely to be the locus of additional nuclear proliferation. Two of the nine known nuclear weapons states are in the IOR (Pakistan and India), and another four are on its periphery (Russia, China, Israel, and North Korea). If Iran continues with its nuclear enrichment program, it might prompt other countries to develop programs of their own, though many experts are skeptical of such predictions of cascading proliferation.[25] If it did occur, however, new nuclear weapons would likely first appear in the Arabian Gulf, or to the west, into the Eastern Mediterranean and North Africa, not in other states in the IOR.

The focus of US efforts, therefore, should be on the security of the existing arsenals in the region, in India and Pakistan. The nuclear weapons states themselves—not the United States—should bear primary responsibility for ensuring that their weapons, dangerous materials, and/or sensitive technologies and know-how remain out of the hands of nonstate actors. The US government should continue to work with these countries, sharing ideas about best practices and helping to establish international standards governing the security of such weapons; but the US military's role in these efforts should be modest.

4. Succeed in counterinsurgency, stability, and counterterrorism operations. This objective from the 2010 QDR was largely superseded by the revised strategic guidance from January 2012. The shift was well along by the summer of 2011. Then–secretary of defense Robert Gates predicted that the US military's focus on counterinsurgency (COIN) was likely to recede in relative importance over the next ten to fifteen years as the wars in Iraq and Afghanistan draw to a close. "The United States is unlikely to repeat a mission on the scale of those in Afghanistan or Iraq anytime soon—that is, forced regime change followed by nation building under fire," he wrote in the May–June 2011 issue of *Foreign Affairs*.[26] Less than a year later, he told Army cadets at West Point that "any future defense secretary who advises the president to again send a big American land army into Asia or into the Middle East or Africa should 'have his head examined.'"[27] By December 2011 President Obama had endorsed the retreat from COIN. In a meeting with the Joint Chiefs of Staff and the nation's combatant commanders, the president turned down the Pentagon's call to maintain a standing force of 100,000 US troops for "stability operations." "By scratching that off the proposed budget," the *New York Times'* David Sanger explains, "Obama's message was clear: America was out of the occupation business."[28] The revised strategic guidance issued the following month publicly affirmed, with emphasis, that "*US forces will no longer be sized to conduct large-scale, prolonged stability operations.*"[29]

This judgment reflects the fact that such missions are enormously costly, are unpopular with the American people, and are unlikely to achieve their stated objectives in a reasonable time frame. Simply put, COIN is armed nation building; and nation building is a fool's errand. Effective counterterrorism does not depend upon the creation of functioning nation-states in distant lands; counterterrorism operations in the IOR, including in Somalia, Yemen, and Indonesia, can continue as they have over the past decade, and do not require large numbers of US troops. Indeed, an obtrusive US military presence is likely to make the problem worse. Effective counterterrorism efforts will leverage the common concerns of the rising powers in the IOR. No nation-state should want to see nonstate actors expand their power and influence. Those who have attempted to use terrorist groups to advance their national security objectives should have learned by now that such efforts will often backfire and are never justified. The US government at all levels should continue to communicate this message.

1. Deter and defeat aggression in antiaccess environments. The US military must retain the ability to operate in vital strategic regions, but there is little evidence that a hostile power could effectively deny access to the IOR, as a whole, or to important subregions within it. Some technologies and doctrine that allow the US military to operate in antiaccess environments in one region can be applied to the IOR, as required. In the case of the IOR, specifically, US aircraft carriers are uniquely suited to be able to surge into a vast area that possesses very few convenient staging areas for large numbers of ground troops, or facilities that could host land-based aircraft.

2. Operate effectively in cyberspace. To the extent that this is a core mission for the US military, there is nothing unique to the IOR that pertains to cyberspace. America could continue to operate effectively in cyberspace with no permanent peacetime presence in the IOR, or it could fail even with dozens of ships patrolling the Indian Ocean, and with tens of thousands of personnel deployed at a string of bases from Mombasa to Djibouti to Singapore to Perth.

RISKS AND UNCERTAINTIES

As with any frontal assault on the reigning orthodoxy, some will argue that the burden of proof is on those calling for change, given that the current strategy has done a reasonably good job of keeping the United States safe and secure. The alternatives to the status quo, they claim, would be far worse. The advocates of primacy seem particularly dismissive of the idea that the country's resource constraints compel it to restrain its foreign policy ambitions.[30]

When considering the risks of the strategic framework outlined here, however, one should also consider the risks of inaction—that is, the risks inherent in maintaining the status quo. When Washington embarked on the unipolar project in the early 1990s, the United States accounted for about a third of the world's economic output, and about a third of global military spending. Today, the United States accounts for nearly half the world's military spending, and less than a quarter of economic output. It defies basic common sense to expect US taxpayers to bear a *larger* share of the burdens of global governance as their share of the global economy declines.

That said, there are some particular areas where US policymakers and military leaders should focus to ensure that this new strategic concept continues to advance US interests. The following discussion highlights a few possible risks, and suggests measures that can mitigate these risks.

Managing the Transition

Historically, major shifts in the distribution of global power have been associated with unrest and violence. In the worst cases, power transitions have precipitated wars between major powers.[31] It is possible that the history of the distant past no longer provides a useful guide to the present and near future, if, as some have suggested, global politics has undergone a profound and durable transformation.[32] Further, the most recent power transition, from Cold War bipolarity to post–Cold War unipolarity, was not associated with a dramatic increase in interstate violence, although it did result in a considerably higher operational tempo for the US military. To the extent that the warnings contained within power transition theory remain valid, Washington can mitigate the risks by selectively disengaging from its Cold War–era commitments, and by doing so as expeditiously as is strategically prudent. This might take a decade, or two or three. But the message to all security dependents should be that the era of American unipolarity is coming to an end.

Devolving Security Responsibilities

Instability or violence might also occur if other countries prove unable or unwilling to cope with their new responsibilities. It is possible that global security in the future will be underprovided relative to what exists today under US unipolarity. This might be mitigated by repurposing existing multinational institutions to enable them to better address security challenges without the US military in the lead. This option is not immediately available to the states of the IOR, which lack a regional security organization along the lines of NATO, the Gulf Cooperation Council, or the Association of Southeast Asian Nations. Conversely, unlike countries in Europe, the Middle East, and East and Southeast Asia, security in the IOR countries is not heavily dependent upon US military power. Still, for many countries in the IOR, a good bilateral relationship with the United States is more important than relationships with each other. That will change as the United States focuses attention on the few core regions that are a vital concern for US security.

Stopping, or Slowing, Nuclear Proliferation

Countries no longer formally protected by the US nuclear umbrella, or that come to doubt US commitments to defend them, might be tempted to acquire nuclear weapons for the purposes of deterrence. However, although there are practical reasons why the leading contestants in the new nuclear weapons state sweepstakes will choose to forgo such weapons in spite of their new strategic circumstances. This is particularly true in the IOR. As noted above (in the section on military missions), non–nuclear weapon states in the IOR would gain little from acquiring such weapons.

Policymakers should also explore creative ways to discourage nation-states from wanting to acquire nuclear weapons, even as they are mindful of the legitimate reasons why those nations might want them (as a deterrent against aggression). Nonstate actors are unlikely to respond to the same inducements, as their motives for acquiring such weapons are likely quite different than for states. In particular, many fear that nonstate actors would be anxious to use them, whereas leaders of states hope that they never have to.[33]

Loss of Influence

A less obtrusive military presence in the IOR might impede the US government's ability to influence key policy decisions there. As a practical matter, however, the US presence has always been quite small, and America has minimal leverage, even over those countries in the region where it has maintained long-standing ties. The tens of billions of dollars in US financial assistance given to Pakistan, for example, have neither convinced Islamabad to support US policies in neighboring Afghanistan nor purchased much goodwill with the Pakistani people. The best way for the United States to acquire and retain influence in the region is to put its own economic house in order, and to serve as a model for nascent democracies.

The United States should open its markets to the countries in the region, and otherwise facilitate the free flow of goods and services to boost prosperity and to bind these countries more tightly together economically, thus reducing the likelihood of conflict.

CONCLUSION: FROM INSOLVENT SUPERPOWER TO RESPONSIBLE LEADING POWER

If ever there was a time for a major shift in US foreign policy, that time is now. The US fiscal outlook remains cloudy at best. Federal spending has exceeded revenues for each of the last ten fiscal years, and deficits are projected to persist under every serious budget proposal. Recent attempts to close the budget deficit have fallen well short of what is required. Still, these near-term challenges pale in comparison with the looming fiscal train wreck, where the government's commitments to retirees, veterans, and the permanently disabled will vastly outstrip any realistic expectation of how to pay for them.

Excessive military spending is not the prime driver of the nation's fiscal incontinence; but it is a factor. Polls suggest that the public is more inclined to cut the military's budget than to forgo promised retirement benefits under Social Security, or to accept cost-saving reforms in the Medicare system. Meanwhile, there is little support for across-the-board tax increases to close the budget gap.[34]

The combination of these factors could contribute to significant military spending cuts during the next decade. More likely is a slow but steady decline in real spending, as modest increases in the DOD base budget are offset by inflation. Even modest cuts, however, could have a detrimental impact on the force if they are not matched with a new approach to where, when, and how US troops are deployed. A recent report by the RAND Corporation's National Defense Research Institute finds "considerable advantages to DOD's establishing a strategic direction in which to accommodate further sizable reductions." The RAND study calls for "a strategic direction [that] limits the risk the cuts may impose or, at the very least, makes that risk explicit to the nation's leaders. By definition, it requires prioritization of defense challenges and of what risks to accept, with force structure and program decisions following."[35]

Not everyone agrees. The defenders of the status quo claim that it is possible, and desirable, for the United States to maintain its role as the guarantor of global security for a very long time. But history and common sense teach otherwise. It is more likely that as America struggles to provide the resources to cover its many and growing global commitments, it will live in a constant state of fear, and it will never be able to overcome its nagging sense of insecurity. It will continue to spend more and more, convinced by its own rhetoric of an approaching near competitor. And as it spends, others will react. Its prospective adversaries—spurred by resentment, hostility, or fear—will develop the means to deter it from taking action against them. Meanwhile, its allies and clients, or those who aspire to be, will cajole and connive it into taking risks on their behalf, though they remain content to dedicate resources to their own domestic pursuits. America will spend even more on its military, on the assumption that it must maintain its edge to discourage challenges from prospective adversaries.

And America will send its troops, ships, and planes to more places, and more often, in order to demonstrate its willingness to act on behalf of others, believing that this will reassure its allies, lest they be tempted to switch sides or chart their own course.

But Americans should not pretend that the nation's military power is limitless. They cannot absolve themselves of the need to prioritize whether, and when, to use their power. They should not convince themselves that others will only cooperate with them if they are paying for their security. Over the course of the next two decades, Americans should endeavor to use their military power less, and to encourage others to use theirs more.

A decisive and deliberate move away from primacy makes sense on its narrow strategic merits, but the economic advantages of burden shedding should also be taken into account. US taxpayers would benefit from the redirection of some financial resources to address the nation's fiscal challenges. Perhaps most important, US troops would also gain, as they would be called upon less often to address security challenges that can and should be handled by others. This strategy would allow the US military to better manage a smaller set of core objectives in an era of dwindling resources.

A strategic shift will happen, whether Americans want it to or not. The best approach is to prepare for the eventuality in a proactive way. This would better position the United States to shape the post-unipolar world than if it retained its current grand strategy with only minor modifications. Washington should begin to take a new global posture in the IOR, the one region of the world where US interests and US military deployments are modest.

NOTES

1. National Intelligence Council, *Global Trends 2030: Alternative Worlds* (Washington, DC: National Intelligence Council, 2012), iii, 8.
2. See especially chapter 5 in the present volume, by James R. Holmes and Toshi Yoshihara. See also Robert Kaplan, *Monsoon: The Indian Ocean and the Future of American Power* (New York: Random House, 2010).
3. US Department of Defense, "Sustaining US Global Leadership: Priorities for 21st Century Defense," January 2012, 1, www.defense.gov/news/defense_strategic_guidance.pdf.
4. Ibid., 5–6, 3.
5. Michael Mandelbaum, *The Case for Goliath: How America Acts as the World's Government in the 21st Century* (New York: PublicAffairs, 2005), 224.
6. "Mullen: Debt Is Top National Security Challenge," CNN, April 27, 2010, http://articles.cnn.com/2010-08-27/us/debt.security.mullen_1_pentagon-budget-national-debt-michael-mullen?_s=PM:US; Olga Belagova, "Mullen Addresses Debt and New National Security Team," *National Journal*, April 28,2011,www.nationaljournal.com/nationalsecurity/mullen-addresses-debt-new-national-security-team-20110428.
7. Quoted by John M. Donnelly, "CQ *Roll Call* Executive Briefing: Defense," December 18, 2012.
8. Gordon Adams, "Budget Agreement Reached! 5 Think Tanks Warn of Things to Come for the Pentagon," ForeignPolicy.com, November 27, 2012, www.foreignpolicy.com/articles/2012/11/27/budget_agreement_reached.
9. See, e.g., Andrew Selth, *Chinese Military Bases in Burma: The Explosion of a Myth*, Regional Outlook 10 (Brisbane: Griffith Asia Institute, 2007); and Andrew Selth, "Chinese Whispers: The Great Coco Island Mystery," *The Irrawaddy* 15, no. 1 (January 2007).

10. See, especially, Robert Kagan, *The World America Made* (New York: Alfred A. Knopf, 2012); and Stephen G. Brooks, G. John Ikenberry, and William C. Wohlforth, "Don't Come Home America: The Case against Retrenchment," *International Security* 37, no. 3 (Winter 2012–13): 7–51. See also chapter 5, by Holmes and Yoshihara.

11. Barry Posen, "Command of the Commons: The Military Foundation of US Hegemony," *International Security* 28, no. 1 (Summer 2003): 5–46.

12. See, especially, Mandelbaum, *Case for Goliath.*

13. Robert Jervis, "International Primacy: Is the Game Worth the Candle?" *International Security* 17, no. 4 (Spring 1993): 52–67. See also Eugene Gholz, Daryl G. Press, and Harvey M. Sapolsky, "Come Home, America: The Strategy of Restraint in the Face of Temptation," *International Security* 21, no. 4 (Spring 1997): 548; Barry Posen, "The Case for Restraint," *The American Interest* 3, no. 1 (November–December 2007): 7–17; John J. Mearsheimer, "Imperial By Design," *The National Interest*, no. 111 (January–February 2011): 16–34; Paul K. MacDonald and Joseph M. Parent, "Graceful Decline? The Surprising Success of Great Power Retrenchment," *International Security* 35, no. 4 (Spring 2011): 7–44; Benjamin H. Friedman and Justin Logan, "Why the US Military Budget Is 'Foolish and Sustainable,'" *Orbis* 56, no. 2 (Spring 2012): 177–91.

14. This problem is known as the "stability/instability paradox," which means that fear of mutual destruction is likely to deter two adversaries from fighting one another, but it might make one side wary of intervening on behalf of a third party in the face of nuclear retaliation from the other. See Robert Jervis, *The Meaning of the Nuclear Revolution: Statecraft and the Meaning of Armageddon* (Ithaca, NY: Cornell University Press, 1989), 19–22.

15. Thomas C. Schelling, *Arms and Influence* (New Haven, CT: Yale University Press, 2008), 36.

16. See, e.g., chapter 5 below.

17. Charles Krauthammer, "The Unipolar Moment," *Foreign Affairs* 70, no. 1 (1990–91): 32.

18. William Kristol and Robert Kagan, "Toward a Neo-Reaganite Foreign Policy," *Foreign Affairs* 75, no. 4 (July–August 1996): 23.

19. Niall Ferguson, "A World without Power," *Foreign Policy*, no. 143 (July–August 2004): 38.

20. Kagan, *World America Made*, 134.

21. Mandelbaum, *Case for Goliath*, 195, 218.

22. US Department of Defense, "Quadrennial Defense Review Report," February 2010, iv.

23. DOD News Briefing with Secretary Gates and Admiral Mullen from the Pentagon, January 6, 2011, www.defense.gov/transcripts/transcript.aspx?transcriptid =4747.

24. Barack Obama, cover letter for "Sustaining US Global Leadership," by US Department of Defense.

25. On Iran and the fear of a proliferation cascade, see Colin Kahl, Melissa Dalton, and Matthew Irvine, "Atomic Kingdom: If Iran Builds the Bomb, Will Saudi Arabia Be Next?" Center for a New American Security, February 2013. On generally overblown fears of proliferation cascades, see Francis J. Gavin, "Same as It Ever Was: Nuclear Alarmism, Proliferation, and the Cold War," *International Security* 34, no. 2 (Winter 2009–10): 7–37; and John Mueller, *Atomic Obsession: Nuclear Alarmism from Hiroshima to Al-Qaeda* (New York: Oxford University Press, 2010), 89–102.

26. Robert Gates, "Helping Others Defend Themselves," *Foreign Affairs* 89, no. 3 (May–June 2010): 2.

27. Quoted by Thom Shanker, "Warning against Wars in Iraq and Afghanistan," *New York Times*, February 25, 2011.

28. David E. Sanger, *Confront and Conceal: Obama's Secret Wars and Surprising Use of American Power* (New York: Crown, 2012).

29. "Sustaining US Global Leadership: Priorities for 21st Century Defense," 6.

30. See, especially, Kagan, *World America Made*.

31. The seminal work is by A. F. K. Organski, *World Politics* (New York: Alfred A. Knopf, 1958). See also Eugene R. Wittkopf, *World Politics: Trend and Transformation* (New York: St. Martin's Press, 1997); and Ronald L. Tammen, ed., *Power Transitions: Strategies for the 21st Century* (New York: Seven Bridges Press, 2000).

32. Richard Ned Lebow, *Why Nations Fight* (New York: Cambridge, 2010); Christopher J. Fettweis, *Dangerous Times? The International Politics of Great Power Peace* (Washington, DC: Georgetown University Press, 2010); John Mueller, *The Remnants of War* (Ithaca, NY: Cornell University Press, 2004).

33. For a different take, see Thomas Schelling, "Thinking about Nuclear Terrorism," *International Security* 6, no. 4 (Spring 1982): 61–77; and John Mueller, *Atomic Obsession: Nuclear Alarmism from Hiroshima to Al-Qaeda* (New York: Oxford University Press, 2010), 159–233. See also Todd Masse, "Nuclear Terrorism Redux: Conventionalists, Skeptics, and the Margin of Safety," *Orbis* 54, no. 2 (2010): 302–19.

34. "Majorities in Both Red and Blue Districts Favor Deep Cuts in Defense Spending," World Public Opinion, July 16, 2012, www.worldpublicopinion.org/pipa/articles/brunitedstatescanadara/719.php.

35. Stuart E. Johnson, Irv Blickstein, David C. Gompert, Charles Nemfakos, Harry J. Thie, Michael J. McNerney, Duncan Long, Brian McInnis, and Amy Potter, *A Strategy-Based Framework for Accommodating Reductions in the Defense Budget* (Santa Monica, CA: RAND Corporation, 2012), ix, www.rand.org/content/dam/rand/pubs/occasional_papers/2012/RAND_OP379.pdf.

CHAPTER 5

OFFSHORE BALANCING IN THE INDIAN OCEAN

Forward or Not at All

JAMES R. HOLMES AND
TOSHI YOSHIHARA

The hour for offshore balancing has struck. Or has it? Adherents to this school of grand strategy beseech the United States to disentangle itself from Eurasia, and to let the European and Asian nations counterbalance the overbearing powers that arise in their midst. If the international system is indeed self-enforcing, Washington can shed the burden of maintaining equilibrium far from American shores. Only to prevent a would-be hegemon or hostile coalition from seizing control of Eurasia, only to protect its independence and territorial integrity, and only as a last resort should the United States again take up arms in Europe or Asia.

Offshore balancing, then, is more about influencing policy than executing it. Earlier in this volume, for instance, Christopher Preble presents a strong case for trimming America's commitments in Eurasia, including along the South Asian rimland. The upshot is that the United States neither needs nor can afford to uphold its security commitments in the region. It should pivot homeward. Preble offers a more restrained, more workable vision than do the offshore balancers profiled below. Still, like advocates of similar leanings, Preble is advising policymakers rather than the executors of policy.

Our audience is the strategic, operational, and tactical leaders who do the bidding of elected officials. Strategy is about the ways and means for fulfilling the political aims formulated by political leaders. As we shall see, offshore-balancing advocates proffer abstract claims rooted in international relations theory, as do many of their intellectual opponents. Having asserted that, say, the Eurasian system is self-regulating and can do without outside supervision, they proceed to recommend that the United States eschew Eurasian entanglements. Again, these are political judgments. Offshore balancers seldom concern themselves with the mechanics of how to perform the balancing function, simply because they hope America never will. By contrast, we ask whether and how a scaled-back US military operating from afar can generate the strategic effects expected of it under US foreign policy as it currently stands.

We doubt it could do so even in traditional theaters, much less in remote South Asia, a region of growing strategic importance to Washington. Those advocating strategic restraint, like Preble, believe that the Indian Ocean region will remain peripheral for the United States. They forecast a future based on extrapolations of current conditions. As Preble argues in chapter 4, the security dynamics in the South Asian littorals are "likely to proceed along the trajectory of the recent past," even over the longer term. But this view is at odds with the emerging policy consensus, because US foreign policy has undergone a tectonic shift over the past decade, culminating in 2011 with the Barack Obama administration's announcement that it would "pivot" to the Western Pacific and Indian Ocean, and thus concentrate policy energy and physical power on the region anew.[1]

American strategy has thus come to embrace more than traditional, relatively accessible theaters like Western Europe and East Asia. The mounting importance of South Asia—a region far less hospitable for US power projection—renders offshore balancing too costly and too hazardous to supply the basis for an Indian Ocean strategy. Again, proponents of this approach downplay the practical impediments to offshore balancing, when they acknowledge them at all. Phrasing their appeals in abstractions obscures nettlesome realities. Acting as an external balancer in faraway South Asia would be far more demanding than exercising hard power in East Asia and Europe. Washington must devise other options.

This is a task of considerable moment. The concurrent rise of India and China is reconfiguring the international system, tugging the strategic center of global power southward from the northern coasts of Eurasia. *Global Trends 2030*, to which Preble lends much credence, singles out India as the player most likely to eclipse China as the "rising economic powerhouse" twenty years hence. Such a power shift would almost certainly introduce agents of change that could unsettle the geostrategic environment. Current trends are probably an unreliable guide for discerning the future. Halford Mackinder's analytical effort to unify China and India as a single geographic entity—an "Asiatic monsoon land"—may finally be bearing fruit.[2] New political, economic, and military realities are shifting the US center of gravity—or buoyancy, if you will—toward South Asia. Indeed, Robert Kaplan prophesies that the "Greater Indian Ocean" may come to represent "a map as iconic to the new century as Europe was to the last one," owing to the region's abundance of natural resources, its position along the nautical frontiers of Islam, and its central location astride critical sea lanes.[3]

In other words, the strategic, political, and economic dynamism of the countries inhabiting the Indo-Pacific rim will exert an almost gravitational pull on US interests. The US sea services stole an intellectual march on Kaplan in 2007, publishing a Maritime Strategy document that portrayed the Indian Ocean as one of two vital theaters for the exercise of US maritime power. This marked a dramatic shift. This document, *A Cooperative Strategy for 21st Century Seapower*, in effect proclaims that the US Navy and its expeditionary force, the US Marine Corps, along with the US Coast Guard, remain the two-ocean force they have been for seven decades, since Congress enacted the Two-Ocean Navy Act of 1940.[4] But the two oceans are different. The uniformed service chiefs evidently consider the Atlantic Ocean a safe expanse. Instead, they instruct the sea services to stage "credible combat power" in the Western Pacific and the Indian Ocean basin (including the Persian Gulf) for the foreseeable future.[5] Washington's strategic gaze is now locked on maritime Asia.

Offshore balancing runs counter to this strategic vision. Strictly applied, it would require Washington to forgo managing the system of globalized trade and commerce in favor of US commercial, political, and military interests. It rejects early action to prevent regional tensions from spiraling into conflict or war. And it displays scant regard for "core capabilities," such as humanitarian and disaster relief, that feature prominently in the Maritime Strategy. By confining US interests strictly to defending US territorial independence against great power adversaries and thwarting would-be Eurasian hegemons, it would vitiate core maritime functions such as multinational trusteeship over the system. Offshore balancing would compel sea service leaders to completely rethink their approach to strategy, and indeed their most basic assumptions about the nature of the international system and how to superintend it.

By design, furthermore, offshore balancing cedes the initiative to prospective aggressors, and thereby primes US leaders to abjure peacetime strategic competition and delay entry into high-intensity wars. Surrendering the initiative would compound the hazards and costs of war for the United States if it ultimately chooses to intervene. US forces would need to fight their way into important theaters in the face of formidable "antiaccess" weaponry and tactics. If littoral powers like China or Iran erected no-go zones along transit routes to the Indian Ocean, the prohibitive costs of forcible entry might deter the United States from intervening—even if offshore balancing dictated it. By sheltering in the Western Hemisphere, then, Washington could well forfeit its capacity to balance in South Asia's marginal waters in any meaningful sense.

Offshore balancing is unrealistic in a South Asian setting for a variety of political and military reasons. It expects potential allies—both long-standing allies that Washington will have abandoned to pursue narrow self-interests, and wary friends like New Delhi that appear ambivalent about close ties with Washington—to maintain base infrastructure or prepositioned hardware, presumably at their expense, and to US standards, in case US forces should someday return. It expects them to grant military-basing rights in perpetuity to a government that openly advertises the flimsiness of its commitment to their defense. We take aim at offshore balancing mainly because it is impractical now that the United States has designated the Indian Ocean as a central theater. It is a strategy founded on dubious assumptions. It amounts to after-the-fact balancing alongside partners who are uneasy working with a United States that is only shallowly committed to the endeavor and thus is employing forces that could prove inadequate to the task.

This strains credulity. Forced to rearm and assume greater regional responsibilities, former friends and allies would prove less amenable to US entreaties than offshore balancers maintain, even if the danger of a rising hegemon bulked large. They would likely seek other forms of insurance to hedge against what they saw as American flightiness. Washington should be careful what it wishes for, if it undertakes the burden-shedding, or "buck-passing," exercise that offshore balancers espouse.[6]

In the next section we review the case put forward by leading proponents of offshore balancing and explore why they argue that Washington should resurrect this older strategic approach. We spend the ensuing two sections identifying impediments to executing an offshore-balancing strategy in the Indian Ocean; we first examine the problem on the strategic plane, and then on the operational plane. The subsequent section presents a strategic alternative to offshore balancing in this remote theater, by tracing the contours of a workable "offshore option." We close by warning that an offshore-balancing strategy in South Asia is no strategy at all. Although its members have fashioned an elegant theoretical model, the offshore-balancing school has fallen behind changing geopolitical and strategic realities.

WHO ARE THE OFFSHORE BALANCERS?

Despite the limitations outlined above, offshore balancers nevertheless cut an outsized figure with policymakers and the educated public. John Ikenberry and Stephen Walt maintain that the United States "just needs to maintain local balances of power to ensure that key areas of the world aren't dominated by hostile powers. . . . Intervening with our own forces should only be a last resort, partly because other countries see US power as potentially dangerous."[7] This represents a seductive vision that comports with American traditions. The United States was an offshore balancer before the term was invented.[8]

What are the chief characteristics of this approach? According to John Mearsheimer, "The central aim of American foreign policy has traditionally been to dominate the Western Hemisphere while not permitting another great power to dominate Europe or Northeast Asia."[9] Robert Art frames offshore balancing as one of two viable alternatives to his preferred strategy of "selective engagement," along with "isolationism." Such "free hand" strategies, writes Art, "shun formal standing commitments to employ America's military power and are as sparing as possible in its use." Both strategies "are feasible in that there are no political barriers to their implementation and in that the resource demands that they make are moderate."[10] At times Art merges the two, depicting offshore balancing as the strategic means to isolationist ends. Today's isolationists, he says, "hold that offshore balancing (keeping all American troops in the United States) is as effective as onshore balancing (keeping American forces deployed forward in Eurasia at selected points) and safer. Indeed, most isolationists are prepared to use American military power to defend only two vital American interests: repelling an attack on the American homeland, and preventing a great power hegemon from dominating Eurasia. As a consequence, they can justifiably be called the most selective of selective engagers."[11]

Art adds another tenet of isolation/offshore balancing. He is careful to note that though this strategy "does not eschew the use of force," it nonetheless "remains at heart a watching and reactive strategy, not, like selective engagement, a precautionary and preventive one."[12] It maintains that balances of power are normally self-regulating. Thus an offshore balancer can afford to monitor events from afar, stepping in belatedly when a hegemon attempts to dominate Eurasia. For Mearsheimer the United States should "avoid the fighting entirely or, if it has to join in, to do so later rather than earlier." This allows Washington to "pay a much smaller price than the states fighting from start to finish" while helping it mold the postwar order.[13]

Offsetting a South Asian hegemon, however, represents a task of a higher order than facing down an ambitious European or East Asian power. If offshore balancers got their way, the United States would sever its alliances, shutter overseas bases, bring home forward-deployed forces, cut defense spending drastically, forgo military missions unrelated to power politics, and monitor events to discern when its help was necessary to check the pretensions of domineering powers. Offshore balancers present their strategic concept as a cost saver for the United States. Yet quitting Eurasia would magnify the costs of returning, potentially many times over. Even Art, a skeptic about this approach, undersells its resource demands. The costs of offshore balancing are moderate only if the United States never actually needs to rebuild its depleted forces to oppose a hegemon. As Spykman points out, the United States cannot perform its balancing function if it cannot apply its power in a contested region. A challenge that would prove difficult in the European and East Asian rimlands verges on being insurmountable in the even more remote, inaccessible Indian Ocean basin.

How to convert offshore balancers' concept into an actionable strategy remains unclear. For specifics we turn to Texas A&M University professor Christopher Layne, who has pushed this strategic concept articulately for more than a decade. Alone among the members of this school, he gives details. And rather than traffic in grand abstractions, he issues policy recommendations that are admirably frank. Thus it is possible to conduct a substantive debate with him. It is worth reviewing his work in some depth to gain insight into the practical dimensions of offshore balancing. He made his case in *International Security* in 1997, expanded his analysis to book length in 2006 as *The Peace of Illusions*, and returned to it in 2009 in the *Review of International Studies*.[14]

Like Art, Layne sees little practical difference between offshore balancing and isolationism in peacetime. Indeed, he forthrightly dubs his grand strategy an "America First" strategy. In so doing he evokes—consciously, one presumes—the isolationist movement of the interwar years. "America First is an imperative," he proclaims, "not a pejorative."[15] For him the "two crucial objectives" for US grand strategy are to keep great power wars from ensnaring the United States and to continually bolster US national power relative to other states. "Offshore balancing," he writes, "would define US interests narrowly in terms of defending the United States' territorial integrity and preventing the rise of a Eurasian hegemon" in an increasingly multipolar world.[16]

Layne juxtaposes his approach against the long-standing strategy he calls "preponderance," whereby Washington provides for allied security in hopes of preserving and expanding economic interdependence and the blessings that interdependence is said to bestow. Overseas engagement, he insists, embroils the republic in conflicts estranged from its true interests. It is better to pull back, exploiting North America's isolated geographic position. Once US forces withdraw, the realist logic of balancing will return to Eurasia, forcing the states whose security is under direct threat to shoulder the "risks and costs of antihegemonic balancing."[17] Except for the most dire circumstances, states can maintain a satisfactory equilibrium without US help. After an adjustment period, during which the US military would shift responsibility to indigenous forces, consequently, "the United States would disengage from its military commitments in Europe, Japan, and South Korea."[18]

As Art notes, a "solid US–Japan alliance is the cornerstone of America's political-military position in East Asia and one of the two cornerstones of America's global defense posture—the other being the NATO alliance in Europe." Offshore balancing would pull the keystones out of this edifice.[19] Layne nonetheless contends that the United States can spare itself the costs and risks of maintaining an informal empire through this more aloof grand strategy. He approvingly quotes a 1993 study asserting that "'imperial' security responsibilities" consume one-half of US defense spending.[20] If so, Washington can renounce its Eurasian commitments and undertake sweeping budget cuts, all without compromising national security.

Although offshore balancing purports to be a school of thought about strategy, many of its proponents more or less openly countenance constraining the ways and means at Washington's disposal. In so doing they bias US policy against intervention in Eurasia. Carl von Clausewitz observes that the value of the political object at stake in an enterprise determines the magnitude and duration of the effort a competitor puts forth on behalf of that object. In other words, the degree of importance the leadership attaches to a goal dictates how many lives and how much treasure it is prepared to expend, and for how long.[21]

But "magnitude" is a relative term, not an absolute one. If offshore balancers get their way and drive down the size of the US military, they will have effectively driven up the magnitude of any campaign in Eurasia. If the costs exceed the expected benefits of the enterprise, advises Clausewitz, the goal should be renounced. Only truly dire circumstances would warrant hazarding most or all of a shrunken US military in combat, particularly in a protracted engagement. Having reduced American means, offshore balancers will have rallied Clausewitzian cost/benefit analysis to their standard—reshaping ends by reshaping ways and means.

STRATEGIC BARRIERS TO IMPLEMENTATION

What would this mean in practical terms for US Maritime Strategy in the Indian Ocean? What would offshore balancing look like in execution? Unanswered questions are legion. As noted above, the combined Indian Ocean / Persian Gulf region is one of two theaters where the 2007 Maritime Strategy vows to station credible combat power for the foreseeable future, not only to sustain regional power balances but also to safeguard free passage through the global commons.[22] Implemented strictly, offshore balancing would obviate important military and nonmilitary functions mandated by the Maritime Strategy, both in the Indian Ocean theater and far beyond.

For the United States, renouncing its forward presence would mean fettering the exercise of its military power. For the historian Alfred Thayer Mahan, sea power was founded on industrial production and foreign commerce, with overseas bases and merchant and naval shipping.[23] In Mahanian terms, offshore balancing would knock one of the main struts—namely, forward bases—out from underneath American sea power. It would strike a second strut, the navy, a sharp blow. America's ability to project power into Eurasia would diminish commensurately—multiplying the costs and dangers if the US leadership were to ultimately decide to exercise its offshore-balancing option.

In passing, Art spotlights this critical shortcoming of offshore balancing as an actionable strategy. He observes that offshore balancers forswear peacetime military deployments, rendering "more difficult the warlike use of America's military power." Under a forward strategy, the United States enjoys "valuable bases, staging areas, intelligence-gathering facilities, in-theater training facilities, and most important, close allies with whom it continuously trains."[24] Bereft of these advantages, Washington would be forced to improvise under perhaps forbidding circumstances—compounding the costs, risks, and frictions inherent in even the best-executed military campaigns. A wait-and-see posture would be perilous, even along the eastern and western Eurasian rimlands, which are relatively close to the United States and are reachable via reasonably direct, unobstructed sea and air routes. Such a posture would verge on being unworkable in South Asia. In short, it is increasingly incongruent with geostrategic reality.

Naval bases, then, are mundane yet indispensable. Nearly a century ago, Rear Admiral Bradley Fiske likened their purpose to "supplying and replenishing the stored-up energy required for naval operations."[25] To stay with his physics simile, the fleet swiftly discharges its potential energy at sea. Smaller warships such as destroyers and frigates, which defend aircraft carriers and other "high-value units" against air, surface, and undersea attacks, refuel under way every three to four days lest they exhaust their bunkers. A virtually inexhaustible fuel source drives nuclear-powered flattops through the water. Thirsty air wings nonetheless demand jet fuel to stay aloft, sustaining sortie rates typical of aerial combat. By no means does nuclear power liberate carriers from their bases. Submarines boast the greatest at-sea endurance in modern navies. During the Cold War, US ballistic-missile submarines routinely undertook seventy-day patrols. Even so, their crews still need food—and they must put into harbor periodically to load it.

A fleet's at-sea endurance, then, is far from infinite. It is exceedingly difficult for the fleet to sustain this stored-up energy—manifest in fuel, stores, spares, and ammunition—over vast distances. Replenishment vessels must themselves be replenished, and often. Explains Fiske, the capacity to refuel under way "subtract[s] *partially* one of the reasons for naval bases" while leaving "the other reasons still existent, especially the reasons connected with machinery repairs"[26] (emphasis added). Combatants feature modest welding, pipefitting, and machine shops, but only a shore depot can perform extensive repairs and maintenance—hence the protracted refits US vessels undergo every couple of years as part of their operational rhythm.

If the US sea services were to leave their forward naval stations—and thus in effect dismantle their land-based logistics network—they would be compelled to develop substitutes. To become more or less self-sufficient, they would need to beef up the fleet's combat punch, letting it fight its way into South Asia; augment the combat logistics fleet that resupplies warships that are under way; and build submarine and destroyer tenders to overhaul damaged vessels and perform depot-level maintenance. This would offset the fleet's loss of base infrastructure—partially and temporarily. In all likelihood such expensive undertakings would render illusory the force cutbacks and budgetary savings touted by offshore balancers. Offshore balancing amounts to hoping that balancing dynamics will prevent the Eurasian order from unraveling so catastrophically that US forces will be forced to return. Yet hope is not a strategy.

Suppose Washington nevertheless embraces the realist vision. At present, US forces are stationed to the extreme eastern and western ends of the grand Asian theater designated in the Maritime Strategy, in Japan to the east and Bahrain to the west. Abrogating US alliances would presumably denude the US military of automatic basing rights not only there but also at the other seaports routinely visited by the US Navy, such as facilities in Diego Garcia, Oman, and the United Arab Emirates. If Washington were to determine that it had to intervene in the Indian Ocean for balancing purposes, it would be compelled to negotiate access to such seaports anew—possibly amid the extreme stresses of war, judging from Layne's criticism of US entry into the two world wars and Mearsheimer's plea for Washington to delay as long as possible before marching to war.[27]

Layne interprets "last resort"—offshore balancers' usual standard for US intervention—sweepingly, strongly implying that even total Axis control of Eurasia during World War II would have posed too small a danger to the Americas to warrant deploying US military forces. If Germany had refrained from declaring war in 1941, he contends, the United States could have kept supplying war matériel to the Allies "indefinitely," regardless of how Allied forces fared on the battlefield without direct US help.[28] Layne discounts the repercussions of an Allied defeat for US security. Offshore balancers of such convictions appear ready to let the Eurasian security situation deteriorate almost past rescue before committing US power to right the balance.

A key assumption held by offshore balancers is that the United States enjoys the luxury of intervening at the times and places of its own choosing. Its freedom of action, they say, derives in large part from prevailing geostrategic circumstances. The most important global centers of gravity are located in Western Europe and Northeast Asia, along the western and eastern fringes of Eurasia. These regions boast enormous manpower and resources that could give rise to a hegemon capable of challenging US security and survival. The Pacific and the Atlantic provide oceanic bulwarks against Eurasian challengers. For its part, the United States can reach both theaters directly, provided it maintains sufficient naval power to project power onto Eurasian shores to check the rise of an ambitious power. Offshore balancing, then, hinges on easy naval access to likely theaters.

Writing during World War II, the Yale professor Nicholas Spykman offered a geostrategic analysis that codified geopolitical traditions dating from the earliest days of the republic. He built a convincing case for the United States to balance in the "rimlands," or coastal regions, of Europe and East Asia.[29] America, that is, could project military power across the Atlantic or Pacific to prevent aspiring hegemons from wresting control away of the Eurasian landmass. In stark contrast to offshore balancers, however, Spykman insisted that the United States must mount a standing, forward defense to avert such an outcome. For him the alternative, hemispheric, defense was "no defense at all," because it would deprive America of beachheads on the Eurasian landmass.[30]

Spykman believed that a hegemon could marshal sufficient maritime resources to reach out across the Atlantic or the Pacific, menacing a New World that was geographically surrounded by the larger, more populous, more resource-rich Old World.[31] To forestall such a nightmare scenario, Spykman beseeched the United States to acknowledge that "the power constellation in Europe and Asia is of everlasting concern to her, both in time of war and in time of peace."[32] US statesmen ought to stand ready, lest the regional balance tilt dangerously toward hegemony. Spykman, then, premised his strategy on managing events in an Old World dominated by the Eurasian rimlands. US strategy conformed to his worldview throughout the Cold War.

Although Spykman and the offshore balancers disagree sharply about how the United States should restore the global power balance, they concur that Western Europe and Northeast Asia are the arenas where the struggle for mastery would unfold. But we now inhabit a post-Spykman world, where the rimland strategy is losing strategic cogency. For reasons we review below, its prospects of success would be uncertain today, even in familiar precincts like East Asia and Europe. Trying to shape events in the Indian Ocean from North America, Hawaii, or Guam—from very far offshore, indeed—would prove more doubtful still. In short, offshore-balancing proponents apply Spykman's geostrategic template to a world that has left it behind. Outdated assumptions beget faulty strategy.

Now consider the US position in the Indian Ocean region. As an "exterior-line" power converging on Eurasia without permanent footholds along the continent's fringes, the United States would find itself compelled to conquer the tyranny of geography from a far weaker and more distant position than it currently occupies. The past is instructive. Nineteenth-century Great Britain seemingly represents an archetype for offshore balancers.[33] But though he paid the Indian Ocean little attention per se, Spykman points out that a "surrounding string of marginal and Mediterranean seas" encloses the Eurasian rimlands, "separat[ing] the continent from the oceans." These waters constitute "a circumferential maritime highway which links the whole area together in terms of sea power." Britain bestrode the world in its imperial heyday because its Royal Navy ruled the "girdle of marginal seas" ringing the Eurasian landmass.[34]

For Spykman, a successful offshore balancer must pursue its strategy along this peripheral thoroughfare, radiating power inland to offset overweening continental powers. The Arabian Sea and the Bay of Bengal bulk large among these Eurasian waters. The Royal Navy, however, boasted an advantage of colossal import by virtue of its naval stations in British-ruled India, which were complemented by strategically placed outposts such as those in Ceylon (now Sri Lanka) and Singapore. London also held narrow between-sea passages such as the Strait of Gibraltar and the Suez Canal, guaranteeing access from the British Isles to the Indian Ocean. If the United States were to embrace the strategy espoused by scholars like Layne, it would deliberately abandon the strategic positions and automatic access enjoyed by the Royal Navy—the rudiments of offshore balancing.[35] Thus offshore balancers draw a false analogy to imperial Great Britain.

Consider the operational hurdles to offshore balancing from American soil. US expeditionary forces would need to cover transcontinental distances simply to reach the theater. Abrogating US alliances would compel them to voyage to the Indian Ocean—in essence a vast, enclosed inner lake south of the Eurasian landmass—without the benefit of permanent way stations in the Mediterranean Sea and the Western Pacific. The nearest US territory to the South Asian theater is Guam, which lies at the midpoint of the "second island chain" that envelops coastal East Asia. If the US fleet were using Guam as a jumping-off point, it would need to venture through hazardous expanses such as the South China Sea and also chokepoints such as the Malacca Strait before commanders could even commence Indian Ocean operations. Simply deploying, then, might exact a high price.

In chapter 4 Preble contends that the United States will likely retain the capacity to ensure unimpeded access to the Indian Ocean region. Not only does he find "little evidence that a hostile power could effectively deny access to the [Indian Ocean region]," but he also believes that the US Navy will boast the technological and doctrinal wherewithal to force its way into the region. Although he is right to assert that the open seas of the vast Indian Ocean are ideal for carrier operations, the problem is that reaching the theater in the first place will become increasingly problematic in the coming years. Indeed, Eurasia's marginal and narrow between-sea passages are increasingly falling under the shadow of regional militaries.

For instance, China's mix of resources, capability, geopolitical interests, and ambition could embolden Beijing to seek preponderance in the Indian Ocean. What if Beijing were the South Asian power that Washington meant to counterbalance? Annual Pentagon reports on Chinese military power predict that the entire South China Sea and the Malacca Strait will soon fall within range of the People's Liberation Army's (PLA's) DF-21D/CSS-5 antiship ballistic missile (ASBM)—if indeed they do not already. The PLA's ASBM represents the world's first ballistic missile able to strike at moving warships hundreds of miles distant.[36] Whether the United States can project adequate power into the Indian Ocean in a brewing crisis or hot war, then, is a question increasingly worth pondering. Fire support from PLA onshore sites could slow Washington's access to the combat theater while imposing heavy losses—even if Beijing chose not to risk its fleet in a toe-to-toe sea fight.

In sum, Layne evidently sees little reason for peacetime balancing, he would make few advance preparations for wartime balancing, and he would wait until an opponent had attained crushing superiority before ordering US forces into battle. Could a US military whose budget had been slashed by half reach important theaters despite enemy resistance, and how much strength would it have to contribute in the first place? Would basing infrastructure maintained by foreign nations—nations that were no longer bound to the United States by treaty and were unable to depend on Washington for support—meet US needs? Such questions demand answers before the US leadership undertakes a strategic realignment of this gravity.

Layne acknowledges such concerns, but apparently only as an afterthought. His answers provide scant comfort for those who have been entrusted with overseeing the military component of offshore balancing: "Although the United States will not maintain an ongoing forward military presence in Eurasia, it should seek to maintain close military contacts with the Europeans and the Japanese—and develop them with India and Russia—and conduct regular joint exercises. Because future geopolitical conditions might necessitate the reinsertion of US military power into Eurasia, the United States should maintain a network of basing rights that can be used for this purpose should it become necessary."[37]

This passage represents the sum total of Layne's acknowledgment that implementing the vision he propounds with such confidence might in reality not be that straightforward. And a strategy that flouts inconvenient realities is a strategy apt to fail.

Furthermore, the author overlooks the diplomatic ramifications of his proposals. He makes no effort to explain why prospective partners and allies would accept such arrangements with what, by definition, would be an untrustworthy US ally—a mercurial protector, committed only to its own territorial integrity and relative power, that is constantly on the lookout for opportunities to escape from the partnership. Washington would presumably negotiate the reentry arrangements Layne describes so vaguely after unilaterally canceling or drastically revising its treaty obligations and implicit commitments to major regional actors. Why former US friends and allies would permit the United States to reoccupy air and naval bases after "cutting and running"—their likely, and fitting, interpretation of US policy—goes unexplained.

Their skepticism would be merited. A Washington intent on offshore balancing would cut and run again once it judged—again, unilaterally—that the geopolitical balance had been restored. Advertising one's unreliability is slipshod alliance management. It also remains unclear why the regional powers would care so much about US intervention in the first place if offshore balancers prevailed in US strategic debates. After all, the budget reductions for which they clamor would enfeeble US military strength. Token doses of US military power could well prove insufficient to defeat hostile action by a hegemon, even assuming that the regional governments did readmit US forces to their bases. To pursue any serious balancing effort, Washington would be forced to rebuild its strength—itself an expensive, time-consuming enterprise—having chosen to start from behind.

Having done so, it would dispatch forces back to Eurasia in numbers on the order of the massive reinforcements that would flow through Japan today if a second Korean War were to erupt. Host nations no longer accustomed to working with Americans in close quarters would probably resent the newly robust, intrusive US presence on their territory. Rapidly reintroducing US assets and personnel under circumstances short of all-out war would surely accentuate such perceptions. Unless friendly nations found themselves on death ground, it is entirely conceivable that their governments would refuse a US expeditionary force access to their soil.[38] Even if national survival were at stake in a hegemonic war—the only dire scenario that would engage an offshore balancer—a potential host nation might only grudgingly permit access at the last possible minute, or, worse, too late.

Preble objects to our suggesting that former allies and friends might not open their doors to US forces. He is certainly right that certain conditions, such as the threat of conquest, would likely compel local players to readmit American forward presence without much hesitation. But he underestimates the complexities of coalition politics. As noted above, deep suspicions and hard feelings owing to perceptions of US abandonment in the wake of an offshore posture would need to be overcome. Regional capitals could also encounter stiff resistance from domestic constituents opposed to readmitting the American military. Working through such intangibles as bruised pride and fear would likely take time, a commodity in short supply in a great power confrontation or conflict.

Nor do the difficulties stop there. Ex-allies may well have taken over, partially dismantled, or entirely closed military bases after Washington vacated them. Such facilities may have decayed or been reconfigured for other purposes. If so, they would be ill equipped to absorb US forces in large numbers and to rearm, resupply, and repair high-technology US warships and aircraft. For instance, the transformation of the Subic Bay Naval Base into a special economic zone attests to the dramatic changes likely to occur after a handover. Since the US Navy withdrew in 1992, commercialization and privatization efforts have rendered Subic

Bay virtually unusable for military purposes. On the US West Coast, similarly, the conversion of the Long Beach Naval Shipyard into a container port verges on being irreversible. Similar fates could await naval stations scattered across the eastern Eurasian seaboard—notably Yokosuka, Sasebo, Chinhae, and Changi—in the event of a US pullout. Getting out of the marginal seas might be easy. Getting back in would be a different proposition entirely. Layne thus slights difficulties of enormous magnitude.

In operational and force-structure terms, offshore balancers call for premising US military strategy on capabilities sure to warm any naval officer's heart. Stephen Walt insists that the US Navy is central to this strategy. The navy would need to "command" the sea in order to project power, mount a forward presence, and safeguard trade routes.[39] (For Mahan, command meant amassing "overbearing power," not only through a strong battle fleet but also through forward naval stations.[40] How Walt would mount a forward presence without bases, let alone win fleet engagements, goes unaddressed.)

Like Walt, Layne advocates "robust nuclear deterrence, air power, and—most important—overwhelming naval power." Shipboard, precision, and standoff weaponry would be at a premium for offshore-balancing contingencies, as would sea-based ballistic missile defenses.[41] One imagines he approves of certain aspects of the emerging Air-Sea Battle doctrine, concerned as it is with moving high-value assets temporarily out of the "antiaccess" threat envelope.[42] But Layne would probably object to the goals the architects of the doctrine hope to achieve. Air-Sea Battle presupposes that US forces would fight their way back to major operational hubs, using them as a platform to wrest back command of the commons. In a major war with China, US air and naval bases along the Japanese archipelago would furnish stepping-stones for follow-on suppression campaigns against Chinese antiaccess forces—stepping-stones without which Air-Sea Battle would fail. In short, even options designed to remedy forward bases' vulnerability to enemy missile salvos would find little place in Layne's brave new world.

An additional practical impediment to offshore balancing, then, would be the imperative to pierce antiaccess measures erected by countries like China. Returning to Eurasia is easier said than done. As noted above, if the United States left Eurasia, its closest base to the Indian Ocean would be on Guam, an island thousands of miles from the theater, whose access is obstructed by convoluted geography and that increasingly falls within reach of Chinese weaponry such as ASBMs and stealth fighter aircraft. Unlike Yokosuka and Sasebo, however, Guam is physically small and lacks the industrial base and infrastructure to support or homeport major elements of the US Seventh Fleet. The majority of US naval forces would still sortie from Hawaii, or even from San Diego and Everett on the West Coast.

Even assuming that the United States could amass sufficient forces swiftly enough to reach the Indian Ocean in wartime, US naval commanders would still need to pass through hostile zones en route to the South Asian maritime theater. With narrow chokepoints at each end, for example, the South China Sea would resemble a death trap if Beijing chose to contest it. Would Beijing grant the US Navy unimpeded access to the Indian Ocean to balance Chinese ambitions there? Would Washington risk its fleet just to reach the combat theater? The likely answer to both questions: No.

Offshore balancing would also corrode deterrence and crisis stability. Retreating to hemispheric defense and dismantling much of today's robust force would substantially reduce the United States' capacity to act as an arbiter of Eurasian affairs. If Washington felt compelled to redress a power imbalance in Eurasia amid a great power war, it would do so as a disadvantaged outsider. The weight of US power would be acutely felt by a revisionist power, especially after a prolonged absence. Indeed, an aspiring hegemon unaccustomed to a nearby US presence would be inclined to exaggerate the likely effects of US reentry into Eurasian geopolitics. Hypersensitivity to external interference might goad such a power into destabilizing actions that it would otherwise never countenance.

Consider the interwar period in the Pacific, when the United States remained mostly over the horizon. Washington hoped to telegraph resolve vis-à-vis Tokyo by deploying naval and air forces to Hawaii and the Philippines as a show of force. Instead, its efforts at deterrent signaling—or what Clausewitz aptly termed "war by algebra," a largely passionless endeavor predicated on building more impressive forces than the adversary—produced the opposite effect.[43] Tokyo was provoked rather than deterred. Rather than see the window of opportunity slam shut, Japanese decision makers rationally chose to strike preemptively, while the naval balance still permitted. Similarly, a rising power that covets regional dominion might confront two stark choices: capitulate to preclude US intervention, or preempt to forestall the United States' attempts to regain its position. Such circumstances would drive a revisionist power to consolidate an impregnable position quickly, before Washington could muster sufficient political resolve and military forces for a decisive intervention. Fait accompli strategies would become the coin of the geopolitical realm.

Clearly, offshore balancing is starkly different from simply assuming an over-the-horizon stance in Eurasia. Its popularity stems from extravagant assumptions about seagoing forces' ability to operate independent of forward bases, amplified by unrealistic assumptions about how easy it is to construct and maintain coalitions with partners that rightly doubt US motives and military capability. Certain aspects of Samuel Huntington's influential "transoceanic" strategy for the Cold War fan this confusion. Writing in 1954, Huntington maintained that a transoceanic navy could tap "base-less" capabilities like carrier aviation, amphibious warfare, and naval fire support to project power inland.[44] Admiral Gary Roughead, the recently retired US chief of naval operations and America's top naval officer, cited this part of Huntington's transoceanic strategy to support his case for an "offshore option."[45] (We will return to the confusion between the offshore option and offshore balancing near the end of this chapter.)

Intrinsic logistics capabilities do constitute a key advantage of seagoing forces—to a point. The US Navy developed hardware and techniques for underway replenishment for World War II. Its capacity to refuel, rearm, and reprovision at sea allowed US task forces to wage war without surcease across vast distances, hammering away at Imperial Japan. But as was detailed above, at-sea replenishment does not obviate the need for naval stations, and thus for the diplomacy that opens foreign bases to US mariners and airmen. Indeed, the Pacific campaign was predicated on seizing forward air and naval outposts from Japan as platforms for projecting power onward toward Asian shores. In no way were these operations "base-less."

Naval forces, then, can operate offshore for awhile at some distance from their bases. But even Huntington's transoceanic Cold War US Navy could not mount prolonged operations off enemy coasts without forward bases of *some* kind. When he used the term "base-less," in fact, he was referring to the US Sixth Fleet—which was composed of units that rotated from homeports *to naval stations in the Mediterranean Sea*, notably Gaeta, Italy.[46] The Sixth Fleet could have accomplished little without European basing rights. This was an unwontedly imprecise choice of words for Huntington. Still less could the US military sustain operations in the Indian Ocean for long without access to installations like Bahrain and Diego Garcia.

It may be prudent, nevertheless, for officialdom and scholars to explore some form of offshore posture. Applying the Mahanian standards of position, strength, and resources—the parameters whereby America's sea power prophet took the measure of strategic sites—Australia offers a more promising candidate for US basing in the Indian Ocean basin than does Bahrain.[47] Bradley Fiske adds that strategic position is the crucial attribute of a distant overseas base. To make the point, he juxtaposes the 1916 Battle of Jutland against the 1905 Battle of Tsushima. Both the British and German fleets retired to their nearby bases in good order after the former battle, showing "in clear relief the efficacy of bases."[48] But conversely, the Russian Baltic Fleet, having rounded Eurasia and Africa, met catastrophe at Japanese hands during the latter battle, in large measure because the Russian men-of-war had nowhere to take shelter.

Because there was "no base or harbor of refuge," notes Fiske, "disaster succeeded disaster in a cumulative fashion, and the Russian fleet was annihilated in deep water."[49] An offshore-balancing US fleet would court similar risks without well-placed naval stations to which to retire for fuel, ammunition, provisions, and repairs.

AN UNAFFORDABLE OPERATIONAL OPTION

The real test of offshore balancing is how US military operations can responsively and effectively restore equilibrium to the international system when a rising challenger deeply unsettles a regional order. Yet fielding a strategy and the military means to reverse a power grab would be extraordinarily taxing for any external balancer. Judging from balancing proponents' commentary, Washington would enter the fray only belatedly, after an aspiring hegemon had already severely disturbed the peace. In Layne's and Mearsheimer's multipolar future, prevention is the business of others. Even if deterrence fails, Washington should sit out the fight if at all possible. The downside to this approach is that the United States would watch from the sidelines until a hegemonic victory seemed imminent. US forces would then need to roll back the adversary's gains, uprooting it from the entrenched positions it had seized through territorial conquest. Given the proliferation of antiaccess capabilities on display today, the United States would find itself hard-pressed to dislodge an opponent without incurring prohibitive costs.

The United States thus would relegate itself to the status of a latecomer attempting to halt a blitz campaign or tip the balance in a protracted war. A concerted effort to fight its way into the Asian theater could come to resemble the slog across the Pacific in World War II. It is noteworthy that the US naval campaign against Japan could have been much bloodier if the Imperial Japanese Navy had adequately consolidated its defenses along the Pacific island barrier, as planners originally intended. Similarly, if Nazi Germany had channeled more resources into its submarine buildup before opening hostilities with Great Britain, the Battle of the Atlantic would have proved an even harsher trial for the Allies. Both campaigns were closely run, despite the triumphal glow that now surrounds them. It presumes too much to believe that future antagonists will commit the same blunders as the Axis states did—presenting compliant enemies.

In all likelihood it would prove less expensive for the United States to stay in the Asian theaters with its current fleet than to try to reconstitute a global force in times of strife. Offshore balancing would likely prove more expensive, not cheaper, than the current force structure and strategy. In the nomenclature employed by the Center for Naval Analyses (CNA) in a recent study, the US Navy would build down from the current, largely forward-deployed "global navy" to a "surge navy" stationed predominantly in US homeports. Such a navy could "get by" with smaller numbers of warships because it would give up the forward-presence, coalition-building, and maritime-security functions envisioned in the report *A Cooperative Strategy for 21st Century Seapower*. It would also "cut back on organic logistics capabilities" needed to sustain operations far from home.[50]

CNA team members explicitly term their surge navy an "offshore-balancing navy." It is worth pointing out that, unlike Layne, they stop short of renouncing bases and terminating alliances in Japan and the Middle East. The US Navy would remain in Japan, the Persian Gulf, and the Mediterranean Sea, but only for ballistic missile defense missions. Even so, US forces would enjoy residual access to foreign bases. The CNA report, consequently, understates the difficulties that a real offshore-balancing navy would encounter when trying to regenerate forces and overseas infrastructure for a system-shattering conflict. The authors observe that such a posture "puts at risk the ability to promptly deny an aggressor any gains" while damaging Washington's credibility as a "coalition leader." In short, the US Navy that remains in hemispheric waters "is a navy that America last saw in the isolationist days between the world wars." Thus idled, the navy "could become prey to budget cutting" as congressional budget-cutters questioned its relevance.[51]

But suppose the United States adopts an offshore-balancing strategy over the objections we raise here. How would Washington reengineer its forces to fulfill its duty as the self-appointed defender of last resort? More specifically, what would an effective offshore-balancing fleet look like? Judging by offshore balancers' criteria, only high-stakes great power wars are worth fighting. System-shattering conflicts like the Napoleonic Wars and World War II are their standard. The United States would need a decisive margin of preponderance to prevail in conflicts of such magnitude.

Consider a wartime scenario. If the United States were contemplating entry despite its offshore-balancing predilections, it would be safe to assume that regional actors had failed to deter aggression on their own, and that the local military balance had tilted sharply toward the challenger. As noted above, revisionist powers will almost certainly anticipate US intervention, laying the groundwork to defeat US efforts to forcibly restore the antebellum order. Such an adversary would contest the approaches to the Eurasian continent with all its might. To force entry under such hazardous circumstances, US naval forces would need to defeat antiaccess efforts, assert local sea control wherever necessary, project (or threaten to project) power ashore, sustain high-tempo operations across oceanic distances, and gird themselves for protracted war. This is a tall order, and it belies the cost savings that Layne expects from offshore balancing. This would be an expensive, trying venture by any measure.

Although standing armies may be largely irrelevant in Layne's world, only substantial numbers of top-end naval assets could force their way into combat zones. Yet forces cannot be scaled down and up as readily and as swiftly as offshore-balancing proponents seem to assume. The fleet must exist when it is needed, or the nation will run grave risks in wartime—as the United States did in the Pacific War, when commanders were forced to improvise a strategy until a new Pacific Fleet could be built and join the fray.

Thus it is "not the most probable of dangers," vouchsafes Alfred Thayer Mahan, "but the most formidable, that must be selected as measuring the degree of military precaution to be embodied in the military precautions thenceforth to be maintained."[52] Mahan extolled the time-tested British approach to calculating interests and probabilities in faraway theaters. He concluded that the benchmark for military preparedness "is the estimated force which the strongest *probable* enemy can bring against you, allowance being made for clear drawbacks upon his total force, imposed by his own embarrassments and responsibilities in other parts of the world" (emphasis in the original).[53]

Using this logic, China—an ambitious, increasingly muscular seafaring nation—represents the standard for US naval preparedness. Indeed, a major shift in the balance of power has already taken place without prompting a serious response from Washington or its regional allies.

The Asian powers' inaction belies claims that it is straightforward to forecast systemic conflicts and respond to them ahead of time. The PLA Navy (PLAN) boasts a growing high-technology fleet whose first aircraft carrier is undergoing sea trials. As long as Beijing limits its interests to maritime Asia, moreover, the navy can count on shore-based fire support supplied by combat aircraft flying from airfields in China, an assortment of short-range systems like diesel submarines and stealthy catamarans packing antiship cruise missiles, and, most controversially, the ASBM, a truck-fired weapon able to target warships under way hundreds of miles distant.

According to Pentagon estimates, ASBM coverage will span the South China Sea, the Strait of Malacca, the entire Bay of Bengal, and parts of the Arabian Sea—even without forward-deploying batteries to South Asia.[54] Recent missile deployments to Guangdong Province in southeastern China suggest that the Chinese Second Artillery Corps, or missile force, is already eyeing the Southeast Asian littoral.[55] In short, land-based weaponry constitutes a force multiplier as well as a protective umbrella for the PLAN fleet in the very expanses where the US sea services must operate to prosecute offshore-balancing missions in the Indian Ocean.[56] ASBM units are joining the Second Artillery now that the system has achieved "initial operational capability."[57] The US military possesses no known defense against this missile. This is the high-stress tactical environment for which the US sea services and their political masters must plan, exercising their Mahanian foresight and making force-structure decisions well in advance.

A surplus of capability, not parity or a shortfall, is the most prudent standard. Even Walt acknowledges that China could make itself a more formidable competitor at sea than was the Soviet Union.[58] The Pacific War and Cold War provide rough benchmarks for the following estimates:

- To clear the seas of antiaccess threats, particularly enemy submarines, the US Navy would need to dramatically augment its fleet of nuclear-powered attack submarines (SSNs) and other antisubmarine warfare (ASW) assets. SSNs will form the vanguard of any surge capability able to pierce antiaccess measures in important waterways like the South China Sea—evading enemy ASW units, sinking enemy submarines, and raiding surface shipping. The PLAN already fields more submarines in the Pacific theater than does the US Navy. China's diesel boats are no match for their US counterparts on a boat-for-boat basis, but its undersea force is improving swiftly and would hold the advantage of fighting on familiar waters in the South China Sea.[59] Without unencumbered access to the seas, the United States would be unable to act meaningfully in a regional power's backyard at an acceptable cost. The US Navy must boast a decisive margin of superiority in ASW, even if allied powers boast competent submarine forces. To build up such a margin, the navy would need to at least double its current inventory of fifty-three SSNs, yielding a fleet that equals or exceeds the number of SSNs deployed during the Cold War.

- The navy should retain the capacity to surge three to four carrier strike groups centered on nuclear-powered aircraft carriers (known as CVNs) into the Indian Ocean in order to command the skies, sink surface combatants, and pummel the enemy's shore defenses. Such a force would be necessary to face down the carrier forces that are taking shape in Asia. Given the training, refitting, and overhaul requirements necessary to keep modern men-of-war at sea, about nine carriers and their escorts would be needed to preserve this surge option. Three to six vessels would be ready for instant deployment under the navy's 3:1 rhythm of workups, major deployment, and extended refit.[60] Although this represents a cut from the current fleet of eleven CVNs, we believe this residual carrier force would suffice. Because a US offshore balancer would shed commitments in far-flung theaters, it could unify the US Navy fleet in the Western Hemisphere. No longer would carrier strike groups make routine peacetime cruises off Eurasia, with the wear-and-tear and dispersal of force that accompany such deployments. A concentrated three- to six-carrier force would pack quite a wallop, outnumbering and outgunning likely adversaries.[61]

- In addition, a fleet of a dozen nuclear-powered guided-missile submarines (SSGNs) armed with land-attack cruise missiles would supplement the offensive by striking at targets ashore. These stealthy, lethal boats would set the terms of a campaign by destroying an enemy's integrated air defenses and other command-and-control facilities. Blinding attacks would clear the way for follow-on suppression operations to permanently deprive the opponent of the capacity to contest US access to and use of the commons. SSGNs are converted *Ohio*-class fleet ballistic-missile submarines (SSBNs) that are nearing replacement. The conversion process changes their armament from 24 submarine-launched ballistic missiles to an imposing 154 Tomahawk land-attack missiles—some 30 more than the US Navy's next-biggest Tomahawk shooter, the *Ticonderoga*-class Aegis cruiser. Four boats have already undergone conversion to SSGN configuration. The remaining fourteen *Ohio*-class SSBNs will become candidates for conversion as replacement SSBNs now under design begin entering service.

- A modest number of expeditionary strike groups capable of inserting and extracting amphibious units would provide commanders with a "disposal" ground force to exert additional pressure on an opponent. The US Marine Corps estimates that it needs at least 33 amphibious-assault ships of various types—preferably 38—to discharge current missions.[62] The lower figure translates into eleven expeditionary strike groups, each of which can transport a marine expeditionary unit totaling around 2,200 personnel. Given the navy's tactical training cycle, between 3 and 8 of these groups are available for deployment at any time. This is an exceedingly lean capability in manpower terms, but it offers a useful metric for an offshore-balancing force. It is hard to see how the United States could make do with less if it is serious about the capacity to surge forces into the Western Pacific or the Indian Ocean. Indeed, the demand for amphibious units might even grow beyond today's requirements if US coalition partners requested that the fleet move their forces around, pose a threat along a new axis, or open new operations in their ground campaigns against the hegemon.

- Perhaps most important, the US Navy would need to substantially augment its combat logistics fleet (CLF) to provide staying power in expeditionary operations of this kind. These vessels would substitute for fully equipped forward bases. A massive fleet of replenishment ships and tenders would be essential to refuel, rearm, resupply, and repair the panoply of warships and aircraft at sea under combat conditions across transcontinental distances. A fleet without adequate under-way-replenishment capacity is a fleet that withers on the vine when deployed to remote theaters without adequate shore bases. Furthermore, the 32 CLF vessels operated by the US Military Sealift Command generally transit to and from combat zones without escort—making them inviting targets for a cunning adversary. Why risk a fleet engagement with the US Navy when its fleet will go away if denied sufficient fuel, ammunition, and stores? Equally glaringly, the navy has let its fleet of destroyer and submarine tenders—specially designed vessels with repair shops for working on combatant ships and, in the case of submarine tenders, on nuclear power plants—dwindle to zero. The navy must rebuild this flotilla of unglamorous but crucial ships to sustain offshore-balancing operations in the Indian Ocean. Offshore balancing will be an ephemeral affair absent such workaday capabilities.

Given the capital-intensive nature of naval construction, the building cycle from design to laying a keel to commissioning to full combat readiness is measured in years, if not a longer period. It takes nearly a decade's lead time to build a nuclear-powered submarine, for example, including the time required to fabricate nuclear fuel and other components for nuclear reactors. In other words, the vessels and equipment enumerated above must be built ahead of time and be made ready for immediate deployment if policymakers sincerely wish to respond effectively to Eurasian conflicts. The precedent of the Pacific War applies.

Moreover, keeping such a massive fleet afloat and at sea would be extremely costly. Even current peacetime naval operations far from Asian homeports can exact a high premium, measured in fuel and worn equipment. Furthermore, a fleet that perpetually stays in home waters or remains moored to the pier rapidly loses its fighting spirit and readiness. Naval commanders would still need to take their vessels to sea in the offshore balancers' brave new world, keeping the fleet in fighting trim through training and local exercises. If the US Navy must remain ready to wage a hegemonic war in distant theaters, it must hone its expeditionary capabilities through long-distance cruises, presumably in the Western Hemisphere.

Naval diplomacy—a latter-day counterpart to the cruise of the Great White Fleet—might be used to justify such preparations. There is ample precedent for such enterprises in the "UNITAS" cruises that the navy routinely undertakes in Latin America.[63] By visiting seaports and working alongside foreign sea services, such ventures foster hemispheric goodwill while building the capacity for combined operations. Whatever the case, it is extremely doubtful that US politicians would permit the fleet to remain inert and thus allow a vast investment to shrivel while risking their own political fortunes. Visibly sustaining readiness would be as much a political as an operational necessity, if only to justify the expense of a great navy. There is nothing cheap, easy, or quick about offshore balancing.

Beyond force structure and operational readiness, arraying the fleet for swift deployment is an important consideration. Naval leaders should think in unorthodox terms about where to station the fleet. If trouble loomed in the Atlantic, for example, ports along the US Gulf Coast would provide a more central location than established bases like San Diego and Norfolk. From there the fleet could readily swing into action in the Atlantic theater or—via the Gulf of Mexico and the Panama Canal—steam into the Pacific theater. Considering the obstacles I have elucidated here, no amount of nimble strategy and acute foresight will enable

Washington to act as an offshore balancer in the Indian Ocean at an affordable cost. Persevering with something resembling the current fleet size, configuration, and basing network appears far more prudent.

AN OFFSHORE OPTION

If not offshore balancing, then what? The United States' bases in Northeast Asia, notably Yokosuka and Sasebo, will likely remain indispensable to its Maritime Strategy in the Western Pacific. They are the only naval bases west of Hawaii that boast world-class physical infrastructure and a highly skilled local labor force specifically tailored to provide the US Navy with logistical support, maintenance, repairs, and resupply. Hardening those facilities against air or missile strikes represents an obvious measure for the US–Japan alliance to take, lest the Seventh Fleet or the Japan Maritime Self-Defense Force be lost while in port.

Farther to the south, Singapore offers a well-situated way station along the sea lines connecting the two halves of the Indo-Pacific region. The city-state is unlikely to agree to host heavy US forces on a permanent basis, and it falls increasingly under the shadow of Chinese weaponry. Despite its ideal geographic position, then, it is a dubious candidate to anchor the US presence in Asia. Forward-deploying small ship detachments—a rotating squadron of Littoral Combat Ships will call Singapore home starting in 2013—accompanied by support staff will help keep open the option of something more ambitious for the future, if circumstances warrant.

However friendly the relations between the world's oldest and largest democracies become, it is doubtful that India will ever grant military basing rights to the United States. Washington, however, can and should press New Delhi to start taking more responsibility for maritime security and defense in South Asia. For instance, the Pentagon's 2012 Defense Strategic Guidance specifically calls on India to act as a "provider of security in the broader Indian Ocean region." The Indian Navy can ease the burden on the American sea services without running afoul of Indians' renowned prickliness vis-à-vis foreign bases in the subcontinent's near abroad. In short, India can help the United States by helping itself, asserting regional leadership while acting as a silent partner in US Maritime Strategy. New Delhi need not ally itself formally with Washington to become a joint custodian of security in the Indian Ocean.

Still, the US military needs its own central position in the Indo-Pacific region to align its force posture with strategy. Whereas US forces in the Persian Gulf could find themselves cut off from the wider Indian Ocean if Iran chose to make mischief in the Strait of Hormuz, Australia lies at the seam between the Pacific Ocean and Indian Ocean theaters, allowing for ready strategic maneuvers between the two oceans while circumventing the maritime bottleneck at the Strait of Malacca.[64] It is remote from potential threats like the Chinese conventional ballistic missile force and other striking arms of the People's Liberation Army. It boasts the resources of a continent-spanning state. Furthermore, US relations with the prospective host nation are excellent.

Prominent Australian officials and scholars evidently find this logic compelling. Some, in fact, have taken to debating the merits of basing US naval forces along their shores.[65] At first Canberra rebuffed the idea of hosting American carrier strike groups. By late 2012, however, Defense Minister Stephen Smith affirmed that HMAS Stirling, the naval station in the western seaport of Perth, will play a growing part in the US pivot to the Pacific in coming years.[66] There are no guarantees, but Smith's words could represent the prelude to an agreement on large-scale forward basing. The Australian option is something Washington must pursue.

Such options are worth exploring if the US leadership opts for a more offshore posture. Adopting a more dispersed basing architecture in maritime Asia would require neither a large military footprint in the Indian Ocean region nor burdensome new security commitments to regional players. In this context we agree with Preble that new access arrangements, including the prepositioning of military equipment at forward locations, and regular rotations of US forces to host nations would be sufficient in peacetime. Withdrawing from the Eurasian landmass yet staying forward would preserve a realistic option for balancing would-be hegemons while discharging the other functions that the framers of the Maritime Strategy deem worthwhile. Art's vision of selective engagement represents the essence of a true offshore option.

OFFSHORE BALANCING = NO INDIAN OCEAN STRATEGY

Strict fidelity to Layne's offshore-balancing strategy yields distinctive implications for the US posture in the Indian Ocean. Given the transcontinental distances and complex strategic geography involved, the Indian Ocean region will prove least susceptible among Eurasia's marginal seas to the effects of offshore balancing. Replicating Great Britain's balancing strategy appears far harder for Washington today than it was for London at the apex of its power. Indeed, Spykman would blanch at the thought of trying to preserve the geopolitical balance in the Indian Ocean from Western Hemisphere homeports. Offshore balancers assume that the United States has the luxury of just-in-time balancing. Such a strategy lies out of reach in the distant Indian Ocean.

From an operational standpoint, it would be hazardous even to reach this body of water—especially if the aspiring hegemon were China, a power wielding significant influence over the eastern approaches to the Indian Ocean. For reasons elaborated above, I doubt that the United States could successfully prosecute an offshore-balancing strategy—even in the European and East Asian rimlands. The sea services should write off the Indian Ocean and draft a new Maritime Strategy if the US leadership opts for such a grand strategy. If Washington adopts such an approach over the objections raised here, tough political decisions lie in store for the Obama administration and its successors:

- First, offshore balancing would herald a decisive seaward turn in US foreign policy and strategy, and thus a decisive break with the joint-warfare ethos that has dominated US military affairs since Congress enacted the Goldwater-Nichols Act in 1986. Disbanding the structures, operational doctrines, and platforms that bind the various services together for joint undertakings would be neither easy nor cheap. It has taken a quarter-century to implement Goldwater-Nichols, if indeed it has been fully implemented. It could take additional decades to usher in this new age of maritime primacy among the armed services.
- Second, to fund this turn to sea power Congress must redirect scarce defense dollars toward the sea services, the operational arm of offshore balancing. Such a dramatic shift in resource allocation would prove enormously wrenching and disruptive in institutional terms after decades when the services enjoyed more or less equal shares of the defense budget. Ferocious pushback and ugly interservice rivalries are inevitable. The US Army and Air Force will not acquiesce meekly in their subordinate status.
- Third, the US Navy must rethink its internal operational and force-structure priorities, sharing emphasis between carrier and amphibious groups, the SSN and SSGN fleets, and the mundane-seeming capabilities found in the CLF and tender fleets. The result, and the silver lining, would be a more balanced way of thinking about naval power. But here, too, any moves that undercut the privileged arms of the US Navy, such as carrier aviation, would likely beget stiff resistance. Even the most coherent policy pronouncements and plans for offshore balancing could run afoul of bureaucratic inertia and institutional prerogatives.

One often gets the sense from foreign policy debates that the term "offshore balancing" is shorthand for "get out of the Middle East." If this impression is accurate, those are the terms on which the debate should proceed. A genuine turn to offshore balancing would jettison a forward strategy that has served well for seven decades. US leaders must not undertake making such a decision without careful forethought.

NOTES

The views expressed in this chapter are the authors' alone.

1. Hillary Clinton, "America's Pacific Century," *Foreign Policy*, November 2011, www.foreignpolicy.com/articles/2011/10/11/americas_pacific_century.
2. Halford Mackinder, "The Round World and the Winning of the Peace," *Foreign Affairs* 21, no. 4 (1943): 602.
3. Robert D. Kaplan, *Monsoon: The Indian Ocean and the Future of American Power* (New York: Random House, 2010), xi.
4. George W. Baer, *One Hundred Years of Sea Power: The US Navy, 1890–1990* (Stanford, CA: Stanford University Press, 1994), 134–35.
5. US Navy, US Marine Corps, and US Coast Guard, *A Cooperative Strategy for 21st Century Seapower*, October 2007, www.navy.mil/maritime/Maritimestrategy.pdf.
6. John J. Mearsheimer, "The Future of the American Pacifier," *Foreign Affairs* 80, no. 5 (September–October 2001): 46. Mearsheimer expands his analysis to book length in *The Tragedy of Great Power Politics* (New York: W. W. Norton, 2001).
7. G. John Ikenberry and Stephen M. Walt, "Offshore Balancing or International Institutions? The Way Forward for US Foreign Policy," *Brown Journal of World Affairs* 14, no. 1 (Fall 2007): 14.
8. Josef Joffe also identifies British and Bismarckian German precedents for offshore balancing, presenting these as templates for twenty-first-century US grand strategy. Josef Joffe, *Überpower: The Imperial Temptation of America* (New York: W. W. Norton, 2006), 127–57.
9. Mearsheimer, "Future of the American Pacifier," 46.
10. Robert J. Art, *A Grand Strategy for America* (Ithaca, NY: Cornell University Press, 2003), 172.
11. Robert J. Art, "The Strategy of Selective Engagement," in *The Use of Force: Military Power and International Politics*, 6th ed., ed. Kenneth Waltz and Robert J. Art (Lanham, MD: Rowman & Littlefield, 2003), 317.
12. Ibid.
13. Mearsheimer, "Future of the American Pacifier," 60.
14. See Christopher Layne, "From Preponderance to Offshore Balancing: America's Future Grand Strategy," *International Security* 22, no. 1 (Summer 1997): 86–124; Christopher Layne, *The Peace of Illusions; American Grand Strategy from 1940 to the Present* (Ithaca, NY: Cornell University Press, 2006); and Christopher Layne, "America's Middle East Grand Strategy after Iraq: The Moment for Offshore Balancing Has Arrived," *Review of International Studies* 35, no. 1 (2009): 5–35. Layne and other offshore-balancing advocates recently restated their views at a conference convened by the Center for Naval Analyses. See Michael Gerson and Alison Lawler Russell, *American Grand Strategy and Seapower* (Washington, DC: Center for Naval Analyses, 2011), www.cna.org/sites/default/files/research/American%20Grand%20Strategy%20and%20Seapower%202011%20Conference%20Report%20CNA.pdf.

15. Layne, "From Preponderance to Offshore Balancing," 124. See also Eugene Gholz, Daryl Press, and Harvey Sapolsky, "Come Home America: The Strategy of Restraint in the Face of Temptation," *International Security* 21, no. 4 (Spring 1997): 5–48. Stephen C. Brooks and William C. Wohlforth cover this debate in *World Out of Balance: International Relations and the Challenge of American Primacy* (Princeton, NJ: Princeton University Press, 2008), 15–16.

16. Layne, "From Preponderance to Offshore Balancing," 112.

17. Ibid., 117–18.

18. It would also pull out of the Middle East, renounce Taiwan, court Russia as a "geostrategic linchpin," and allow the Asian powers to balance against China. Layne, *Peace of Illusions*, 187–89.

19. Robert J. Art, "The United States and the Rise of China: Implications for the Long Haul," in *China's Ascent: Power, Security, and the Future of International Politics*, ed. Robert S. Ross and Zhu Feng (Ithaca, NY: Cornell University Press, 2008), 279.

20. Layne, "From Preponderance to Offshore Balancing," 87, 94, 97–109, 111, 112, 116.

21. Carl von Clausewitz, *On War*, ed. and trans. Michael Howard and Peter Paret (Princeton, NJ: Princeton University Press, 1976), 92.

22. US Navy, US Marine Corps, and US Coast Guard, *Cooperative Strategy for 21st Century Seapower*.

23. Alfred Thayer Mahan, *The Influence of Sea Power upon History, 1660–1783* (1890; repr., New York: Dover, 1987), 71.

24. Art, "Strategy of Selective Engagement," 317–18.

25. Bradley A. Fiske, *The Navy as a Fighting Machine*, intro. Wayne P. Hughes Jr. (1916; repr., Annapolis, MD: Naval Institute Press, 1988), 268.

26. Ibid., 269.

27. This is a reasonable reading of Layne's views on the timing of US balancing strategy. For instance, he commends US actions in 1939–41 as an example of offshore balancing while suggesting that the United States could have abstained from direct involvement in World War II altogether. Even outright German conquest of Eurasia would not have posed a mortal threat. This suggests that he would be willing to let conditions degenerate into open war—indeed, to near-defeat for friendly Eurasian powers—before actually siding with them against an aspiring hegemon. Layne, *Peace of Illusions*, 184–85.

28. Layne, *Peace of Illusions*, 161–63.

29. Nicholas John Spykman, *The Geography of the Peace*, ed. Helen R. Nicholl and intro. Frederick Sherwood Dunn (New York: Harcourt, Brace, 1944); and Nicholas John Spykman, *America's Strategy in World Politics: The United States and the Balance of Power* (New York: Harcourt, Brace, 1942).

30. Spykman, *America's Strategy in World Politics*, 457.

31. Spykman, *Geography of the Peace*, 19, 22, 33, 60.

32. Ibid., 19, 22, 33, 60.

33. Benjamin Schwarz and Christopher Layne, "A New Grand Strategy," *The Atlantic*, January 2002, www.theatlantic.com/past/docs/issues/2002/01/schwarzlayne .htm.

34. Spykman, *Geography of the Peace*, 38.

35. Ibid., 24–25.

36. US Office of the Secretary of Defense, *Annual Report to Congress: Military and Security Developments Involving the People's Republic of China*, 2010, www.defense .gov/pubs/pdfs/2010_CMPR_Final.pdf.

37. Layne, *Peace of Illusions*, 189–90.

38. Sun Tzu, *The Art of War*, trans. and intro. Samuel B. Griffith (New York: Oxford University Press, 1963), 129, 212. Death ground connotes life-or-death circumstances—peril so dire that national leaders will do almost anything to survive.

39. Stephen M. Walt, "Keynote Address," Current Strategy Forum, Naval War College Newport, RI, June 8, 2011.

40. Mahan, *Influence of Sea Power upon History*, 138.

41. Layne, "From Preponderance to Offshore Balancing," 113.

42. See, e.g., Andrew F. Krepinevich, *Why AirSea Battle?* (Washington, DC: Center for Strategic and Budgetary Assessments, 2010), www.csbaonline.org/ wp-content/uploads/2010/02/2010.02.19-Why-AirSea-Battle.pdf.

43. Clausewitz, *On War*, 76.

44. Samuel P. Huntington, "National Policy and the Transoceanic Navy," Naval Institute *Proceedings* 80, no. 5 (May 1954): 483–93.

45. "Chief of Naval Operations Adm. Gary Roughead Delivers Remarks at University of Chicago Conf on Terrorism & Strategy," October 12, 2010, www.navy .mil/navydata/people/cno/Roughead/Speech/101012-UofChicagoremarks%20 FINAL.doc.

46. Huntington, "National Policy and the Transoceanic Navy," 483–93.

47. Alfred Thayer Mahan, *Naval Strategy* (Boston: Little, Brown, 1911), 132–36.

48. Fiske, *Navy as a Fighting Machine*, 272.

49. Ibid., 272–73.

50. Daniel Whiteneck, Michael Price, Neil Jenkins, and Peter Swartz, *The Navy at a Tipping Point: Maritime Dominance at Stake?* (Washington, DC: Center for Naval Analyses, 2010), esp. 4–17, 33–36, www.cna.org/sites/default/ files/research/The%20Navy%20at%20a%20Tipping%20Point%20D0022262 .A3.pdf.

51. Whiteneck et al., *Navy at a Tipping Point*, 36.

52. Mahan, *Interest of America in Sea Power*, 180–81.

53. Ibid., 193.

54. For instance, Pakistan recently implored China to construct a naval base at its port of Gwadar. If Islamabad is ready to grant access to Chinese warships, it would hardly refuse access to missiles meant to protect the port. US Office of the Secretary of Defense, *Annual Report to Congress: Military and Security Developments Involving the People's Republic of China*, 2010, 30–32, www.defense. gov/pubs/pdfs/2010_CMPR_Final.pdf; Farhan Bokhari, "Pakistan Turns

to China for Naval Base," *Financial Times*, May 22, 2011, www.ft.com/cms/ s/0/3914bd36-8467-11e0-afcb-00144feabdc0.html.

55. See Mark Stokes and Tiffany Ma, "Second Artillery Anti-Ship Ballistic Missile Brigade Facilities under Construction in Guangdong?" *Asia Eye*, Project 2049, August 3, 2010.

56. For a more complete assessment of the operational dynamics involved, see James R. Holmes and Toshi Yoshihara, "Mahan's 'Active Defense' Is Turning Offensive," Naval Institute *Proceedings* 137, no. 4 (April 2011): 24–29.

57. Ronald O'Rourke, *China Naval Modernization: Implications for US Navy Capabilities—Background and Issues for Congress* (Washington, DC: Congressional Research Service, 2011), 8-14, www.fas.org/sgp/crs/row/RL33153.pdf.

58. Walt, "Keynote Address."

59. For a capsule summary, see "World-Wide Nuclear-Powered Attack Submarines," GlobalSecurity.org, www.globalsecurity.org/military/world/ssn.htm; and "World-Wide Conventional Submarines—2010," GlobalSecurity.org, www .globalsecurity.org/military/world/ss.htm.

60. Though it is not an iron law of naval operations, a US Navy thumb rule holds that three hulls are needed to keep one at sea and fully combat-ready: one is on deployment, another is working up for deployment through exercises and periodic maintenance, and the last is in extended shipyard overhaul and completely unavailable. Consequently, commanders can count on no more than two-thirds of the navy's full strength—and usually less.

61. China's People's Liberation Army (PLA) Navy conducted sea trials for its first carrier, the retired Soviet flattop *Varyag*, in August 2011. Estimates of the final Chinese carrier fleet range from two to four indigenously built ships. The *Varyag* will likely remain a training vessel, so we chose the top-end figure of three and sized the US carrier contingent accordingly. (So long as the PLA Navy limits operations to maritime Asia, holding down the wear-and-tear on its ships, it may be able to improve on the US Navy's 3:1 ratio, keeping two or even three of four PLA Navy carriers ready for immediate service.) With their bigger air wings, US CVNs will remain more than a match for their Chinese counterparts on a one-to-one basis for the foreseeable future. Consequently, a three-carrier US task force would enjoy considerable superiority over a three-carrier Chinese force.

62. Eleven of these would be big-deck amphibious helicopter carriers (LHA or LHD), with the remainder divided between smaller amphibious platform dock (LPD) and dock landing ship (LSD) hulls. Most ESGs are composed of an LHA or LHD, an LPD, and LSD, and assorted escort ships. Juan Ortiz, "Amphibious Ship Programs," presentation delivered May 21, 2008, Headquarters Marine Corps Website, http://hqinet001.hqmc.usmc.mil/i&L/v2/ LP/LPD/LPD.../PPO%20Brief.ppt. See also "Report of the Committee on Armed Services, House of Representatives, on H.R. 1540," 112th Cong., 1st Sess., May 17, 2011, 36, http://armedservices.house.gov/index.cfm/files/ serve?File_id=7cb6f96d-b253-4ee4-aec1-9f342b8374b3.

63. "UNITAS," Federation of American Scientists Website, www.globalsecurity.org/military/ops/unitas.htm.

64. Caitlin Talmadge, "Closing Time: Assessing the Iranian Threat to the Strait of Hormuz," *International Security* 33, no. 1 (Summer 2008): 82–117.

65. See, e.g., Rory Medcalf and Andrew Shearer, "PM Faces Challenge of Deeper Alliance," *The Australian*, March 7, 2011, www.theaustralian.com.au/news/world/pm-faces-challenge-of-deeper-alliance/story-e6frg6so-1226016729247.

66. David Wroe, "Australia to Deepen US Ties by Boosting Bases," *Sydney Morning Herald*, November 14, 2012, www.smh.com.au/opinion/politics/australia-to-deepen-us-ties-by-boosting-bases-20121113-29ait.html#ixzz2JrG6PeQv.

CHAPTER 6

Cooperative Security in the Indian Ocean Region

RODGER A. PAYNE

Cooperative security is often recommended as a viable grand strategy for US foreign policy by contemporary liberals and neoliberals, but the relevant literature suggests that academics, government officials, and policy analysts do not always agree about what it means or requires. In fact, perhaps more than any other grand strategic concept, cooperative security has long been seen as a work in progress, even by its backers. Understandings of both "cooperation" and "security" have evolved over time, and when brought together can imply a very wide range of potential meanings.[1] Thus, before specifically considering how cooperative security might be employed to advance American interests in the Indian Ocean region (IOR), perhaps as part of the so-called Asian pivot, it is essential to determine precisely what proponents hope to achieve when they support this grand strategy. The remainder of this introduction thus offers a brief explanation of the evolution of cooperative security as a grand strategic concept.

To begin, cooperative security has almost always implied a somewhat ambitious set of multilateral military practices, often proposed in preference to US unilateral action.[2] In traditional policy circles, supporters propose that states act collectively through international institutions, to coordinate "the deterrence and defeat of aggression."[3] All states share a strong interest in world peace, proponents assert, so the community of states should work together to preserve peace and avoid war. One leading scholar of international relations, who does not recommend this grand strategy for the United States, basically describes cooperative security as collective security plus other forms of military-related interstate cooperation, including arms control and disarmament efforts.[4] By this definition, the Persian Gulf War coalition was a near-perfect application of the strategy. Dozens of countries acted in a coordinated manner in 1990 to implement a United Nations Security Council (UNSC) resolution authorizing the use of "all necessary means" against Iraq, which had invaded Kuwait the previous summer. During the early years of the global war on terrorism, many analysts advocated that the United States and other members of the international community should similarly embrace cooperative security measures against the newly prioritized common threat. For example, G. John Ikenberry wrote in 2002 that the threat from transnational terrorism should be addressed by cooperative security featuring a "pragmatic orientation" that would stress "alliances, multilateral cooperation and a commitment to building order around practical and mutually beneficial rules and institutions."[5] A defense analyst explained the specific kinds of security cooperation that might be required: "Numerous nations must mount and coordinate intensive efforts to ... tighten border controls, police remote regions, screen financial transactions, and freely share sensitive intelligence with other states."[6] According to this view of cooperative security, states pursue collaborative military action in certain situations because they share an important interest in reducing third-party security threats. Of course, as the prelude to the 2003 Iraq War demonstrated so clearly, it can be very difficult to build the kind of broad military coalition that was assembled in 1990 and early 1991 to defeat Iraq.[7] Thus, in practice, this relatively standard conception of cooperative security is more often reflected in less contentious policies, such as arms control and disarmament initiatives.

Indeed, arms control figured prominently in the immediate post–Cold War period as the new security relationship between the United States and Russia was often explicitly described in terms of cooperative security. The conclusion of the Cold War seemed to signal the end of a zero-sum competitive security environment between two former superpower rivals. The new cooperative security relationship allowed for the prospect of positive-sum security collaboration, including bilateral efforts to reduce shared threats from the dangerous nuclear weaponry that each had deployed over the decades. Thus, the Strategic Arms Reduction Treaty (known as START) that these countries signed in 1991 exemplified this understanding of cooperative security because it eliminated thousands of nuclear weapons from the American and Russian arsenals. In the prior few years, the United States, the Soviet Union, and their Cold War partners had also successfully achieved the Intermediate-Range Nuclear Forces Treaty, which eliminated this class of weaponry altogether, and the Treaty on Conventional Armed Forces in Europe, which reduced a large portion of the tanks, heavy artillery, and combat aircraft deployed between the Atlantic Ocean and the Ural Mountains. Ultimately, many cooperative security thinkers of that era broadly imagined an ongoing "commitment to regulate the size, technical composition, investment patterns, and operational practices of all military forces by mutual consent for mutual benefit."[8]

Throughout the 1990s and early 2000s, the notion of cooperative security was taken up by a number of policymakers around the world who obviously intended the idea to have utility outside great power relations. These efforts additionally served to broaden the notion of security well beyond traditional geostrategic and military concerns. Perhaps most prominently, former Australian foreign minister Gareth Evans advocated the pursuit of cooperative security to address the kinds of intrastate security threats that were of greatest concern in the 1990s.[9] Evans and others emphasized the potential ability of the United Nations to prevent and/or respond to internal conflicts linked to nationalist and ethnic violence, or to address related problems such as the plight of millions of political refugees and internally displaced peoples. In due course, the UNSC adopted a number of Chapter VII–based enforcement resolutions (pertaining to the chapter of the United Nations Charter titled "Action with Respect to Threats to the Peace, Breaches of the Peace, and Acts of Aggression"), both before the Persian Gulf War and throughout the following decade, that seemed to reflect a new common understanding of the threat to international peace and security. These resolutions generally responded to internal conflicts and triggered the use of multilateral security instruments, including the imposition of economic sanctions or the deployment of UN peace-keeping forces. Virtually by definition, the UNSC employs a cooperative security perspective when it identifies and acts to counter such threats.

As states have debated and implemented various multilateral security initiatives in reaction to an array of threats and interrelated problems during the past twenty-five years, many policy analysts and government officials have argued for numerous procedural and substantive elements that have yielded a transformed (and arguably more "progressive") understanding of cooperative security.[10] The evolution of this grand strategy has been a truly global phenomenon, and it is tied to many international normative and institutional design developments that cannot be discussed here. To provide a measure of their scope, many analysts argue that the idea is "enshrined in every major OSCE [Organization for Security and Cooperation in Europe] document" and that the December 2003 European Security Strategy is fundamentally a cooperative security text.[11] In these contexts, cooperative security no longer merely implies arms control or multilateral action to achieve a common purpose. Rather, security is now frequently presumed to be indivisible, meaning that insecurity in any one state or region should be considered a common security concern.[12] Instability, violence, and other transnational threats can literally spread to neighboring states or regions and beyond, though indivisibility obviously also has normative implications.[13] Genocide, ethnic cleansing, and weather catastrophes, even in remote or powerless regions, are now potentially viewed as global security concerns.

Moreover, genuine cooperative security is thought to require shared and even consensual decision-making practices. In the words of the Cooperative Security

Consortium core group, an early 1990s collection of prominent policymakers and scholars, "cooperative security is a strategic principle that accomplishes its purposes through institutionalized consent."[14] Lack of multilateral approval was thus a key problem when the George W. Bush administration assembled its "coalition of the willing" to attack Iraq in 2003. Nongovernmental organizations (NGOs) and intergovernmental institutions are now independent voices that are taken seriously in security discussions. Their participation has helped assure the broadening of the security agenda and can promote more open and transparent decision processes. Thus, though weaponry and warfare remain central security issues, especially the proliferation of weapons of mass destruction (WMD) and their potential use by transnational terrorists, today's expanding security agenda includes also the so-called human security concerns of ordinary people, such as poverty and economic inequality, environmental calamity, and hunger.

As employed throughout this chapter, cooperative security refers to the idea that nation-states, ordinarily working through intergovernmental institutions and often with NGO partners, collaborate with one another consensually to seek solutions to an array of common security problems and threats.[15] The security agenda extends beyond traditional geostrategic and military issues—such as international and intrastate war, terrorism, and the risks associated with the proliferation of WMD—to encompass other burgeoning threats to global peace and stability. As the Obama administration recently declared, these include "inequality and economic instability, ... damage to our environment, food insecurity, and dangers to public health."[16] Finally, proponents of cooperative security view security as indivisible, meaning that insecurity in one state or region should be viewed as a common security concern.

The balance of this chapter considers how cooperative security can be—and often is—employed in the IOR to achieve American national and global interests.

COOPERATIVE SECURITY AND US INTERESTS IN THE INDIAN OCEAN REGION

Much of the public discussion about the so-called Asian pivot has centered upon the military implications for US foreign and security policy. Indeed, Obama administration officials typically use "rebalancing" as a substitute word for "pivot" to describe American intentions and actions, seeming to imply with this terminology the classic realist concern with confronting or containing great power rivals before they become hegemonic within a region. In the Asia-Pacific region, the obvious concerns are the rise of China (and ultimately India) and the concomitant need to limit their influence in the long term. The United States is planning to move more of its military assets to Asia and is already attempting to strengthen regional alliances and defense relationships and increase the number of military training exercises in the region. For example, an additional 2,500 US Marines will train with Australian forces, Littoral Combat Ships are newly deploying to Singapore, and some bomber forces are moving from the Middle East to Asia. Perhaps most significantly, the United States intends by 2020 to deploy 60 percent of its ships in the Pacific Ocean region versus 40 percent in the Atlantic. Currently, the split is about 50/50.[17]

Despite these changes in military deployments and the apparent focus on great power competition, then–secretary of state Hillary Rodham Clinton emphasized the diplomatic, political, and especially the economic dimensions of the US strategic pivot. Indeed, Clinton essentially denied the importance of the realpolitik commonly thought to be undergirding the rebalancing policy and suggests that a liberal agenda apparently consistent with cooperative security is instead at the heart of the strategy: "The President's visits to Burma and the East Asia Summit highlighted the democratic values and diplomatic engagement that power the pivot. None of this is about containment. It's all aimed at advancing a rules-based order in the Asia-Pacific that will drive peace and prosperity for decades to come."[18] Consistent with this rationale, the State Department frequently claims to be working to place economics at the center of US foreign policy priorities, which implies an altogether different meaning of the word "rebalancing." The United States apparently intends to deemphasize the importance of military power in its foreign and security policy. As part of this effort, the Obama administration has sought new trade agreements and advocated for an improved investment climate in the region.[19] Additionally, as Deputy Secretary of State William J. Burns has noted, the strategic pivot includes efforts to support "Asia's promising regional institutions," such as the Association of Southeast Asian Nations and the East Asia Summit, because they could play a "critical role in developing common rules of the road and systems that can help address increasingly complex and transnational challenges, like non-proliferation, maritime security, and humanitarian and natural disasters."[20] Put differently, the strategic pivot to Asia already seems to imagine an important role for cooperative security.

This section considers how cooperative security might help the United States and its partners address the most important threats and challenges facing the IOR. The initial subsection discusses the security threats that have dominated global debate during much of the past decade—WMD proliferation and transnational terrorism. Next, the analysis considers how cooperative security strategy might address a classic international relations problem: great power rivalry. The final two subsections consider nontraditional security threats related to global climate change and economic development.

Nuclear Proliferation Threats

In the foreseeable future, the United States expects the Indian Ocean regional powers India and Pakistan to maintain and perhaps upgrade their nuclear weapons capabilities, and anticipates that Iran will continue to seek nuclear weapons. Additionally, other states seeking biological, chemical, missile, or nuclear capabilities—potentially including Burma, North Korea, and Saudi Arabia—will likely use the Indian Ocean as a critical transshipment route. The UN has reported, for example, that Iran and North Korea have shared ballistic missile technology, though they seemingly employed air cargo trade.[21]

India's first nuclear test dates to 1974, but it did not develop a weaponized nuclear arsenal until after 1998, when both India and Pakistan conducted multiple atomic tests. These states continue to dispute the status of Kashmir, and since 1947 that conflict has been a significant factor in three of the four wars waged between the now-nuclear-armed rivals. Iran's nuclear program has been the subject of great attention over the past decade, of course, but no hard evidence yet suggests that it has enriched uranium to weapons grade levels. Nonetheless, Iran's nuclear status will be an ongoing and central concern for policymakers for the foreseeable future. The United States worries that it will pose a significant threat to Israel, the most important American ally in the Middle East, and fears that Iran's ruling mullahs will not accept the logic of nuclear deterrence. Iran's links to transnational terrorism also explain heightened US concern. North Korea has long been viewed as a rogue state by the United States, and its nuclear and missile programs are viewed by the United States as threatening to important allies like Japan and South Korea. Obviously, if either Iran or North Korea develops an intercontinental missile capability, it could ultimately pose a threat to more distant potential targets such as the US homeland.

A cooperative security approach to WMD threats emerging from this region should be multidimensional. First, the United States could continue to work with states in the IOR, and with other great powers and like-minded states, to strengthen multilateral arms control and disarmament initiatives. India and Pakistan are not members of the Nuclear Non-Proliferation Treaty (NPT), and Iran breached important elements of the nonproliferation regime by failing to report all its activities, including the construction of nuclear enrichment facilities. In the near term the United States should continue to support multilateral efforts through the UNSC, the International Atomic Energy Agency, and other institutions to ensure Iranian compliance with its commitments under the NPT. The logic of cooperative security likewise suggests the prospect of a negotiated agreement with Tehran, perhaps as part of a comprehensive settlement of long-standing disputes involving trade, diplomatic relations, and security policy.

Additionally, the United States might want to take seriously the desire occasionally expressed by some Indian officials for that country to enter the NPT as a nuclear weapons state. Although such a move could establish an undesirable precedent, the United States and its multilateral collaborators could consider various means of implementing this plan in conjunction with broader treaty reform. One proposal, for example, would extend the cutoff date for nuclear status from 1968 to 1974, though this is complicated by the fact that India has always considered its 1974 atomic detonation a "peaceful nuclear explosion." Moreover, Pakistan would likely never agree to join a nonproliferation regime that legitimizes India's bomb while stigmatizing its own nuclear weapons. In any case, India could be made a more important partner in strengthening the nonproliferation regime.

Of course, Indian officials have long scolded the United States for having an inconsistent and hypocritical record on arms control and disarmament. They typically refer to Article VI of the NPT, which requires member states "to pursue negotiations in good faith on effective measures relating to cessation of the nuclear arms race at an early date and to nuclear disarmament, and on a Treaty on general and complete disarmament under strict and effective international control." Because the United States spent decades increasing the size and capability of its nuclear arsenal, including a long period after the NPT language was drafted, India views the NPT as a discriminatory treaty, locking in two distinct tiers of nuclear status, though the treaty was not meant to create these as permanent.

The most credible commitment the United States could make to nonproliferation, arms control, and disarmament would entail fulfillment of President Barack Obama's so-called global zero statement, made in Prague in April 2009: "I state clearly and with conviction America's commitment to seek the peace and security of a world without nuclear weapons." Hundreds of current and former government and military officials—from the United States and many other nations—have likewise called for a world without nuclear weapons, but states have not yet agreed to a precise pathway toward accomplishing this objective. As an interim and incremental measure, some policymakers and analysts call for US ratification of the Comprehensive Test Ban Treaty, which failed to attain Senate consent in October 1999. Others advocate regional nuclear-weapons-free zones, an idea that the United States has previously opposed because of the desire to maintain ambiguity concerning the arsenals aboard American naval vessels.

The United States could seek other arms control measures to counter WMD proliferation risks. For instance, the United States could engage other states to strengthen the Biological Weapons Convention (BWC). An eleventh-hour US decision in 2001 scuttled a negotiated verification protocol to the BWC and that decision was reaffirmed by the Obama administration in 2009. The Cooperative Threat Reduction program (long known as Nunn-Lugar, for its original legislative backers in the US Senate) could likewise be replicated for Indian Ocean states seeking to comply with the BWC, the Chemical Weapons Convention, the NPT, or even a comprehensive future nuclear or conventional disarmament plan. Over the next decade, the United States could also attempt to engage allied states to ratify the Additional Protocols to the NPT. Neither Egypt nor Israel has agreed to these standards, for example, though they have been the two largest recipients of American foreign assistance for several decades. Israel is not a member of the NPT and is unlikely to change its policy without a comprehensive Middle East peace settlement.

Multilateral economic sanctions, coercive weapons inspections, and counterproliferation military operations, including conceivably "preemptive" attacks on WMD facilities, can be compatible with a cooperative security strategy. Ideally, the members of the UNSC would agree about the significance of a particular proliferation-related threat and about the proper collective course of action. The UNSC is uniquely positioned to legitimate international order and thus potentially to broaden the scope of cooperation, increase burden sharing, and thereby make multilateral efforts more effective.[22] For example, it seems likely that the comprehensive multilateral economic sanctions regime against Iraq, coupled with the coercively induced weapons inspections regime, largely disarmed Iraq of its WMD programs in the 1990s.[23] Then again, the prolonged Iraq sanctions regime almost certainly had high human costs—even conservative estimates of the humanitarian consequences calculate that the sanctions contributed to more than 100,000 civilian deaths during the decade.[24]

The burden-sharing implications of potential counterproliferation operations can be quite important. The most recent Iraq war has cost the United States more than $3 trillion by some estimates.[25] In contrast, the UNSC-approved 1991 Persian Gulf War, which was mentioned above as an almost ideal application of cooperative security strategy, and which involved more than 500,000 US troops and associated equipment, cost only a small fraction of that total. Most important, the overwhelming majority of the $61 billion war cost was paid by contributions from the Gulf states (primarily Saudi Arabia and Kuwait), Japan, and Germany in 1990 and 1991. In total, international payments toward US expenses amounted to $53 billion, or 86.9 percent of the war costs.[26] Such burden sharing for future international commitments could be particularly important if US defense budgets shrink significantly as a result of deficit reduction efforts.

The most problematic measures to address WMD proliferation risks, from the perspective of cooperative security, would be policies perceived as wholly unilateral or independent US initiatives. The nuclear-proliferation-related sanctions employed by the United States against India and Pakistan after their 1998 nuclear tests were basically unilateral. More important, the decision to use force in the 2003 Iraq war was made primarily in Washington, even though the Bush administration assembled a coalition of willing partners, including Great Britain. In this latter case, despite this assent, policies were viewed as autonomous and not reflective of authentic cooperative security. Of course, cooperative security does not impinge on what Article 51 of the UN Charter calls "the inherent right of individual or collective self-defense" against armed attack. Thus, the United States can devote additional resources to homeland or missile defense—and work with its partners to deter or defeat potential external aggression, even in areas that the Pentagon considers antiaccess environments.

Finally, the logic of cooperative security suggests the need for procedural reform in the promising Proliferation Security Initiative (PSI), which was launched by the United States in 2003 as a global effort to interdict vessels suspected of trafficking in WMD, related materials, or delivery systems. More than 100 countries have endorsed the PSI Statement of Interdiction Principles, but the ideas might gain even more traction if they are formalized as an international norm via treaty or in a resolution passed by the UNSC, as difficult as that might be. A cooperative security approach to the PSI should be consistent with the stated goal to strengthen and expand the policy.

Ongoing Terrorism Threats

Terrorist organizations, including al-Qaeda associated movements (AQAM)—working independently, or in affiliation with various ethnic, religious, and nationalist factions within Afghanistan, Iran, Pakistan, Somalia, Yemen, or other regional states—may precipitate crises through bold attacks on urban centers, government buildings, military assets, or other high-profile targets. Willing state partners could provide financial support or a safe haven for terrorists, though AQAM will likely continue to prey primarily on weak and failing states. Terrorist activity could threaten the political stability of states with significant Islamic populations, even in relatively orderly countries. A large US footprint in the region potentially radicalizes these movements and coalitions and makes it easier for them to recruit new members.

As noted in the introductory section, many international security specialists argue that a wide variety of anticounterterrorist and counterterrorist policies require extensive multilateral cooperation in order to be effective. Since the terrorist attacks of September 11, 2001, the United States and many other states have indeed worked together to develop or strengthen an extensive array of collaborative security policy instruments, including the use of military force, intelligence assets, law enforcement, and financial tools. As of June 2013 America had about 68,000 troops deployed in Afghanistan who are explicitly part of the nearly fifty-nation International Security Assistance Force, a UNSC-backed peace enforcement operation related to nine UNSC resolutions. The United

States is also an important cooperating partner with the United Nations Assistance Mission in Afghanistan (UNAMA), though its role is primarily related to humanitarian and reconstruction operations as well as political and peace processes. Given cooperative security's broad conception of security, efforts to promote and monitor good governance, human rights, and the rule of law can be viewed as security functions, as are counternarcotics efforts. The United States provides 22 percent of UNAMA's budget, the same share it provides for the regular UN budget.

However, the history of the past decade reveals that the United States has not always operated in a manner consistent with the ideals of cooperative security. Even longtime American allies have overtly opposed particular dimensions of the global war on terrorism, especially with regard to the holding and treatment of alleged terrorist captives at the detention facility at Guantánamo Bay, Cuba, the claimed inapplicability of the Geneva Conventions to terrorism suspects, and, of course, the launch of the 2003 Iraq war. Although many specific disputed policies have been altered or ended in recent years, and some wounds have healed with time, American actions and policies will continue to be challenged if they are viewed as unilateral, primarily self-interested, or outside the bounds of international law. Indeed, if the United States strictly followed the logic of cooperative security, military operations would seem to be limited to traditional legal acts of self-defense and collective defense against aggression, plus UNSC-authorized enforcement operations. Counterinsurgency (known as COIN), stability, and counterterrorism operations employed in Afghanistan to support ongoing UN Chapter VII operations would withstand this standard. However, unilateral counterterrorism operations conducted with military force in many global locations would be more problematic.

International norms, however, can evolve over time. In the controversial 2002 *National Security Strategy* document, the Bush administration asserted a need for new international legal and normative standards related to defining "preemptive" versus "preventive" war. After all, terrorists, perhaps supported or sponsored by rogue states, might launch deadly suicide strikes without warning. Old standards of international law would seem to be inapplicable when attacks are committed by nonstate actors, are not preceded by an observable military buildup, and conceivably could involve nuclear or biological weapons. What state should suffer the retaliatory blow if transnational terrorists complete a surprise attack with WMD? Largely because of these concerns, the United States continues to claim an ability to "preempt" terrorist plots based upon actionable intelligence. Although many states sought to uphold long-standing international norms about the use of force in the debate preceding the Iraq war, the norm limiting preventive action has arguably evolved over the past decade to reflect many of the United States' concerns.[27] It now appears that some previously precluded preventive uses of force are recognized as legitimate, though most states prefer collective decision making about the nature of the threat and the preemptive response.

Recent and ongoing United States actions in Pakistan are potentially instructive. Although no European government formally condemned the May 2011 Navy SEAL operation in Abbottabad that ended in the death of Osama bin Laden, German chancellor Angela Merkel faced some criticism at home and across the continent for declaring that she was "glad that it was successful, the killing of bin Laden."[28] Some international lawyers questioned the legality of the operation, equating the outcome to the assassination of a political figure rather than the wartime targeting of a military leader. Worse, many analysts have expressed concerns about the apparent infringement of Pakistani sovereignty by the operation, which was reportedly not cleared in advance and evidently required an assertion of extraterritorial jurisdiction. On a broader level, many Pakistani officials have long challenged the legality of US drone attacks inside their state's territory. Conceivably, apart from the legal implications, the unpopularity of the so-called drone war could pose a threat to the stability of Pakistan's government, given that it is unable to stop ongoing US strikes inside its borders.

From a cooperative security perspective, the United States should endeavor to gain the widest possible support for its antiterrorist and counterterrorist operations in the IOR. In practice, this means assuring diplomatic and political collaboration, even if the actual policies on the ground, in the air, at sea, or at a distant computer terminal are undertaken by American personnel. Ideally, the cooperation would be assured through international institutions featuring genuinely shared decision-making procedures and not merely reflect US construction of ad hoc coalitions of nations willing to embrace the American view of particular situations and solutions. The latter, again, might be viewed as unilateral or independent, and thus as illegitimate by other members of the international community.

Finally, the United States could continue to pursue a variety of other creative ideas to address terror-related threats that would be consistent with cooperative security. For example, the United States should be able without controversy to continue its practice of building up the security capacity of partner states, depending upon which capacities are built and larger contextual factors. Weak, failing, and failed states often need many nonmilitary capabilities that could well be promoted through cooperative security, including certain kinds of security assistance, such as law enforcement and counterterrorism training. The United States could also pursue arms registries and a new arms control regime in partnership with other states to limit access to short-range ballistic missiles by nonstate actors such as the Taliban or Hezbollah. The United States could also work with other states to develop defensive systems that defend against such threats.

Great Power Rivalry

China and India are likely to become much more powerful states in coming decades. They also have a history of competitive relations, which means that great power tensions in the region could increase over time. War between them is unlikely at any given moment, but it is conceivable, potentially even as an unintended outcome after an escalation of Indian–Pakistani tensions. Pakistan has long-standing military, technical, and economic ties to China. All these states are also currently linked to the United States—Pakistan is a critical state for the ongoing war in Afghanistan, China is a leading economic partner, and India is a key player on transnational questions of energy, climate change, and nonproliferation.

Additionally, American sea services are committed to maintaining credible combat power in both the Persian Gulf–Indian Ocean region and in the Western Pacific. The Chinese military presence in the IOR will probably increase and will potentially require expanded access to land-based facilities. The Indian Navy is poised to grow as well, with intent to assert greater regional influence. In the coming decades, China, India, and possibly other great powers may deploy nuclear-powered and/or nuclear-armed submarines as well as aircraft carriers in the Indian Ocean. These regional powers are also likely to maintain or increase their reliance upon natural resources from the Persian Gulf region and Africa. Economic and population growth are the driving forces for increased resource consumption, and this region will likely continue to experience substantial new demand. Conceivably, competition for supply will motivate many foreign policy decisions for each of the regional powers.

Clearly, for a multiplicity of reasons, opportunities for misperceptions and crisis escalation among the great powers will increase in the IOR. Nonetheless, cooperative security strategies provide an opportunity for great powers to negotiate and agree to transparent international norms covering a broad range of interactions and should thus encourage the great powers to pursue nonviolent and even collaborative solutions to the kinds of problems that might otherwise trigger competitive and dangerous behavior. States will have a strong shared interest in developing alternatives to many raw materials, particularly new energy resources. Conceivably, US participation could facilitate India and Pakistan arriving at a meaningful solution to their dispute over Kashmir. Other long-standing and seemingly intractable disputes in international politics have been resolved or mitigated by a negotiated settlement of differences. The Northern Ireland peace process, culminating in the final 2007 agreement, is a leading example and is fully consistent with cooperative security strategy.

Moreover, cooperative security strategists from various states could develop and strengthen international rules involving the maritime forces of the United States, China, India, and possibly other great powers operating in the IOR.

Conventional arms control measures might be the preferred method of limiting many risks. The United States could attempt to limit "antiaccess" environments by seeking arms control for particular kinds of weapons systems, such as medium-range ballistic missiles with precision-guided maneuvering warheads. Of course, the United States will face charges of hypocrisy if it tries to preserve a capacity for itself that it wishes to outlaw for others. Additionally, confidence-building measures could be embraced to reduce the likelihood of interstate conflict. For instance, states could commit to transparency by revealing their deployments and operations, including war games. Conceivably, states could make long-term commitments to collective military force configurations. It is also within the realm of the possible to imagine states agreeing to establish joint naval bases in the IOR. More likely, they might agree to establish midterm to long-term collaborative naval operations. Military-to-military exchanges and observational exercises might prove beneficial. States of the region could also negotiate a norm modeled after the 1972 deal between the United States and the Soviet Union known informally as the Incidents at Sea Agreement. In the past few years, India and Pakistan, India and China, and the United States and China have established bilateral military "hotlines" in order to promote communication and reduce the risk of misunderstandings during crises. These channels could be extended multilaterally and potentially to additional states in order to promote cooperative security in the region. The Association of Southeast Asian Nations' Proposed Elements of a Regional Code of Conduct in the South China Sea could serve as a meaningful starting point, though China has been accused of stalling a process that has been in the works for many years.

Climate Change Threats

The United States and the rest of the world could negotiate significant reductions in carbon emissions to head off climate change. Although such an approach is clearly compatible with cooperative security, this section ignores that issue and focuses on the likely reality that the world will not be able to prevent at least some climate change in this century. As a study for the UN's *Human Development Report* office recently noted, the South Asian region is "highly sensitive to the consequences of climate change. It is known to be the most disaster-prone region in the world supporting a huge population of more than 1.3 billion." The report concluded that "climate change is a grave and immediate issue for South Asia" and that states in the region are expected to suffer increasingly frequent natural disasters such as monsoons, serious food insecurity, and reduced access to safe drinking water.[29] Many states in the region will face human health emergencies and other humanitarian disasters. From Bangladesh to India and Pakistan, states are likely to lack the capacity to address crises wrought by climate change.

Empirical academic research on the relationship between so-called environmental scarcities and security finds that population growth, inequitable access to resources, and reductions in the quality or quantity of renewable resources can reduce economic activity and lead to mass migrations of peoples searching for resources or economic opportunities. These problems, which are important factors in the weakening of states, can then exacerbate ethnic or deprivation conflicts.[30] Most likely, the United States and other members of the international community will in the coming decades face a series of conflict-linked challenges in the IOR. Cooperative security strategists should emphasize the importance of monitoring the areas hit hardest by environmental scarcities in order to be able to implement appropriate preventive diplomacy, conflict resolution, and/or intervention techniques.

Additionally, by the logic of cooperative security, the poverty and hunger linked to climate change should be viewed as important global security threats in their own right. Thus, if the United States pursues this strategy, it will be challenged to provide assistance to victims of environmental scarcities and natural disasters throughout the IOR. Preventively, the United States could work with other states to build effective regional and national capacities to assure the uninterrupted supply of food, water, and other basic necessities of life. However, the United States might be expected, in complex humanitarian emergencies, to help provide the kind of assistance that the international community contributed following the December 2004 earthquake and tsunami in the IOR, the 2005 earthquake in Kashmir, and the July 2010 monsoon rains and flooding in Pakistan. An even stronger obligation to act is implied by the so-called responsibility to protect (R2P), a relatively new international normative initiative meant to establish something like an obligation for the international community to protect populations at risk living in weak, failing, and failed states if their governments are unable or unwilling to provide basic protections for them. Thus, the United States and other countries might need to be prepared for the possibility that states hit by natural disaster could react in a manner not unlike Burma's government in May 2008 following a devastating cyclone that killed 78,000 people and left another 56,000 missing. The ruling generals initially refused large-scale assistance, and aid workers could not enter the country for several days after the disaster.

The international community's response to recent revolutionary turmoil in a number of Arabic states in northern Africa and the Middle East suggests both the broad importance of R2P and its inherent limitations. To be sure, the limited humanitarian intervention in Libya authorized by the UNSC in order "to protect civilians and civilian populated areas under threat of attack" reflected an apparently successful cooperative security action in support of the R2P principles.[31] However, the lack of significant international response to recent violence in Bahrain and Syria (at least through late September 2013) indicates that the decisions to uphold R2P will likely be ad hoc and involve political calculations inconsistent with cooperative security and the R2P principles. Nonetheless, given its position as a uniquely powerful member of the international community, the United States may be asked to lead many additional R2P initiatives in the future. These kinds of cooperative security operations, of course, would be subject to negotiation, and the United States has a veto in the UNSC, which would assure that any Chapter VII–related force commitment decisions would be subject to American approval.

Economic Security

Cooperative security can help promote a strong, innovative, and growing US economy in an open international economic system that encourages opportunity and prosperity. The ongoing globalization of the international economy indicates a high level of economic interdependence built upon the kinds of deeply intertwined trade and financial relations that are broadly consistent with cooperative security strategy. The World Trade Organization and the regional trade entities— supported by the World Bank, the International Monetary Fund, and regional development banks—have promoted an open international system with relatively free-flowing investments, goods, and services. The so-called Washington Consensus was potentially threatened by the financial crisis of 2008, but its fundamental norms were not abandoned.

China and, increasingly, India have been major beneficiaries of economic globalization. China has averaged about 9 percent annual economic growth for decades, which has helped lift hundreds of millions of people out of poverty and has made China the second-largest economy in the world. India's economy recently cracked the top ten, as measured by gross domestic product, and it will likely surpass France, Italy, Germany, Britain, and even Russia by 2025. India has averaged nearly 8.5 percent growth since 2004 (and more than 7 percent since 1997), reducing its poverty rate by 10 percent. This is especially significant given that India has more people living at the global poverty level than the entire continent of Africa. Because advocates of cooperative security are concerned about poverty and view security as indivisible, the economic success stories for China and India are also success stories for the United States and the world.

Not everyone views economic prosperity in this manner, of course. Recessions can spawn economic nationalism and calls for neomercantilist strategies, which would likely result in policies antithetical to cooperative security. States might pursue policies to satisfy unhappy laborers, whose economic activity has been essentially delinked from the globalization of capital. Absent dramatically altered global migration policies and practices, labor is still mostly bound within nation-state boundaries. Millions of manufacturing jobs have been permanently exported from the United States to China, India, or other states. This creates protectionist urges, which could be magnified during the next economic downturn. Corporate profits have been strong, but economic growth has been somewhat weak and unemployment levels have remained very high. According to the logic of cooperative security, global economic problems should be resolved via inclusive multilateral negotiations.

CONCLUSIONS: RISKS AND UNCERTAINTIES

To a great extent, a commitment to cooperative security is a commitment to a value-laden security strategy. The strategy has long been associated with liberal and antimilitarist ideas like arms control and disarmament, and it embraces collaborative and consensual decision making with other members of the international community. Moreover, security is seen as both substantially inclusive—human rights abuses, inequality, and poverty are important threats to security—and indivisible, meaning that the great powers like the United States should be quite concerned about the insecurities of weak and vulnerable states and peoples everywhere. Cooperative security practices are developed in a context that is sensitive to the interests of other states, intergovernmental organizations, and NGOs.

As this chapter has argued, cooperative security can address many of the primary and secondary security objectives of the United States and its allies and partners. First and foremost, cooperative security achieves these goals by emphasizing multilateral negotiation and collaborative institutional responses to specific security threats and challenges. In addition to arms control and disarmament measures, a number of coercive security policies can be undertaken cooperatively in order to counter the proliferation of WMD or transnational terrorism. These same sorts of mechanisms can also help prevent great power competition and conflict or respond to the threats associated with long-term climate change. Cooperative security is also a foundation for the kind of economic cooperation that has long been associated with prosperity and development.

The greatest risks posed by cooperative security involve the tension between unilateral and collaborative understandings of threats and responses. In many foreseeable circumstances, the United States will be tempted to define problems in a way that will lead to autonomous decisions and unilateral actions. Effective cooperative security should be built upon genuine multilateralism and consensual decision making. The United States will face charges of hypocrisy if it seeks to address and resolve relatively lower-priority problems collaboratively and with negotiated soft power mechanisms but employs more assertive, unilateral, and hard power military strategies to mitigate high politics threats and challenges. In other words, the United States should be as interested in cooperative measures to confront WMD proliferation and antiterrorism as it is to address global poverty and pollution.

Of course, US decision makers have long made decisions with global interdependence in mind. They have taken into account the perspectives of other states and intergovernmental organizations and have often consulted with interested parties before announcing policy choices. However, this is somewhat different from genuinely collaborative and consensual decision making. The UNSC is perhaps an instructive model, because a veto by any of the five permanent members (P5)—China, France, Russia, the United Kingdom, or the United States—effectively ends multilateral efforts in that forum. In the IOR, it is not difficult to imagine that the UNSC will fail to address virtually any security threats involving China, particularly if any other member of the P5 stands in opposition to its policies. Likewise, even a renewed crisis between India and Pakistan would make for difficult days at the UNSC, given the two states' historic and contemporary allies and security partnerships. If UNSC action is desired, either these states must clearly share a common interest in defining a threat or taking action, or potentially disgruntled veto states must have their top concerns assuaged. At a minimum, P5 opponents must be convinced to register any opposition privately and to abstain from vetoing widely desired action. Diplomatic language can be carefully crafted to assure maximum agreement, and some favored policy choices must be abandoned in order to achieve consensus. Though few other institutions have this sort of decision-making procedure, cooperative security strategy imagines states seeking this sort of a consensus through appropriate institutional arrangements. Moreover, because of the centrally important role of the UNSC on the questions of threats to international peace and security, this decision-making body will be very influential in crafting cooperative security strategy.

Even without these great power disagreements, the UNSC can prove to be an impossible venue for addressing threats in short order. US leaders worry that collaborative bodies are not able to respond to situations quickly enough to address urgent problems or crises. Historically, intergovernmental institutions have often failed to respond to threats in a timely fashion. In the post–Cold War era, the UNSC essentially failed for completely different reasons to act quickly to mitigate massive humanitarian emergencies in Rwanda and in Darfur (Sudan). If security is truly indivisible, then these were massive international security failures. Yet many states in the international system are unwilling to further weaken state sovereignty to authorize what they see as intrusive external interventions. Not every P5 state is equally committed to the R2P principle, for example, and thus acts of genocide, complex humanitarian emergencies, crimes against humanity, ethnic cleansing, and other horrific acts have occurred in the post–Cold War world while the international community dithered. Demanding fealty to collaborative, multilateral, and preferably consensual decision-making procedures can be a recipe for stalemate and tragedy.

NOTES

1. For a more detailed discussion, see Rodger A. Payne, "Cooperative Security: Grand Strategy Meets Critical Theory?" *Millennium: Journal of International Studies* 40, no. 3 (June 2012): 605–24.

2. For a discussion, see Barry R. Posen and Andrew L. Ross, "Competing Visions for US Grand Strategy," *International Security* 21, no. 3 (Winter 1996–97): 21–30. Advocates often emphasize the use of nonmilitary instruments of state power to attain national goals as well.

3. Posen and Ross, "Competing Visions for US Grand Strategy," 23.

4. Robert J. Art, *A Grand Strategy for America* (Ithaca, NY: Cornell University, 2003), 107.

5. G. John Ikenberry, "American Grand Strategy in the Age of Terror," *Survival* 43, no. 4 (Winter 2001–2): 20.

6. Carl Conetta, "Terrorism, World Order, and Cooperative Security: A Research and Policy Development Agenda," Project on Defense Alternatives Briefing Memo 24, September 9, 2002, www.comw.org/pda/0209coopsec.html.

7. Of course, the deterrent purpose of collective security is seriously undermined if states are unwilling or unable to make sweeping advance commitments to act against international aggression.

8. Ashton B. Carter, William J. Perry, and John D. Steinbruner, *A New Concept of Cooperative Security* (Washington, DC: Brookings Institution Press, 1992), 6. Jeffrey A. Larsen and others have employed this definition, though Carter, Perry, and Steinbruner actually defined "cooperative engagement" in the quoted material. See Jeffrey A. Larsen, "An Introduction to Arms Control," in *Arms Control: Cooperative Security in a Changing Environment*, ed. Jeffrey A. Larsen (Boulder, CO: Lynne Rienner, 2002), 4.

9. Gareth Evans, "Cooperative Security and Intra-State Conflict," *Foreign Policy*, Autumn 1994, 3–20.

10. See ibid.; and Payne, "Cooperative Security."

11. Wolfgang Zellner, "Cooperative Security: Principle and Reality," *Security and Human Rights* 21 (2010): 64. The United States is a member of the OSCE. See Javiar Solana, *A Secure Europe in a Better World: European Security Strategy* (Brussels: European Union, 2003), www.consilium.europa.eu/uedocs/cms Upload/78367.pdf.

12. Andrei Zagorski, "The OSCE and Cooperative Security," *Security and Human Rights* 21 (2010): 58.

13. See, e.g., Barack Obama, "Remarks of Senator Barack Obama to the Chicago Council on Global Affairs," April 23, 2007, http://my.barackobama.com/page/content/fpccga.

14. Avery Russell, "Cooperative Engagement: The New Imperative of International Security," *Carnegie Quarterly*, Summer 1994, http://carnegie.org/fileadmin/Media/Publications/PDF/Cooperative%20Engagement.pdf.

15. This definition is compatible with the operational understanding employed by the US military. See, e.g., US Joint Forces Command and US European Command, Department of Defense, *Military Contribution to Cooperative Security (CS) Joint Operating Concept Version 1.0*, September 19, 2008, iii.

16. White House, *National Security Strategy*, May 2010, 1, www.un.org/ga/search/view_doc.asp?symbol=S/RES/1973%282011%29.

17. Elisabeth Bumiller, "Words and Deeds Show Focus of the American Military on Asia," *New York Times*, November 10, 2012, www.nytimes.com/2012/11/11/world/asia/us-militarys-new-focus-on-asia-becomes-clearer.html?pagewanted=1&_r=0.

18. Hillary Rodham Clinton, "Remarks at the Foreign Policy Group's 'Transformational Trends 2013' Forum," US Department of State, Office of the Spokesperson, November 29, 2012, http://translations.state.gov/st/english/texttrans/2012/11/20121130139341.html#ixzz2Ex4nrS90.

19. E.g., the Trans-Pacific Partnership is a new free trade deal that seeks to promote regional economic integration as well as to boost American exports to the region.

20. William J. Burns, "Asia, the Americas, and US Strategy for a New Century," remarks at World Affairs Councils of America National Conference, Washington, November 4, 2011, www.state.gov/s/d/2011/176667.htm.

21. BBC News, "N. Korea and Iran 'Sharing Ballistic Missile Technology,'" May 14, 2011, www.bbc.co.uk/news/world-asia-pacific-13402590.

22. Michael N. Barnett, "Bringing in the New World Order: Liberalism, Legitimacy, and the United Nations," *World Politics* 49, no. 4 (July 1997): 526–51.

23. Jacques Baute, "Timeline Iraq: Challenges & Lessons Learned from Nuclear Inspections," *IAEA Bulletin*, 46, no. 1 (June 2004): 64–68, www.iaea.org/Publications/Magazines/Bulletin/Bull461/46102486468.pdf. See also Fareed Zakaria, "We Had Good Intel—the UN's," *Newsweek*, February 9, 2004.

24. Matt Welch, "The Politics of Dead Children: Have Sanctions against Iraq Murdered Millions?" *Reason*, March 2002, http://reason.com/archives/2002/03/01/the-politics-of-dead-children/print.

25. Joseph E. Stiglitz and Linda J. Bilmes, "The True Cost of the Iraq War: $3 Trillion and Beyond," *Washington Post*, September 5, 2010, www.washingtonpost.com/wp-dyn/content/article/2010/09/03/AR2010090302200.html.

26. See US Department of Defense, Final Report to Congress, *Conduct of the Persian Gulf War*, appendix P, April 1992, 725, www.ndu.edu/library/epubs/cpgw.pdf. Additional funds were committed and may have been reported after April 1992.

27. See Peter Dombrowski and Rodger A. Payne, "Global Debate and the Limits of the Bush Doctrine," *International Studies Perspectives* 4, no. 4 (2003): 395–408; and Peter Dombrowski and Rodger A. Payne, "The Emerging Consensus for Preventive War," *Survival* 48, no. 2 (2006): 115–36.

28. "Merkel Comments on Bin Laden Killing Draw Criticism," Spiegel Online International, May 4, 2011, www.spiegel.de/international/germany/celebrating-death-merkel-comments-on-bin-laden-killing-draw-criticism-a-760580.html.

29. Ulka Kelkar and Suruchi Bhadwal, *Fighting Climate Change: Human Solidarity in a Divided World*, Occasional Paper, South Asian Regional Study on Climate Change Impacts and Adaptation: Implications for Human Development (New York: *Human Development Report* Office, United Nations Development Program, 2007–8), 38, http://hdr.undp.org/en/reports/global/hdr2007-2008/papers/kelkar_ulka%20and%20bhadwal_suruchi.pdf.

30. See Thomas F. Homer-Dixon, *Environment, Scarcity, and Violence* (Princeton, NJ: Princeton University Press, 2001); and Ashok Swain, "Displacing the Conflict: Environmental Destruction in Bangladesh and Ethnic Conflict in India," *Journal of Peace Research* 33, no. 2 (1996): 189–204.

31. United Nations Security Council, Resolution 1973, March 17, 2011, www.un.org/ga/search/view_doc.asp?symbol=S/RES/1973%282011%29.

CHAPTER 7

FROM HUB TO HINGE

A Strategic Framework to Promote US Security Interests in the Indian Ocean

MICHAEL AUSLIN

A primary challenge for US policy in the next generation will be to integrate the Indian Ocean region (IOR) into the broader US security framework in the vast Indo-Pacific region. US strategy should have two major ordering approaches: first, an enhanced military presence that presents a credible force posture to deal with both steady state conditions and possible conflict contingencies; and second, a newly crafted set of overlapping and mutually reinforcing alliances, strategic partnerships, and access-granting relationships that will help share burdens, allow operational and planning flexibility for US forces, and create a community of interests underpinning a liberal security regime.

This strategy not only seeks to respond to security trends and issues unique to the IOR but also to approach US security policy to the region within the larger context of US responsibilities and interests in the realm stretching from the Persian Gulf to the Western Pacific. In particular, the strategy should attempt to set "first-order" patterns of security cooperation and the effective encouragement of liberal norms in order to provide security in the IOR (and the extended Indo-Pacific commons) and prevent great power conflict. Second-order concerns include building effective regional and country security capacity; ensuring that violent, IOR-based extremist organizations do not destabilize general security and stability; and countering the proliferation of weapons of mass destruction (WMD).

The result of the strategy will be to provide a new security architecture for the IOR where none currently exists, ultimately building up a community of liberal interests among leading states. It will also extend the United States' influence and flexibility of action through the IOR to the two long-standing areas of US presence and concern: the Persian Gulf and the Western Pacific. Integrating the IOR into hemispheric plans will allow for a more rational allocation of resources and will likely uncover new synergies among existing US security partnerships.

A new strategic framework is needed for one simple reason: The post–World War II liberal international order is weakening due to the relative diminution of strength in leading democratic states, the rise of autocratic powers that are gaining power projection capabilities, and the continuing destabilizing effect of arms races around the globe. The apparent belief by authoritarian states that they will be able to assert their interests against other countries is adding to a belief that the liberal international order is losing both moral suasion and the willingness of longtime supporters, such as the United States, to maintain their ongoing commitments to maintaining stability. Long-accepted norms of international behavior have shifted quickly in eastern Asia, for example, and the sudden focus on the IOR on the part of China, the United States, Australia, and other countries points out the likelihood that the IOR commons will become an increasingly contested region in the future due to its strategic location, long-standing rivalries, and the potential for further growth.[1]

This framework also fits with and embellishes the Obama administration's so-called rebalance to Asia that has been articulated during the past several years. This "pivot," as it was originally called, also was one of the major components of the January 2012 Defense Strategic Guidance. This document sought to shift the United States away from the post-9/11 era of large-scale, ground-based conflict in the Middle East, and instead attempt to secure American interests in the Pacific and the Middle East through "flexible" and "leaner" forces that operate with a smaller footprint. The forward presence envisioned by the Defense Strategic Guidance also privileges the Air-Sea Battle concept that the US Air Force and US Navy have crafted to respond to the changing balance of power in the Western Pacific.

Part of the administration's approach is to seek out new partnerships and greater access for US forces; early specifics include the moving of up to 2,500 US Marines for rotational training in Darwin, Australia, and the forward porting of up to four new US Navy Littoral Combat Ships in Singapore. In the Obama administration's outreach to Southeast Asia, there is the germ of an effort to forge a potential new set of relationships based on common security interests. Logically, deepening US engagement with countries such as Malaysia and Indonesia naturally "moves" Washington into the IOR, and makes an extension of security and political relationships into the region a natural next stage.

Yet a third driver of US policy toward the IOR is the near-term and midterm defense budget environment in the United States, which will see a cut of up to

$1 trillion over the next decade. This will affect all services equally, reducing the readiness of US troops whether deployed or in training, defer maintenance, and limit the funds available for the modernization of US forces. Senior US leaders, including President Obama, took pains to state that "sequestration," as the automatic budget cuts totaling $500 billion are known, would not affect the American presence in the Pacific or interfere with the emerging rebalancing strategy. However, the effects of budget cuts were already clear by 2013, including the cancellation of military exercises such as Red Flag, the reduction in travel by senior US officers throughout the region, sharply limited intellectual engagement activities such as conferences, and the reduced flying and steaming time for both the US Air Force and US Navy. Senior leaders increasingly found themselves having to prioritize which activities or exercises would give the greatest return on investment, thereby leaving out some US allies and partners.

The budget pressures undoubtedly will have an increasingly noticeable effect on the US presence in Asia, including the IOR. Coming just at the time when the Obama administration has focused on the rebalance, the budget realities call into question both the ability of the United States to maintain the same level of relationships it has developed for decades and also its ability to expand its presence and work with new partners. From this perspective, then, an enhanced US presence in the IOR is both called into question by sequestration and also driven by the reality that the United States will need to rely precisely on relationship building in order to have the type of presence it wants in the IOR and the broader Asia-Pacific region. Thus, any new initiatives such as those for the IOR will need to take place in an environment where the traditional US presence may be a comparatively smaller factor than in the past, while innovative partnerships form the foundation cooperation.

The IOR straddles the world's most strategic communications waterways and is affected by the growing uncertainty and sense of insecurity in the broad Indo-Pacific region. US security commitments, including formal alliances and interest in stability, will almost certainly draw US forces into any instability or conflict. Therefore, a strategy to maintain and enhance security in the IOR is part of a larger US global strategy.

However, what is needed is a conceptual shift away from sole reliance on US alliances, the traditional "hub-and-spokes" model. This post–World War II architecture linked the United States to Thailand, South Korea, Australia, Japan, and the Philippines. Although those commitments should be maintained, a new strategic framework will move from "hub" to "hinge," recognizing that the IOR is the hinge linking together the Indo-Pacific region, if not the whole Eastern Hemisphere. Therefore, the future US strategy should be to focus on the hinge while making a seamless connection of the hinge to the existing US security architecture of alliances and Persian Gulf–area presence.

THE STRATEGY'S ASSUMPTIONS

This strategy assumes that the United States will remain the world's most power-ful and capable military force through 2025. However, it also makes four further assumptions. First, the US military will see a decline in steady state readiness due to the budget cuts of $1 trillion from 2009 through 2023. In addition, the aging of navy and air force platforms and weapons systems in particular and a reduction in the number of ships and planes in the force as a whole will make the US military presence less effective than before and impose cost calculations on US command-ers for everything from mission sets to annual exercises and military diplomacy activities. As a subassumption, this strategy assumes that there will be a reduced F-35 force from the program of record numbers (i.e., fewer than 1,735 air force F-35s) and a significantly reduced next-generation bomber fleet from air force estimates of 70 to 80 planes. A further subassumption is that the number of navy support vessels will decline relative to the number of surface combatants, but that more than the current planned 32 Aegis-capable destroyers will likely be built. A final subassumption is that the number of available US aircraft carriers (known as CVNs) is likely to remain below the congressionally mandated level of 11 CVNs due to ongoing budget constraints and maintenance needs. This will lead to a con-comitant decline in US presence in the IOR and the wider Indo-Pacific region, along with increased questioning about the credibility of the United States' com-mitments to its friends and allies.

Second, the greatest effect of this relative decline in US presence and capabil-ity in the IOR will be political. Uncertainty about US capabilities and intentions will lead to a rising sense of insecurity on the part of smaller nations and those who fear the rise of China. American allies will carefully watch US military activi-ties in the region to ascertain if budget cuts are reducing American credibility and effectiveness. Some smaller partners may begin hedging and decide to draw closer to China, if the United States seems unwilling or unable to maintain its pres-ence. China and other states that seek to increase their influence in the region, if not actively challenge norms of regional and international behavior, will likely be emboldened by the apparent decline in the United States' will and capacity. Finally, terrorist groups and other disruptive nonstate actors will take advantage of the perception that there is an increase in uncertainty or instability in the IOR to attempt further activities.

Third, there is likely to be an increase in the linkages among liberal actors both inside and outside the IOR in response to the perception of US decline and the rise of China. India, both as the single most powerful IOR actor and the only major democracy in the region, will likely attempt to explore deeper rela-tions with Japan, Australia, and possibly Indonesia as a way to diversify its foreign relationships and find partners that can help maintain stability in the region. At the same time, the IOR-located nations of the Association of Southeast Asian Nations (ASEAN)—including Indonesia, Malaysia, Singapore, Thailand, and Burma—may begin consulting together on security issues related to the Indian Ocean and how that is connected to broader ASEAN initiatives to enhance stability in Southeast Asia.

Fourth, no country in the IOR will develop its military capacity enough to be considered the regional hegemon or to be able to assert its interests with little or no risk. India will continue to develop its maritime and air power, but will also remain primarily land focused due to continuing instability emerging from Pakistan and unsettled border questions with China. Indonesia will slowly develop the capacity to regularly patrol its extended archipelagic waters, but it will not be able to project power in any meaningful way into the Indian Ocean. Australia will maintain a modern naval and air fleet, but its limited size will compel Canberra to focus the deployment of its assets close to the continent and strategic waterways in the approaches to Indonesia.

THE INDIAN OCEAN'S GEOSTRATEGIC ENVIRONMENT

This strategic concept responds to the growing interconnectivity and insecurity in the IOR over the short term to midterm, and over the midterm to long term, in the following ways. First, it seeks to maintain the US forward presence and enhance the set of security relationships that Washington has with the IOR nations in order to blunt the growing sense of competition in the region's common areas. India was the world's largest importer of arms from 2006 to 2010, and it plans on spending $50 billion to upgrade its military through 2015.[2] It is doing so due to continued friction with Pakistan and also with a clear sense of concern that China's military development will result in greater Chinese influence throughout the Indo-Pacific region. Pakistan may now be the state with the world's fourth-largest nuclear arsenal, and it actively supports disruptive terrorist organizations, including al-Qaeda.[3] China's continuing relationship with Burma, despite recent moves by Yangon to normalize relations with Washington, provides it with strategically located access points on the Bay of Bengal, whereas its long-standing ties with Pakistan give it similar possibilities to increase its presence in the Arabian Sea.

Other than its bases on Diego Garcia, the United States has no permanent presence in the Indian Ocean and therefore must extend its already-stretched forces to maintain regular patrols. Any surge requirement in the Indian Ocean would task US forces and possibly present political difficulties to national decision makers. Therefore, this strategic concept seeks to ensure that the United States does two things: (1) build on an existing set of relationships to bring new partners into a larger security architecture, and (2) expand the scope of US access points in the region that can reduce planning uncertainty and serve to allow the United States to preposition supplies or even base forces for short periods during periods of crisis or instability. In short, the strategic concept works to maintain the current balance of forces in the IOR while preparing the ground for a more substantial, long-term change in the region's security environment.

Second, this strategic concept aims to build a long-term security architecture dominated by liberal states that will provide stability and baseline security in the IOR commons. The reality over the next generation likely will be that liberal states will come to recognize the nascent community of interests they share. Their general desire to uphold recognized norms of interstate behavior, freedom of navigation, diplomatic solutions to territorial and other disputes, support for civil society, relative openness to free trade, and civilian control of the military will be challenged by the growing strength of authoritarian regimes and in addition by potential domestic political instability in newly liberalized states.

The security architecture envisioned by this strategic concept will provide a balance to the growth of the Chinese military and the increased power projection capabilities of the People's Liberation Army (PLA) Navy and the PLA Air Force. It will respond precisely to the uncertainty created by the PLA's activities in the IOR commons, which is linked to a more assertive attitude toward the South China Sea. Moreover, increasing India's security relations with the United States and other liberal nations may offset New Delhi's concerns about its relative isolation in facing Islamabad. This would further work to reduce geostrategic pressure in the region. A more joint response to ongoing terrorism threats would also serve to reduce the operating freedom of nonstate actors and possibly blunt the possibility of nuclear proliferation from nuclear powers like Pakistan to terrorist groups.

In the long term, a more liberal-oriented security structure can also be used to address the weak governance that plagues many nations in the region, in part by encouraging greater interaction between stable, liberal states and those at risk of instability. Finally, by increasing stability and confidence among a host of regional actors, this strategy can promote intraregional trade, thereby increasing wealth, driving durable trade ties, and making politicians responsive to the benefits of tying their countries into the liberal IOR network.

As indicated in the other chapters of this volume, the goal of this strategy is not for the United States to become the primary security provider in the IOR, nor for the United States to take on new security responsibilities or attempt to forge an unrealistic set of alliances. Rather, it is to recognize that Washington shares the same interests in stability and openness in the IOR as do all the nations of Asia that rely on the trade routes passing through the region, along with the potential for widespread conflict if tensions get out of hand. Given the stabilizing role that the United States has traditionally played along with the variety of actors in the Indo-Pacific region, this strategy attempts to create a more self-conscious community of interests that will work cooperatively and jointly to identify threats and potential disruptions and to create working relationships to address them before they become realized.

MEETING US NATIONAL AND REGIONAL SECURITY OBJECTIVES

This strategy meets US national and regional security objectives in the following ways. First, it enhances US military and diplomatic presence in the IOR. This will benefit steady state maritime security by sending a message that the United States remains committed to preserving stability in the IOR, even in a time of budget cutbacks. It will encourage the US ally Australia to become more focused on operations in the IOR and will also let China know that any activities it undertakes in the region will need to be cooperative and nonconfrontational. It will also put pressure on terrorist groups and nonstate actors, which will need to reckon with a recommitted US presence and an enhanced ability to respond to attacks, threats, or other disruptive behavior. Altogether, the results of implementing this strategy will help maintain certainty in the minds of shippers, insurers, fishermen, and the like that freedom of navigation will be protected and that each group will be able to continue its activities free from the fear of disruption, which will further promote trade and investment in the region.

Second, this strategy will provide the foundation for building a set of relationships among liberally inclined nations in the IOR and beyond that will further promote stability and growth. Encouraging greater Indian interaction with Australia will bring leading IOR democracies together for wide-ranging discussions on joint security issues as well as joint exercises, activities, and the like. Reaching out to Indonesia to help it build its own maritime security capacity as well as enabling it to play a role in interacting with Australia and Indonesia will also develop a community of liberal interests. Both the US Navy and the Royal Australian Navy (along with each country's air force) can play leading roles in helping to build capacity among friendly nations for improving training, humanitarian assistance and disaster relief ability, patrolling duration, information sharing, and the like. Further, this strategy can be employed to help create a more robust intelligence, surveillance, and reconnaissance (ISR) regime in the IOR, working not only with Australia but also with India, Indonesia, and other nations to pool and share information, identify potential threats or disruptions, and provide the ability for more flexible responses and planning.

Third, this strategy links the above-noted activities to the US interest in maintaining stability in the broader Indo-Pacific region and throughout the global commons. Having a more comprehensive linking of ISR, operations, joint exercises, capacity building, and the like with allies and partners stretching from the Western Pacific to the Persian Gulf region will provide US policymakers with greater ability to identify threats that can disrupt commerce in the global commons. It will also allow for better matching of resources to ends such as extended patrolling, information gathering and analysis, sharing information with partners, and identifying realistic burden sharing among allies and partners. This strategy therefore makes the IOR the hinge in the US presence in the global commons, recognizing that stability and cooperative behavior in the region are the prerequisite for global economic stability, the prevention of great power friction between China and India, and limitations on the freedom of action of terrorist groups and would-be nuclear proliferators.

APPLYING THE STRATEGIC CONCEPT TO THE INDIAN OCEAN

Implementing this strategic concept would require significant changes in existing military, intelligence, economic, and diplomatic policies and activities. Perhaps the most fundamental adjustments would occur in the military sphere, although a comprehensive shift in its overarching approach to the Indo-Pacific would require a range of initiatives internal and external to the region.

Military Mission Areas

This strategy should encompass four key military mission areas. First, there should be enhanced patrolling and port calls across the IOR. Although budget cuts will affect overall steaming time, the US Navy should designate tier one security partners in the IOR, such as India and Indonesia, and identify key strategic nodes where port visits and presence missions will be focused. Elements of the Pacific Fleet should transit regularly from the Western Pacific into the Indian Ocean to such nodes, patrolling the seas lanes leading to the Persian Gulf. This should be combined with an attempt to make even limited port calls throughout the region in order to build up public awareness of the US presence. Indeed, this was one of the elements of the "rebalance" to Asia highlighted by then–defense secretary Leon Panetta at the 2012 Shangri-La dialogue in Singapore. Concurrent with this, the US Air Force should conduct similar transits and visits to air bases throughout the region, focusing again on US tier one partners that have developed air forces, such as Australia, India, and even those countries as far east as Singapore. In particular, both navy and air force units can conduct local officer training and provide basic medical services, for example, as part of a "military diplomacy" approach with those nations that will then be most likely to share their knowledge and experience. Australia, Malaysia, and India would be considered at the top of this list.

Second, there should be a building up of ISR assets in the IOR. The US Navy should work with India, Indonesia, and Australia to discuss ways of increasing ISR coverage of the eastern Indian Ocean/Bay of Bengal area that leads into the Strait of Malacca. These assets may be land- or sea-based and jointly owned or operated. In addition to this, the US Air Force and US Navy should increase autonomous ISR capacity in the region, utilizing both Global Hawks and Broad Area Maritime Surveillance (when fully operational). These can be combined with lower-altitude platforms, such as Fire Scouts, when needed to respond to specific situations. Increasing maritime air patrols along waterways leading to vital passage points or contested areas will also send a message about the United States' commitment to maintain domain awareness as a perquisite to stability. As a subset of this, a joint IOR information center should be set up to combine the various streams of intelligence for analysis, building off the model maritime information center in Singapore.

Third, there should be more use of the Littoral Combat Ship and other smaller surface craft for antipiracy/antiproliferation patrols in conjunction with larger surface platforms for wider area coverage. This would bring to the Indian Ocean a measure of the operational flexibility provided by the Proliferation Security Initiative in Northeast Asian waters. Regular patrols with allied and partner nations will enhance overall security and likely deter nonstate actors from considering the IOR an open field for their activities.

Fourth, there should be an increase in the number of US military-to-military contacts with Indonesia and India, preferably in conjunction with Australia and US allies like Japan and South Korea. Given budget shortfalls, this is an activity that could even be spearheaded by US allies invested in providing public goods in the region, with US support as available. This mission area is vital in order to improve interoperability in the future. It should include educational and training interaction, expanded joint exercises, and the discussion of doctrine development. Both the US Navy and US Air Force should be part of this bolstering of friendly military ties and confidence-building measures in areas such as search and rescue, humanitarian assistance and disaster relief, and the like. This effort eventually could be extended to more comprehensive joint exercises and regular officer exchanges among the countries in the region. Washington's ability at some point in the future to step back from the leading role in this endeavor would be one indicator of an enhanced community of interests in the region.

Enabling Capabilities and Concepts

To most credibly execute this strategy, the US Pacific Command (PACOM) will need to forward base more US ships and planes, and the US Department of Defense (DOD) will need to approve shifting global assets so as to provide a more robust Indo-Pacific presence. Sequestration will already involve such a shifting of assets, in order to maintain the president's commitment to his rebalancing, but long-term plans will need to be developed to ensure that there are even greater access points for US forces that can be used for short periods.

Despite assertions by then–defense secretary Panetta that 60 percent of the US Navy's advanced F-35 stealth fighters will be based in the Pacific, budget cuts and resource limitations in the coming years will make it difficult to increase the US presence in the region, especially if other Middle Eastern contingencies demand the use of US military assets. Nonetheless, due to basing limitations in the IOR, which are unlikely to change (see the next subsection), if such plans become a reality, more of the ships, submarines, and planes to be used in the IOR will need to be based in the Western Pacific, particularly in Japan, but also with greater access to partner nations. This will allow for a larger steady state force that can provide an enhanced presence throughout the IOR, as well as a more rapidly deployable surge force during times of tension, crisis, or conflict.

PACOM should consider the forward porting of at least one more aircraft carrier to complement the USS *George Washington* in Yokosuka, Japan. Along with its carrier air wings, another carrier would allow for a greater, more persistent presence in the IOR. Again, this will be difficult to do with only ten US aircraft carriers through at least 2015, but long-range planning should attempt to take advantage of the eventual deployment of the *Gerald Ford*–class next-generation aircraft carrier. Similarly, more advanced fighter wings of F-22s and F-35s stationed in Japan would permit more visits to IOR countries for training, officer exchanges, and so on. Airborne ISR assets should also be increased so as to allow for greater coverage of the region. Moreover, given the growing regional focus on submarines throughout the IOR and the Indo-Pacific region, the US Navy should base no less than three-quarters of its nuclear-powered attack submarines in the region, with regular patrolling through key areas of interest. Having a credible numerical as well as qualitatively superior submarine force will be increasingly important to US strategy in the IOR. Moreover, the deployment of US Marines to Darwin, Australia, also opens up the possibility of a greater presence of amphibious forces in the region that can work with counterparts in Southeast Asian countries bordering the IOR as well as India itself.

The key enabling concept is to build up the US steady state presence in the IOR and the Indo-Pacific region (where many assets will be based) in order to provide enhanced operations, interaction with regional partners, and credible deterrent capability against disruptive threats. This may not address questions related to the western IOR, and the African littoral, but the first step in following the expanded IOR strategy should be to conceive of the broader Indo-Pacific region as an integrated operating theater where the United States can leverage existing alliance relationships and the nascent multilateral structure represented by initiatives such as the East Asia Summit.

Regional/Subregional Implementation

Part of the regional implementation is provided in the enabling concepts section above, that is to say, the need to increase assets in the IOR and the Indo-Pacific region, forward basing more qualitatively superior platforms, both naval and air, closer to the areas where they can be employed with regularity and also surged when necessary. However, there are at least two further implementation priorities.

The first priority is to ensure the survivability of US forces in the Indo-Pacific that will be crucial to maintaining stability in the IOR. This includes hardening key existing facilities—the most important ones being Kadena Air Force Base, Anderson Air Force Base, and Diego Garcia—and also other airfields and command-and-control centers for US forces in the region. Added to this, the United States and its allies need to increase ballistic missile defense capacity in order to protect naval assets (bases) and command-and-control centers.

The second priority is to increase US access throughout the region. This is different from the question of a dispersal of assets, which requires further basing capacity. The likelihood of increasing US bases is slim, for two reasons. First, the budgetary environment will likely not permit a significant investment in new bases. Second, the difficulty of securing basing rights on non-US territory limits the realistic chances of building significant new bases that could better balance US forces throughout the region. This raises the question of whether narrower access agreements may be the better path to take in order to implement the IOR strategy discussed in this chapter.

Access agreements could be crafted to allow for the right of use of bases during crises, as well as for cross-servicing agreements or prepositioning of supplies. Candidates could include Australia (especially Christmas Island), Indonesia, and Vietnam, all of which are strategically located, either within the IOR or close to the vital sea lanes leading to it. Such access agreements are inherently vulnerable to domestic political pressure, and US forces might find themselves without permission to use facilities in times of need. These agreements also skirt the politically fraught question of granting basing rights to Americans. Access agreements that included stepped-up US training of host forces or other goods-providing activities could make it easier to get approval for this approach. This would then allow for the dispersal of forces when needed as well as for providing numerous entry points into the IOR.

Relations with Nondefense Activities and Other US Government Institutions

This strategy is designed to build up US political influence in the IOR and the Indo-Pacific region concurrent with US military capacity. On the ground, US embassies will play a key role in maintaining regular, positive relations with those countries with which America seeks to enhance its relations (see the next section). Close consultation with US diplomats in the region will provide current information on the domestic and foreign policies of partner states, thereby allowing for better DOD and PACOM planning. The State Department can play a significant role in negotiating and maintaining access agreements, as well as in building up closer diplomatic relations with allies and potential partners.

Similarly, the US intelligence community will play a major role in providing non-DOD intelligence about political and military issues in the IOR, and representatives of the intelligence community should be collocated at military bases to ensure the timely exchange of information. Specific ISR tasking may be better suited for non-DOD agencies, and clear lines of communication should be established to allow for the provision of information necessary to seamless decision making at PACOM or in Washington.

The US House and US Senate armed services committees can play important roles in helping to ensure the implementation of this strategy and in discerning the strategic thinking of DOD on the importance of maintaining stability in the IOR. Similarly, the House and Senate foreign affairs and foreign relations committees can play similar roles in clarifying the importance of the IOR in general to US economic growth and to regional stability. This will ensure that appropriate resources are devoted to implementing an IOR strategy like the one described in this chapter.

Relations with Key Regional Players and International/Regional Organizations

For the purpose of implementing this strategy, enhanced relations with a number of regional actors is a prerequisite. This will also lead to them adopting expanded roles in the formation of a security framework for the IOR and the Indo-Pacific region.

At the regional level, the key US partners in this strategy should be Australia, India, and Indonesia. Given the strong and long-standing United States–Australia alliance, the Canberra–Washington relationship should be primary in setting agendas and goals for enhanced IOR security, joint activities, information sharing, and future operations. The two allies should then reach out to Jakarta and New Delhi to begin the process of discussing regional challenges, basing opportunities, information sharing, and joint activities. US Navy and Royal Australian Navy ships should begin the process of expanding joint patrols and visiting key waterways, while both countries' air forces should increase their joint training. Existing information sharing between Canberra and Washington should be upgraded to view the IOR as part of the larger Indo-Pacific region where overall domain awareness is the goal.

Next, the Indian Navy should be encouraged to join with its US and Australian counterparts for training along the lines of the current Malabar maritime exercises. India's plan for the rapid growth of its maritime and air forces over the next decade makes this strategy a perfect opportunity to normalize regular training exercises and low-level operations (patrolling, etc.) among the three countries. Exchanges of senior naval officers, port visits, and even sponsorship of Maritime Strategy conferences can help build stronger links between the Indians and the US and Australian navies. Similarly, India should be encouraged to further develop and share its naval doctrine with its two allies in order to improve their mutual understanding of India's primary maritime-related security goals and concerns.

At the same time, the United States and Australia should reach out to Indonesia, to help it build capacity in what is still largely a coastal patrol navy. Given the size of the Indonesian archipelago, any support that Washington or Canberra can give to Jakarta may make a large difference in helping Jakarta improve its ability to patrol its numerous straits and waterways, as well as providing an avenue to more effectively work with regional actors to promote maritime stability by undertaking joint patrols and increasing its maritime awareness capacity. Discussions about the future force structure of the Indonesian Navy can help discern possible strategic decisions in Jakarta, and both allied navies can help Jakarta think through its developing naval doctrine. Joint training with littoral elements of the US and Australian navies can play a significant role in developing Indonesian capabilities and building confidence in a more robust partnership.

Extraregional partners should also be brought into this nascent security architecture. Treating the IOR as part of the larger Indo-Pacific maritime security zone leads to including other US allies in this partnership-building exercise. In particular, Japan should be invited to participate in joint training and exercises, information sharing, and officer exchanges. After the eight-year refueling mission of the Japan Maritime Self-Defense Forces in the Indian Ocean, few other allied navies have had as much experience operating in the IOR. Japan and Australia also have well-established maritime ties, and the prospect of three long-standing allies working to embrace India and Indonesia can give a regionwide flavor to the strategy. At a more local level, Singapore and Malaysia should also be invited to participate in information sharing (something Singapore is already set up to do), training, officer exchanges, and joint patrols.

In essence, this approach would link major powers such as Japan and Australia with emerging and strategically crucial states like India, Indonesia, and Malaysia. Creating a community of maritime security interests among them will help in improving the flow of information on WMD proliferation, suspected terrorist activity, and nascent naval rivalries. It may also help in increasing security access for US naval and air forces, as discussed above, and provide further options for building ISR capacity in the region.

RISKS AND UNCERTAINTIES

As with any new strategy, various risks and uncertainties are connected with the process of adopting this IOR strategic framework. A major concern will be the question of adequate resources. With a declining US defense budget and a generally restrictive budgetary environment expected over the next decade or more, the US government will be hard-pressed to uphold all its global commitments. A strategy like this is in essence an insurance policy designed to prevent the deterioration of stability in a crucial region where conflict or crisis would almost certainly draw in the United States, with exorbitant expense. However, investing in this strategy will also be expensive. The tasks of hardening physical facilities, increasing operational tempo, and forward basing top-line US assets will absorb significant amounts of a dwindling defense budget.

Separate from the monetary aspect, concentrating assets in the IOR and the Indo-Pacific region will raise the question of whether the United States has enough manpower and matériel to complete ongoing operations in Afghanistan through 2014 or enough strategic depth to respond to unforeseen contingencies such as those witnessed recently in Libya. Major crises, such as those that might be precipitated by a nuclear Iran, would require massive amounts of US military assets. Having a preponderance of available forces in the Indo-Pacific region could complicate planning and operations (though increasing the US presence in the IOR could also allow for greater operational flexibility throughout the Middle East). Not having significant forces in Europe or elsewhere available to respond quickly to humanitarian or other needs would result in criticism of an IOR/Indo-Pacific heavy force posture.

A second risk is that enhancing the United States' IOR posture would antagonize China and therefore lead to precisely the type of aggressive behavior that this IOR strategy is designed to mitigate. In the light of the United States' current presence in East Asia, Beijing could see this strategy as an attempt to encircle China or intimidate the People's Liberation Army from undertaking more blue-water deployments or air-based operations. In a cyclical response effect, increasing the US focus on the IOR could lead China to invest in precisely the numbers and types of weapons systems that will allow it to project power more capably and also lead to a deterioration of stability over time. The United States would then be forced either to pull its presence back, which would be interpreted as surrendering to Chinese demands, or to double down with increased forces (if possible) and local agreements, thereby increasing the Chinese sense of vulnerability.[4]

These are already fears expressed by Beijing in response to the Obama administration's rebalancing strategy. Combined with the recent return to power of Japan's conservative Liberal Democratic Party, Beijing is likely to interpret any attempt to enhance the US presence throughout the Indo-Pacific region as aimed at Chinese interests. Therefore, engaging the Chinese in further dialogue regarding the US IOR plan will almost certainly fail to assuage their fears. Operationally, indeed, it could compromise the strategy by removing the very uncertainty that it is designed to instill about the placement of US forces and the doctrine guiding their employment in the IOR. Nonetheless, it remains in US and allied interests to attempt to increase their presence and military cooperation in light of recent tensions over territorial possessions in the East and South China seas, as well as more general concerns about the scope of China's military buildup.

A third risk is that concentrating more US effort on the IOR will lead to a sense of insecurity on the part of America's long-standing East Asian allies, particularly Japan and South Korea. They may interpret a focus on the IOR as signifying a gradual disengagement by the United States from their region (though stressing the importance of maintaining the IOR's stability to sea lines of communication, etc., may help mitigate this fear). It may make it more difficult to work with Tokyo and Seoul on issues such as status-of-forces agreements or host nation support if it is believed that these agreements subsidize US operations in the Indian Ocean. Seeing more US assets devoted to the IOR may also encourage domestic groups in both South Korea and Japan that wish to see a further reduction of US forces in the region. However, the fact that most US IOR-focused assets will likely still be based in East Asia may prevent this from happening.

Finally, this strategy may be too forward-leaning for non-US allies such as India and Indonesia. Both may fear getting entangled with US security goals and losing their independence. Both may also fear antagonizing China and thereby worsening their security situation.[5] For both these countries, then, the United States will need to play the long game, patiently and steadily building trust and a set of working relationships to allow for greater joint activity, information sharing, and even operations. Stressing the importance of maintaining stability in the IOR, tying it to the long-term growth of India and Indonesia, and encouraging both to play naturally larger regional roles may further help to mitigate fears and build vested domestic interest groups that seek to improve their relations with the United States.

The end result may be a more self-consciously connected IOR, with nascent cooperation on security and political issues. These relationships, and the transregional networks in which they are embedded, could then most directly be integrated into a larger Indo-Pacific political and security framework. Strengthening an explicit focus on the interconnection between trade and stability, and the cooperative mechanisms that can foster both, will be a decades-long process, but one in which the actors can learn from experience in Southeast Asia and leverage ties with Asia's most developed nations, along with the United States.

NOTES

1. Michael K. Green and Andrew Shearer, "Defining US Indian Ocean Strategy," *Washington Quarterly* 35, no. 2 (2012): 175–89, www.csis.org/files/publication/twq12springgreenshearer.pdf.

2. Sam Perlo-Freeman, Julian Cooper, Olawale Ismail, Elisabeth Skons, and Carina Solmirano, "Military Expenditure" in *SIPRI Yearbook 2011: Armaments, Disarmament and International Security* (Stockholm: Stockholm International Peace Research Institute, 2011), 157–229.

3. Jayshree Bajoria and Eben Kaplan, "The ISI and Terrorism: Behind the Accusations," Council on Foreign Relations, www.cfr.org/pakistan/isi-terrorism-behind-accusations/p11644.

4. Richard Weitz, "Asia Overreacts to US Military Pivot," *The Diplomat*, http://thediplomat.com/2012/01/25/asia-overreacts-to-u-s-military-pivot/.

5. Daniel Bodirsky, "US–Indonesian Relations: A Balancing Act." *Geopolitical Monitor*, www.geopoliticalmonitor.com/us-indonesian-relations-a-balancing-act-4684/.

PART II

≋

EVOLVING RECENT US POLICIES INTO THE FUTURE

CHAPTER 8

THE INDIAN OCEAN

Protecting Access to a Volatile Powerhouse

TERESITA C. SCHAFFER

Two big trends define today's geopolitical changes: the centrality of Asia in global power relations; and, within that, the rise of India and China. These transform the place of the Indian Ocean in the US strategic framework. Historically, the United States has treated this ocean as a transit zone between two areas of much greater strategic interest: East Asia and the Persian Gulf. In the next two to three decades, the United States should regard it instead as a volatile powerhouse, increasingly contested among regional and global powers. The primary US strategic goal should be to ensure unfettered access in a peaceful environment. The Indian Ocean is one of the world's major sources of both growth and risk; it will increasingly also be the key to securing both Asia and the Persian Gulf.

This chapter's judgment that the Indian Ocean region is of great importance to US national security is shared by most of the authors in this volume, with the notable exception of Christopher Preble. To achieve its strategic goal, the United States needs to start with a strong relationship with India, and shape *coalitions for security* throughout the region. America's budget cannot afford, and its political relationships in the region will not sustain, an approach that requires it to establish major new facilities. Nor will the relationships among the countries in the region lend themselves to working through a single leading international organization. The United States needs a network of formal and informal coalitions that is strong enough to discourage efforts by its competitors to dominate the region or impede its access. It is in the unique position of having cooperative relationships with almost all the major players. Its leadership will be essential to achieving the desired result—but it must be exercised with some care, so as not to crowd other countries, notably India, that prize their own leadership role. And though this chapter posits a security-driven strategy, security cannot be achieved without expanding economic development.

In contrast to the strategies proposed in their chapters by Holmes and Yoshihara, Ladwig, and Martel, this approach relies heavily on diplomatic and economic cooperation, closely integrated with military presence and relationships. The relationship with India will be the centerpiece of any realistic Indian Ocean strategy. In that respect, this study agrees with Preble's recommendation for developing a new and stronger security relationship with India, though I would argue that the economic relationship and the growing harmony between Indian and US policies toward the broader Indo-Pacific region are at least as important. Moreover, the United States must also focus more attention and resources on the smaller countries whose maritime ties with China have been expanding in recent years. While acknowledging the importance of transnational security threats in the Indian Ocean region, this approach, unlike that of Winner, does not treat those threats as the drivers of regional relationships. Too many of the region's countries, starting with India, would be uncomfortable with a model that relied on their signing on to a global threat concept coming out of Washington. This approach will require rethinking how the United States uses its financial, development, military, and diplomatic resources in the region. It will be most effective if the US government, and especially its military institutions, deals with the Indian Ocean region as one unit.

A STRATEGIC FRAMEWORK

The center of gravity of US foreign policy and strategic thinking has been shifting eastward for nearly half a century. This is well documented by both policy statements and polling data.[1] The rise of India and China is a product of the 1980s and 1990s. Both countries had emerged as major economic growth poles in the world before the global financial crisis that began in 2008. The crisis has affected both countries, and as this volume goes to press, it is uncertain when they will resume their rapid growth trajectory. But despite the problems in evidence, especially in India, both countries are likely to remain important global economic centers. Both have also embarked on major military investment programs. China is already accepted as a global power. India seeks that status, and it regards China as its major strategic rival. India is of much less concern to China.

The two countries' impact on the United States is completely different, however. India's ties with the United States have been dramatically transformed since the Cold War, with cool and distant ties giving way to the beginnings of a serious strategic relationship. India and the United States now recognize that their interests in the Indian Ocean and in Asia are quite closely aligned. The leading area of

US–Indian military cooperation has been the Indian Ocean, which India regards as its major defensive perimeter.

The United States' relations with China have been constructive and even cordial during much of the two decades since the end of the Cold War. However, Chinese and US interests are not well aligned. As China's economy and capacity for power projection continue to expand, its willingness to accept a leading US role close to its shores will diminish, and its interests are likely to diverge further from those of the United States. In particular, China is widely believed to be at least preparing for the possibility of denying US access to sensitive areas in its vicinity.

China's engagement in the Indian Ocean region has increased markedly in the last decade. Its trade has sharply increased with all the South Asian countries.[2] Its aid, almost entirely focused on infrastructure, is also up in these areas, as well as in Burma and Eastern Africa. In Southeast Asia, Singapore and other countries nurture their ties with China but would prefer that China not be the only major country in the region with a strategic presence. China is building ports in Sri Lanka (Hambantota) and Pakistan (Gwadar), providing major funding for airport improvement in Male (the Maldives), and creating access arrangements at many other points around the Indian Ocean littoral.

Chinese maritime activity in the Indian Ocean is also up. Since late 2008 China has been engaging with antipiracy efforts in the western Indian Ocean. It took part in antipiracy exercises that included Pakistan in March 2013, and has coordinated its antipiracy activities with Japan and India. At the same time, reports of Chinese submarine activity in the Indian Ocean have rung alarm bells in Indian defense circles.[3] Although the evidence for this is disputed, Indian strategic observers have long argued that China is building up some kind of intelligence observation facility in Burma.[4] Observers dispute the military significance of all these developments, but even if one discounts the notion of bases in Burma, the trend toward greater Chinese involvement in the Indian Ocean—civilian and military—is clear.

India has traditionally been the biggest player in the Indian Ocean, but a minor actor further east. However, its economic and security engagement with East and Southeast Asia has increased markedly since it first announced its "Look East" policy in the late 1980s. India now conducts regular military exercises with Japan, Singapore, Vietnam, and occasionally China. It has conducted trilateral exercises with Japan and the United States. Its trade with East Asia, and especially with China, has grown even faster than its overall trade.[5] India's higher profile east of the Indian Ocean has come at the price of some heightened tensions with China. Although India is careful to stress its desire to engage with China, China took sharp exception when an Indian company engaged in a commercial search for oil in the South China Sea in a concession granted by Vietnam.[6]

In light of these trends, the environment for the United States in important parts of the Western Pacific is likely to become less welcoming and perhaps even hostile in the next two decades. Conversely, improved US ties with India have made the Indian Ocean environment more favorable, a trend that will continue as India's power increases. China's growing presence in the Indian Ocean will affect the dynamics there in the next decade or two. India is already watching with deep misgivings as China builds infrastructure to support its military presence, laying the groundwork for what could become a permanent presence in India's "front yard." Both India and the United States have a powerful interest in preventing a possible future Chinese bid for primacy in the Indian Ocean, and in discouraging a Chinese policy that seeks to restrict US or Indian activities in adjacent areas. And further east, notably in the South China Sea, India has been a strong and outspoken supporter of freedom of navigation, in harmony with the United States.[7] US and Indian interests in this area will continue to be aligned in important respects.

DANGERS AND OPPORTUNITIES IN THE INDIAN OCEAN

A cursory look at the Indian Ocean region today makes it clear that, in contrast to the conventional view—and in contrast to the arguments made by Winner and Preble—this region is strategically important to the United States in its own right. India, the predominant littoral power, is a significant source of long-term global economic growth, despite its current economic difficulties. The Persian Gulf is the world's major energy exporter. Virtually all the oil and gas it exports reaches the international market across the waters of the Indian Ocean, whose energy trade will increase with the economic expansion of India and China. Moreover, the region is home to some of the major threats to these same interests, notably including piracy (in the ocean's eastern and western waters) and terrorism.

At least four large powers are active in the area: the United States, India, Japan, and China. The region also includes several midsized powers with more modest global reach, notably Australia, Indonesia, Pakistan, and Iran. This lineup includes two hostile dyads—India/Pakistan and India/China—and two countries, China and Iran, whose strategic interests diverge from those of the United States and are likely to diverge even more sharply in the relevant time frame.

Among these countries, the one whose position in the Indian Ocean is changing the most is China. It is expanding its presence both at sea and along the littoral. Its interests, and potentially its presence, span the entire Indian Ocean area. Its primary strategic concerns lie further east—in the South China Sea, for example, where it has been quick to assert territorial claims that have been contested by some of the Southeast Asian countries. But its strategic footprint in the Indian Ocean has also expanded. China's interests are both defensive—protecting the sea lines on which it depends, especially for energy—and at least potentially offensive—establishing a permanent presence that would permit it to restrict the margin for maneuvering of India, and arguably also that of Japan and of the United States. We can expect China and India to have relations marked by both hostility and cooperation, with competing political and economic interests in the littoral countries and periodic saber-rattling.

The modern strategic rivalry between China and India goes back five decades, but with the increase in China's engagement in the Indian Ocean region and India's engagement in the rest of the Indo-Pacific area, it has taken on a new character. The likelihood of open war between India and China is low, but periodic tensions between them are a near certainty, given their competitive situation. C. Raja Mohan argues in *Samudra Manthan: Sino-Indian Rivalry in the Indo-Pacific* that this competition—on the sea, and in their relations with the littoral countries along both the Indian Ocean and South China Sea—will intensify. It has already reached the point of a "strategic dilemma," with defensive efforts by one state triggering an arms buildup by the other. Moreover, the India–China dynamic is strongly influenced by the relationship that each of them has with the United States.[8]

The second hostile dyad, India and Pakistan, runs a somewhat higher risk of war, especially conflict arising out of miscalculation. Although they have had disputes over one maritime boundary and have had some naval action in their past wars, their confrontations have been overwhelmingly land based. However, an active military engagement between these two would endanger the whole region. Moreover, they have taken very different approaches to international military cooperation. Historically, Pakistan has been a "joiner," participating in the US Cold War alliance system and, more recently, in the antipiracy task forces in which the United States is involved. These linkages have reinforced Pakistan's ties with powerful outside countries, from which Pakistan has sought support in its rivalry with India. By contrast, independent India's foreign policy was founded on the principle of nonalignment, and thus the idea of alliances or even membership in common military organizations was considered out of keeping with India's quest for "strategic autonomy." As we will see below, these different approaches and the two countries' underlying rivalry have complicated efforts to bring them together on security issues. But provided the United States works with both countries in its approach to the Indian Ocean, the United States' choice of strategy will not impede its ability to conduct crisis diplomacy between India and Pakistan, if the need arises. This ability would be determined primarily by the bilateral US relationships with the two countries.

Iran's current involvement in the Indian Ocean region is primarily in the northwestern quadrant—in the Persian Gulf area, where it has a pronounced rivalry with the major Arab powers; in Pakistan, with which it has tense relations;

and in India, for which it is an important oil supplier and with which it has politically important but sometimes schizophrenic relations. A US Indian Ocean strategy should enable America to manage China's growing presence and to ensure that its relationships in the Indian Ocean region are counterbalanced by a strong network of ties. The strategy should seek to prevent China from becoming a clear threat to US interests and a danger to peace. It should sidestep the India/Pakistan dispute as much as possible. The United States should also aim to prevent Iran from creating threats to US interests, either by Tehran working with nonstate actors in the short term or by creating a hostile environment through its political relationships in the longer term. The same kind of network building can serve all these purposes.

Deterring the proliferation of nuclear and other weapons of mass destruction will remain a global US objective. However, this issue should not be addressed primarily at the regional level. US nonproliferation policy has been built around global instruments, primarily the Nuclear Non-Proliferation Treaty (NPT) and the various export control groups. Within the region, India and Pakistan have nuclear weapons that are outside the NPT framework. India has an agreement with the United States that authorizes safeguarded civilian nuclear cooperation, and the Nuclear Suppliers Group (NSG) has granted it a waiver for these purposes. The NPT is, not surprisingly, very controversial in India and Pakistan. The United States–India civil nuclear agreement is at least equally controversial in Pakistan, and to a lesser degree among other countries in the region. Importing this set of controversies into the Indian Ocean strategy, as Payne suggests, would result in a stillborn Indian Ocean policy. These are objectives that the United States must pursue through bilateral and global means. An Indian Ocean strategy will, however, help the United States to address the transit of nuclear materials, especially to Iran and other would-be nuclear states in its neighborhood. Here the idea of coalitions for security will be very important.

The next tier of security interests, piracy and terrorism, is commonly considered substrategic. But these interests deserve to be considered strategic threats— even though the use of "strategic" weapons is not necessarily a suitable response. The danger to shipping from piracy and the danger to world peace from terrorism give them an impact far beyond the immediate damage any given incident can cause. They also impose a significant economic cost by adding to the time required to ship cargoes across the Indian Ocean. Finally, they also represent an opportunity to pull the countries of the region together in a common cause.

Weak governance is another substrategic security threat. It affects the region unevenly. Some states in the region have only tenuous control of their territory and have a substantial terrorist presence (e.g., Pakistan); some are strong states with significant weak areas (India, Sri Lanka, Thailand). Weak governance makes partnerships and cooperative relations more volatile. Because the Indian Ocean strategy depends on these, it will be important to strengthen US policies that can help countries strengthen their governance.

The third set of important US interests in the Indian Ocean is economic. These present both challenges and opportunities. This is a region of both high and low growth.

India and much of Southeast Asia have dynamic economies, substantial trade with the United States, and powerful reasons to work together to maintain peace in the region and preserve full and open access for themselves and for the United States. These growing economies, moreover, are highly dependent on the Indian Ocean for their continued economic progress. Much of their international trade is seaborne. Indeed, in the case of India, the security leadership's awareness of the importance of seaborne trade is beginning to shift the center of gravity of its national security models away from its land-centric past and toward a balance between land and sea.

Economic dynamism will form the glue that holds together not just the United States' relations with the key countries in the region but also the coalitions on which its strategy will depend. The economic ties between them have increased significantly in the last two decades; a good example is the free trade area recently concluded between India and the Association of Southeast Asian Nations (ASEAN).

These countries' dynamic growth as well as the economic expansion of China and East Asia are likely to lead to a significant increase in energy flows to, from, and across the Indian Ocean. India and China are the two most rapidly growing energy markets in the world. Virtually all of India's new sources of energy require shipment across the Indian Ocean. The National Petroleum Council's 2008 Oil and Gas Study projects major increases in shipments across the Indian Ocean by 2030. Indian Ocean countries—including India—are among the largest suppliers of refined products. An estimated 50 percent of the international coal trade travels through these waters as well.[9] The high percentage of the energy trade transiting the Indian Ocean makes this ocean critical to US interests. A disruption in the Indian Ocean trade would massively disrupt global energy markets, regardless of the relatively small percentage of US energy supplies that come through these waters.

Non-energy trade does not have the same strategic punch, but is nonetheless an important dimension of US strategic interests in the Indian Ocean. This, too, is driven by economic growth, and is likely to increase in the next two decades.

The other end of the economic spectrum—the economically fragile and even failing states around the Indian Ocean littoral—intensifies the danger from weak governance that I mentioned above. Moreover, this is a region prone to natural disasters. Since the turn of the twenty-first century, it has suffered one major earthquake (in Gujarat, India), a dramatic Tsunami (affecting the entire eastern part of the region), epic floods (in Pakistan and Sri Lanka), and a destructive cyclone (in Burma). US military and civilian disaster relief planning already recognizes the importance of preparing in advance for such eventualities. Besides the humanitarian impact—which is enormous in this densely populated area—humanitarian relief is an area where the United States has unique skills. It is also a powerful way of organizing cooperation among the countries of the region. India's work with the United States in responding to the 2004–5 tsunami, for example, had a powerful impact on the disaster—but also on India's thinking about its future strategic posture vis-à-vis the Indian Ocean and about the potential for active cooperation with the United States. In other words, disasters can be a vehicle for coalition building.

BUILDING BLOCKS FOR COALITIONS

Creating an enduring strategy for the Indian Ocean region will require the United States to carefully construct and maintain coalitions supportive of US interests and objectives. Any regional coalition will of necessity begin with India, the pivotal power in the region, and expand to overlapping bilateral and multilateral arrangements regarding the full range of security issues challenging regional stakeholders.

The Centerpiece: India

The starting point for an Indian Ocean strategy is India, the region's largest country by far, and owner of its largest navy. Any strategy that attempted to sidestep or marginalize India would be doomed to failure. Such a posture would poison United States–India relations. It would also significantly impair the United States' ability to develop cooperation with the other states on the subcontinent. The "containment" idea that Martel examines is both unrealistic and harmful.

India served as the security arbiter of the Indian Ocean region in the days of the British Raj. Independent India still considers its preeminence in the region from Bab-el-Mandeb to Malacca as central to its security posture. During India's early years of independence, its security thinking focused mainly on the land, and especially on its northern borders, including its lifelong dispute with Pakistan and its troubled relationship with China. As was noted above, its relations with the United States were thin and strained, and it looked on the US presence in the Indian Ocean as a potential threat to its own role there.

The transformation of India's economy and foreign policy since 1990 has dramatically altered its strategic outlook. First, India's strategic thinkers now increasingly stress the strategic importance of resuming and extending India's dynamic growth. Second, and closely related, the growing demand for oil that comes with economic expansion has raised the consciousness of India's policymakers and politicians alike about the importance of the maritime dimension in the country's security doctrine. And third, the growing India–United States relationship, and especially the increasingly important security relationship, has changed India's view of the US naval presence in the Indian Ocean; for India's security managers, this is now a benign or even favorable feature of US policy. India has become an explicit and outspoken defender of freedom of navigation in the South China Sea, and it has worked with the United States on safe passage through the Malacca Strait. All these changes have made the "security manager" role that India expects to play much more realistic, and have opened up the possibility of India carrying it out in a cooperative relationship with the United States.

A strategy of shaping coalitions for security starts by nurturing and intensifying the strategic partnership that the United States and India have been developing in the past two decades. The ingredients for this are already in place: a stepped-up pace of high-level consultations, regular military-to-military contacts, including both bilateral and larger exercises in the Indian Ocean and further east; strategic dialogue with defense officials; an intense foreign policy dialogue on East Asia; and increasingly active, but largely private, trade and investment.

These two countries come to the new partnership with different histories. Despite the strong similarity of their strategic perspectives on the region, they have had difficulty with some areas of multilateral cooperation that are very important to the United States, notably antipiracy. They still face the challenge of creating a model for partnership that works for both. They will need to manage expectations as they undertake the long-term task of creating and working with the different coalitions that will figure in their approach to the Indian Ocean.

Both Pakistan and China are wary of the expanding US partnership with India. This should not deter the United States from the approach suggested here, but it does underscore the importance of also maintaining close strategic relations with Pakistan and China, and of ensuring that the overall network of multilateral organizations involved in this "coalitions" approach provides opportunities for both to participate.

The Multilateral Landscape

The Indian Ocean strategy proposed here would reinforce security and open access to the ocean and its shores through a program of cooperative activities, including both civilian and military components, that would involve the United States and the countries of the region bilaterally and in various multilateral settings. The result would not be a single coalition of Indian Ocean countries, but several overlapping ones, which would create patterns of cooperation within the region and with the United States and would increase everyone's stake in an open and peaceful region. US and Indian officials have separately used the phrase "an open, inclusive architecture" when speaking about East Asia. It applies with equal validity, though with a slightly different group of countries, to the Indian Ocean region.

Many of the specific activities that would implement the proposed strategy are not new. What is distinctive about this approach is the idea of linking US military institutions, bilateral relationships, and participation in international organizations so as to provide a strong diplomatic and military foundation for the United States as a regular participant in the life of the Indian Ocean region, in cooperation with the countries located there.

The following brief, illustrative list focuses on four types of activities, which are discussed in greater detail below:

- *Action organizations* with a specific, operational purpose—notably antipiracy and humanitarian relief. These are the most important international mechanisms for coalition building, but they have important gaps in participation, which the United States needs to address on a priority basis.
- *Regional multilateral organizations*, usually with the United States as a participant, and typically with an economic focus. These are important arenas for deepening US engagement and for developing a more general sense of community among the countries active in the Indian Ocean. The United States is not a leader in all of them, and is not a member of some. Working with other countries in leadership positions will reinforce America's policy message that it seeks inclusiveness and is not trying to marginalize China and Iran. The important thing is to establish a pattern of broad participation in regional organizations.
- *Bilateral diplomacy* is an essential underpinning for the multilateral activities listed above. An essential ingredient, however, is an increased focus on the smaller Indian Ocean countries that are preparing to build new facilities with Chinese help, and presumably with Chinese access in mind. These include Sri Lanka, Bangladesh, and some of the East African countries. The United States needs to give these countries more high-level attention, and to avoid using them as "object lessons" for nonstrategic (and locally unpopular) aspects of US foreign policy.
- *"Military diplomacy,"* both bilateral and regional: The US military commands that share responsibility for the Indian Ocean have a rich menu of conferences, exercises, and other mechanisms for bringing together the countries within their areas of responsibility. They need to focus some of these efforts on Indian Ocean–wide activities.

In addition, the United States should look hard at whether its present three-way command structure in the Indian Ocean is valuable enough to be worth the inevitable confusion it causes among the region's countries.

Action Organizations

The most important multilateral building blocks for the coalitions that would serve this strategy are the mechanisms designed for common action among the countries of the region. Concrete concerns and activities tend to be more powerful vehicles for building a commitment to common action than more general associations.

Two especially important ones are the *multilateral military task forces* established under the Combined Maritime Forces. Combined Task Force (CTF) 150 was established in 2001 to conduct counterterrorism work and maritime security operations in the western Indian Ocean region. CTF-151, established in 2009, has an antipiracy focus, and was established in accordance with United Nations Security Council Resolution 1816, which authorized "states cooperating with [Somalia's] transitional Government . . . for a period of six months, to enter the territorial waters of Somalia and use 'all necessary means' to repress acts of piracy and armed robbery at sea, in a manner consistent with relevant provisions of international law."[10] The United States, the United Kingdom, Australia, and a number of NATO countries are members of both, as is Pakistan.[11]

These task forces are focused on counterterrorism and antipiracy, problems shared by most of the region's countries, and certainly by all those that are plausible partners in any US strategy. At the same time, they also point out the challenge of working with hostile countries in the region.

The task forces include some of the important players, but not all. In particular, India is not a member. It has developed a closer liaison relationship with the two task forces in the past couple of years, especially on antipiracy operations.[12] The United Nations authority under which CTF-151 was established should make it more attractive to the Indian government from the policy perspective. Conversely, the fact that Pakistan is a member of the task force, and takes periodic rotations in command, is clearly a problem for closer Indian engagement with it. China, like India, is outside the task force, but it is interested in closer coordination. For India, this creates both a reason to avoid being left out and a heightened wariness about getting too deeply enmeshed in the structure.

Regional mechanisms for *disaster relief* should also be high on our list of coalition-building mechanisms. All the regional organizations discussed below have created at least rudimentary relief coordination systems. Not surprisingly, the stronger organizations (most of which have a predominantly East Asian character) have created stronger disaster relief machinery, but even the South Asian Association for Regional Cooperation has made progress in this area. India's experience working with the United States' tsunami relief effort in Sri Lanka and Indonesia had a profound impact on India's security managers, as noted above, and is regularly cited as a prime example of India's engagement with its Indian Ocean neighbors.[13] This suggests that further exercises and consultations built around disaster relief may be an effective way to build a sense of community in this region, and to include the US military in it.

Looking further ahead, the literature on *climate change* suggests that the Indian Ocean region will be powerfully affected by changes in sea level, in global temperature, and in rainfall. The estimates of crop loss, flood danger, changes in water supply, and disaster-related population movement for India alone project at least a loss of several percentage points of growth in gross domestic product every year. These developments will weigh even more heavily on countries that are poorer and growing more slowly.[14] This kind of "slow-onset disaster" has not generated as much international cooperation as headline-grabbing disasters, because it appears not as a crisis but as a long, slow adjustment to normal life. This would argue for a significant increase in US efforts to consult with countries in the region about how they will respond to problems induced by climate change.

The Region's Multilateral Forums

The United States should also expand its engagement with the region's multilateral consultative mechanisms. Whereas the United States has a leadership position in antipiracy and humanitarian mechanisms, it has less prominence in other regional organizations. US policy here should be to deepen its involvement. The United States should welcome and encourage leadership by countries whose security priorities are broadly compatible with its own. Inclusiveness is important as well. Chinese and Iranian participation in some of the relevant multilateral organizations would be a plus, and would insulate US efforts against the charge of trying to stir up hostility against these countries. The US goal should not be to exclude China from regional economic coordination mechanisms, which in any case would be unrealistic, but to strengthen access and security for the United States.

In general, multilateral organizations in the Indian Ocean region are weak, and membership is fragmented. The following are the most important regional organizations with which the United States needs to engage. Two include security in their mandate; the rest are economic in their focus.

THE INDIAN OCEAN NAVAL SYMPOSIUM The Indian Ocean Naval Symposium (IONS), a gathering of naval chiefs from the Indian Ocean area, was created in February 2008 by India and is the only military group designed to include all the Indian Ocean littoral countries. It has held three meetings in alternate years—in India, in Abu Dhabi, and in South Africa—with technical or preparatory meetings in the off years. Neither the United States nor China was invited to the inaugural meeting, but the US naval commander in the Persian Gulf participated extensively in the second meeting, and the United States now participates as an observer. Australia is scheduled to chair IONS in 2014.

IONS's purpose is in line with the kind of coalition-building efforts the United States should be supporting—to "promote a shared understanding of the maritime issues facing the littoral states of the Indian Ocean," to "strengthen [their] capability," and to establish cooperative mechanisms and interoperability. Interestingly, a think tank sponsored by India's Defense Ministry states that IONS was loosely modeled on the Western Pacific Naval Symposium, in which the United States plays a central role. The fact that it was created at Indian initiative is another point in its favor; because India is wary of joining new international organizations, it is more likely to be an active participant in an organization that bears its own stamp. Pakistan is listed as a member.[15]

THE INDIAN OCEAN RIM ASSOCIATION FOR REGIONAL COOPERATION The Indian Ocean Rim Association for Regional Cooperation (IOR-ARC), with nineteen members from around the Indian Ocean littoral, is devoted to expanding its members' economic ties. It is not very active, but its comprehensive membership makes it a moderately useful base to touch. Its dialogue partners include Japan, several European countries, and the United States.

ASEAN AND ITS VARIOUS FORMAL DIALOGUES ASEAN is the strongest of the multilateral organizations in the Indian Ocean region, and it has spawned dialogues with a string of nonmembers, including the United States, China, and India. ASEAN itself is oriented more toward East Asia, but as India and to a lesser extent Sri Lanka expand their trade with East Asia, the dialogue mechanisms in which they participate become more important as coalition builders in the Indian Ocean region. ASEAN maintains a formal dialogue with a growing number of nonmembers, including China, Japan, South Korea, India, and the United States.

THE ASEAN REGIONAL FORUM The ASEAN Regional Forum (ARF) was created to foster political and security dialogue among ASEAN's members and their partners. It includes twenty-seven members, from Pakistan at one end to Canada and the United States at the other. The United States has attended ARF meetings in recent years. The presence of Pakistan and China makes this a useful consultative mechanism to supplement IONS.

THE ASIA-PACIFIC ECONOMIC COOPERATION FORUM The Asia-Pacific Economic Cooperation forum (APEC) is formally an association of "economies" rather than "countries," focused on the Pacific Basin. It includes a number of members on the eastern side of the Indian Ocean. The United States and China are both members. India had applied for membership. APEC instituted a ten-year moratorium starting in 1997, but has not yet resumed admitting new members. The United States has been concerned that adding another large member would be a distraction at a time when APEC was having difficulty focusing on its trade liberalization agenda, though it may now be reexamining this issue. Indian membership would be useful from many perspectives, however, including Indian Ocean strategy. The question of Indian membership should be reexamined.

SOUTH ASIAN ASSOCIATION FOR REGIONAL COOPERATION The South Asian Association for Regional Cooperation (SAARC) includes India and its immediate neighbors on the subcontinent, Sri Lanka and the Maldives, plus Afghanistan. Both the United States and China have recently become observers. SAARC is a weak organization. It includes both India and Pakistan, but partly as a result, it has two rules that limit its ability to speak for the region: All significant decisions must be unanimous, and the organization does not discuss bilateral issues in its formal meetings. However, it has taken some useful cooperative steps on trade; it has an embryonic climate change and disaster relief program; and it provides a forum for consultation.

THE GULF COOPERATION COUNCIL The Gulf Cooperation Council (GCC) includes those countries on the Arabian Peninsula that have coastlines on the Persian Gulf. The United States' interaction with the GCC has focused chiefly on Persian Gulf security, but that is a critical dimension of the proposed US Indian Ocean strategy.

Bilateral Diplomacy: The Smaller Countries

To support a coalition-building strategy, the United States also needs to be actively engaged on the bilateral level. The United States has an active diplomatic dialogue with the larger powers of the region—India, China, the ASEAN countries, and Pakistan. Relations with India, as noted above, are central to an Indian Ocean strategy. Consultative mechanisms exist in all these countries for strategic dialogue; the challenge for America is to use this dialogue to deepen its strategic understanding.

To support its proposed strategy, however, the United States also needs to provide more diplomatic weight and "air time" to its dialogue with the smaller countries of the region, especially those where China and Iran have been developing special relationships. Of particular importance are Sri Lanka, Bangladesh, and some of the countries of East Africa.

This suggests three challenges for the United States' bilateral management of its relations with the smaller Indian Ocean countries—policy focus, resources, and time and attention.

POLICY FOCUS Smaller countries often become symbols of US policy issues outside the security area. Recent examples include human rights issues in Burma, allegations of war crimes in Sri Lanka, and the Bangladesh government's campaign against the microfinance pioneer and Nobel laureate Muhammad Yunus. Obviously, these are policy issues that the United States needs to treat seriously, but without making them the exclusive focus of policy—to the detriment of its security interest in balancing China's growing presence in the Indian Ocean. There is no neat textbook solution to this problem. What is recommended here is that the United States explicitly include long-term Indian Ocean security in the policy debate, and that strategy for its other goals (e.g., human rights) include an Indian Ocean dimension as well.

RESOURCES The most tangible tools the United States uses to its deepen relations with the smaller Indian Ocean countries are military and aid resources. The military resources required are not great—the US International Military Education and Training program, access to regionwide activities (more on this below), and occasional exercises and visits. The problem lies in the legislative restrictions on military cooperation.

Funding for economic assistance will be under severe pressure in the next few years, and the US government will need to make a strong national security argument to support aid appropriations. The United States also needs to cultivate new forms of economic support: public–private partnerships, for example, especially for infrastructure. The United States needs to advertise some of the most attractive features of US assistance. For example, unlike China, the United States normally provides grant assistance, and project construction is done with local labor.

TIME AND ATTENTION In some ways, the most important scarce resource is senior-level attention, including high-level visits in both directions. If the United States expects to be taken seriously as it develops coalitions to support secure access to the whole Indian Ocean region, both its senior civilian and military officials will need to find time to visit the region's smaller countries as well as the big ones.

"Military Diplomacy"

The military commands sponsor a rich array of cooperative activities, and these will continue to be an important element of the US presence. They are also critical to building coalitions for security. Logistical conferences, educational and training opportunities, and exchanges and exercises (both bilateral and multilateral) are all ways of building common understandings and showcasing both US capacity and US leadership.

Regardless of whether the United States decides to adjust its current command structure, all its military commands that have Indian Ocean responsibilities should plan at least one activity every year that explicitly brings together military representatives from all over the Indian Ocean region, with a focus on some aspect of their common security interest. This could be either an exercise or a conference; it might focus on counterterrorism, or piracy, or disaster relief.

The US Institutional Structure

The Indian Ocean straddles lines of responsibility and chains of command throughout the US government. For the military, the Central Command, Pacific Command, and Africa Command each has a piece of the Indian Ocean. The boundary between the Central and Pacific commands was created with the understandable objective of permitting different commanders to develop their own, separate, personal relationships with the military leaders of two countries hostile to one another. The structure unintentionally reinforces that hostility. The more recently created Africa Command does not factor into regional hostilities, but it adds to the difficulty foreign authorities have in dealing with the US military. Similar divisions exist in the State Department, the US Agency for International Development, and on the National Security Council staff. Each agency has a slightly different set of boundaries.

Realigning all US government institutions to bring the Indian Ocean together would almost certainly be far too disruptive to be worthwhile. However, if the United States is serious about having an Indian Ocean strategy, this strategy development effort needs a "home" somewhere in the US government. Because an Indian Ocean strategy affects the military more than it does the civilian agencies, this suggests that the military structure is the one that most needs to find a way to reflect the importance and integrity of this region. One could imagine several options: giving the Indian Ocean to one of the existing commands, with, for example, overlapping responsibilities for some of the littoral countries; or merging two or even three of the commands for naval purposes; or creating liaison relationships with multiple commands for some of the larger countries of the region. There may be others. The officials concerned, especially in the Department of Defense and the National Security Council, should revisit the present organizational structure and liaison arrangements to determine how best to reflect a "one Indian Ocean perspective" in day-to-day policymaking and in the United States' relationships with the littoral countries.

SUMMING UP: THE WIDER INDO-PACIFIC PERSPECTIVE

In late 2011 the Obama administration began speaking formally about a shift in its strategic and foreign policy perspective. With this shift—which has been variously known as the "pivot to Asia" and the "rebalancing"—the administration was embracing a shift in policy emphasis toward Asia. Early signs of this shift had come in 2010, when administration spokesmen began systematically referring to US policy that looked at India "in the context of Asia."[16] The "rebalancing" extended this policy to the allocation of some US military resources, some based in the region and especially those based in the United States but earmarked for overseas contingencies. Analysts close to the administration described this shift as a return from the resource patterns that had characterized the war on terrorism to something approximating the previous "normal."[17] It can also, however, be seen as the logical conclusion of the steady increase in Asia's economic importance, and in its publicly perceived importance, during the nearly seventy years since the end of World War II.

This volume's effort to define an Indian Ocean strategy fits in well with the rebalancing. Each of the proposed strategies recognizes that the United States can no longer treat the Indian Ocean region simply as "the space between" the Persian Gulf and the Pacific. The particular approach in this proposal, with its emphasis on diplomacy and on building cooperative coalitions, is valuable for another reason. At the end of World War II and especially after the collapse of the Soviet Union, US policy was built on the assumption that the world would recognize the overwhelming power of the United States and would willingly fit into a US design for the international order. The United Nations, the US alliance structure, the nuclear nonproliferation structure, the Bretton Woods institutions, and many other aspects of the international political, financial, and economic architecture reflect this. None of the organizations that constitute this architecture was created exclusively by the United States, but the mark of US design was strong, and broadly speaking, these were institutions that reflected some of the most important US priorities.

Today the United States remains the single most powerful country in the world, but it clearly needs to use a defter approach in crafting international arrangements with which it and other countries can live. Diplomacy will be more important for the future of US national security, and the US style will need to shift toward persuasion and consensus building—thus, this proposal's emphasis on coalition building and diplomacy. This approach will help US policymakers gain the most from the tremendous assets and sources of power that the country still enjoys.

NOTES

1. See, e.g., President of the United States, *The National Security Strategy of the United States of America* (Washington, DC: White House, 2006), www.state.gov/documents/organization/64884.pdf; President of the United States, *National Security Strategy* (Washington, DC: White House, 2010), www.whitehouse.gov/sites/default/files/rss_viewer/national_security_strategy.pdf; and Chicago Council on Global Affairs, "The United States and the Rise of China and India: Results of a 2006 Multinational Survey of Public Opinion," October 2006, 13–29, www.thechicagocouncil.org/UserFiles/File/POS_Topline%20Reports/POS%202006/2006%20Full%20POS%20Report.pdf.

2. See Teresita C. Schaffer, "India Next Door, China over the Horizon," in *Strategic Asia 2011–2012: Asia Responds to Its Rising Powers, China and India*, ed. Ashley Tellis, Travis Tanner, and Jessica Keough (Seattle: National Bureau of Asian Research, 2011): 285–312.

3. Ananth Krishnan, "Chinese Anti-Piracy Fleet to Join Pakistan Exercise," *The Hindu*, February 17, 2013, www.thehindu.com/news/international/chinese-anti-piracy-fleet-to-join-pakistan-exercise/article4425442.ece; Rahul Singh, "China's Submarines in Indian Ocean Worry Indian Navy," *Hindustan Times* (New Delhi), April 7, 2013, www.hindustantimes.com/India-news/NewDelhi/China-s-submarines-in-Indian-Ocean-worry-Indian-Navy/Article1-1038689.aspx.

4. For a skeptical view, see Andrew Selth, *Burma's Coco Islands: Rumours and Realities in the Indian Ocean*, Working Paper 101 (Hong Kong: Southeast Asia Research Center of the City University of Hong Kong, 2008), www.scribd.com/doc/155246952/Burma-s-Coco-Islands.

5. Teresita Schaffer, "Indo-US Relations: The Trade Factor," September 7, 2012, http://southasiahand.com/wp-content/uploads/2012/09/India-US-Trade.pdf.

6. Ananth Krishnan, "China Warns India on South China Sea Exploration Projects," *The Hindu*, September 15, 2011, www.thehindu.com/news/international/article2455647.ece.

7. See, e.g., Indrani Bagchi, "ASEAN Nations Lap Up Navy Chief's South China Sea Comment," *Times of India*, December 18, 2012, http://timesofindia.indiatimes.com/india/Asean-nations-lap-up-Navy-chiefs-South-China-Sea-comment/articleshow/17668261.cms.

8. C. Raja Mohan, *Samudra Manthan: Sino-Indian Rivalry in the Indo-Pacific* (Washington, DC: Carnegie Endowment for International Peace, 2012), esp. 211–35.

9. National Petroleum Council, "Topic Paper 2: Cultural/Social/Economic Trends," in *Global Oil and Gas Study*, July 2007, http://downloadcenter.connectlive.com/events/npc071807/pdf-downloads/Study_Topic_Papers/2-DTG-CulturalSocialEconomic.pdf; Amit A. Pandya and Rupert Herbert-Burns

with Junko Kobayashi, *Maritime Commerce and Security: The Indian Ocean* (Washington, DC: Stimson Center, 2011).

10. United Nations Security Council, "Security Council Condemns Acts of Piracy, Armed Robber off Somalia's Coast," Press Release, New York, June 2, 2008, www.un.org/News/Press/docs/2008/sc9344.doc.htm.

11. Website of Combined Maritime Forces, http://combinedmaritimeforces.com/.

12. Interestingly, an article in the journal of India's best-known defense think tank argues for closer Indian association with the multilateral antipiracy efforts. See R. S. Vasan, "Case Study of MV Suez and Anti Piracy Operations: Lessons for India and Pakistan," *Journal of Defence Studies* 5, no. 4 (2011), http://idsa.in/system/files/jds_5_4_rsvasan.pdf.

13. For a more detailed discussion of this, see *Asia's Response to Climate Change and Natural Disasters: Implications for an Evolving Regional Architecture*, Report of the CSIS Asian Regionalism Initiative (Washington, DC: Center for Strategic and International Studies, 2010), http://csis.org/files/publication/100708_Freeman_AsiasResponse_WEB.pdf, especially pp. 61–99.

14. See Teresita C. Schaffer, *India and the United States in the 21st Century: Reinventing Partnership* (Washington, DC: Center for Strategic and International Studies, 2009), 197–207.

15. Website of the Indian Ocean Naval Symposium, http://ions.gov.in/?q=about_ions; Gurpreet S. Khurana, "Indian Ocean Naval Symposium (IONS): Where from . . . Whither-Bound?" Institute for Defense Studies and Analyses, February 22, 2008, http://idsa.in/idsastrategiccomments/IndianOceanNavalSymposium%28IONS%29_GSKhurana_220208.

16. See, e.g., William J. Burns, "India's Rise and the Promise of US-Indian Partnership," speech at the Council on Foreign Relations, Washington, June 1, 2010, www.state.gov/p/us/rm/2010/136718.htm.

17. Christopher Clarke, presentation at "A Critical Assessment of US Rebalancing to Asia," Carnegie Endowment for International Peace, Washington, December 14, 2012; the author's private conversations with State Department and Defense Department officials.

CHAPTER 9

Combating Transnational Security Threats in the Indian Ocean

A Focused US Regional Strategy

ANDREW C. WINNER

The primary challenges to US interests in the Indian Ocean region are the set of transnational security issues: terrorism; the proliferation of weapons of mass destruction (WMD); the intersection of these two issues; and various types of illegal trafficking, including in small arms and people, piracy and maritime crime at sea, and natural disasters. Other US interests in the Indian Ocean as a whole involving state-on-state security dilemmas or freedom of navigation can best be supported by organizing an Indian Ocean strategy that more directly and effectively addresses transnational security issues. A strategy focused on transnational security issues will draw in those states that may become rivals and provide venues and opportunities for interaction in support of common goals that can reduce suspicions. In addition, such a strategy could assist in the creation of much-needed security institutions in the Indian Ocean region without the potential downside of any new bodies being perceived as security alliances directed at particular states. In short, such a strategy could help avoid exacerbating security dilemmas.

Those US interests that involve discrete parts of the Indian Ocean, such as the need to counter Iranian antiaccess capabilities in and around the Strait of Hormuz, are best addressed through existing, regionally based, or bilateral strategies and policies. Attempting to wrap US concerns vis-à-vis Iran in an Indian Ocean framework would not add value to Washington's diplomatic leverage, nor would it increase the capabilities available to respond to Iranian provocations. By contrast, transnational threats in the Indian Ocean region could potentially be more effectively and efficiently addressed with a broader regional approach that could also involve extraregional players. US interests in combating transnational threats are relatively long-standing and have received increased emphasis in the post–Cold War US national security strategies. This increased emphasis, particularly on the issue of the intersection of WMD and terrorist groups, has received strong bipartisan support in Washington, and this focus has been reiterated in the Obama administration's January 2012 defense guidance document that outlined the rationale for the "pivot" to the Asia-Pacific region.[1]

Therefore, this strategic concept argues for focusing US strategy in the Indian Ocean region on US activities and building the capabilities and capacity of the region's states to address transnational threats. Because, by their nature, transnational threats cannot effectively be countered unilaterally (except in limited, extraordinary circumstances), this strategic concept advocates building new relationships and strengthening the existing web of bilateral and multilateral security enterprises in the Indian Ocean region with those states that maintain military and/or maritime law enforcement forces in the Indian Ocean. It also seeks to bolster regional implementation capacity for global initiatives that address transnational issues, such as nonproliferation and counterproliferation regimes and ongoing global initiatives to combat transnational terrorism.

For the United States over the next ten to fifteen years, no issues other than transnational issues require an Indian Ocean–wide approach. Even those state-based security threats to US interests that exist in the Indian Ocean are not Indian Ocean–wide or do not require a strategy beyond what the United States is doing either bilaterally or in a subregional context. For example, Iran is a serious maritime issue because of its ability (and threats[2]) to block the Strait of Hormuz to commercial and military traffic, but existing policies and plans are adequate to that threat, and an Indian Ocean–wide analytic lens does not add clarity nor does an Indian Ocean–wide strategy provide added leverage to obtain US objectives in this area. One could argue that the US military bases, access, and infrastructure that would be necessary to address any future Iran-related contingencies rely heavily on the Indian Ocean, but that is not the same as making an argument that a US Indian Ocean strategy should be based on that reliance.[3] In fact, the growth of US military access and basing arrangements in the Indian Ocean has been based on a shifting set of priorities and requirements in the region, beginning during the Cold War as the United States became more dependent on oil from the Persian Gulf and as Soviet activity in the region increased.[4]

Similarly, concern about a crisis, or even war, between nuclear-armed India and Pakistan is not helped by approaching it with an Indian Ocean–based policy framework. Past large-scale wars between India and Pakistan have primarily involved ground and air forces. US involvement in Indo-Pakistani crises and conflicts has been confined to diplomacy and the cessation of military assistance to one or both sides. It is difficult to see a scenario where the complex strategic interaction between the United States, India, and Pakistan is clarified or ameliorated significantly by putting it into an Indian Ocean framework. At best, an Indian Ocean transnational strategy might provide a situation whereby India and Pakistan could be drawn together to work with a broader grouping to address a particular maritime transnational issue. However, given that the two major issues—terrorism and WMD proliferation—are extant issues between those two states, such an eventuality is unlikely. Finally, though both India and Pakistan have plans to add a submarine-based element to their nuclear forces, the importance of that portion of their triad—once deployed—relative to other delivery systems will remain small.

The increase in China's maritime activities in the Indian Ocean is often pointed to as a state-based issue requiring an Indian Ocean–wide approach by the United States. Indeed, a number of the strategic concepts outlined in the earlier chapters of this volume have as a central focus countering or addressing the increasing Chinese presence and capabilities in the Indian Ocean region. However, Chinese maritime activities in the region have a significant number of hurdles to overcome before they could constitute a threat to the United States or its core interests.[5] It is not clear that Chinese maritime actions in the region are ever going to be of sufficient scope to significantly change the region's maritime power alignment. The possibility that a growing Chinese presence in the region could cause misperceptions and therefore increase the chance of military clashes is addressed, in part, by the strategy proposed in this chapter.

UNDERLYING ASSUMPTIONS

One major assumption underlying this strategy is that there will not be a state-on-state war involving the great powers in the Indian Ocean region in the next dozen or so years. In line with current stated policies, the United States will decrease and eventually end large-scale military operations in Afghanistan. It is assumed for the purposes of developing this strategic construct that some combination of conventional and nuclear deterrence will keep both Israel and Iran on one hand, and India and Pakistan on the other, from engaging in any large-scale conventional or nuclear conflicts, although both pairs of antagonists will likely continue to engage in proxy wars and provocations with one another that may involve either supply or attack vectors utilizing the Indian Ocean.

A second assumption is that China will continue to increase its economic and military, particularly military maritime, presence in the Indian Ocean region. China's increasing military presence in the region may spark minor tensions, but these tensions will not result in any open hostilities with the region's states or other external powers with maritime military forces in the region. Absent a conflict over Taiwan, China will not directly challenge the ongoing US military presence in the broader region; nor will its military presence in the region be significant enough during the coming decade and more to challenge India's ability to protect its territory or interests in the region. China's increasing economic activities in the region are neither as directly related to military power as has been claimed by some, nor are they necessarily directly correlated with political alignment or dependency on the part of the region's littoral countries.

A third assumption is that the existing transnational security issues that have been identified in the Indian Ocean region will persist and indeed will likely worsen due to a combination of environmental factors and a lack of regional capacity to address the issues in any systematic and lasting way.

DIRECT RESPONSE OF THE STRATEGIC CONCEPT TO THE INDIAN OCEAN'S GEOSTRATEGIC ENVIRONMENT

The Indian Ocean region will have an increasingly complex security dynamic over the next ten to fifteen years. This will be caused by a mixture of four elements. The first is the persistence in the region of transnational security issues, all of which will continue and likely increase in intensity and frequency over time. The second is the fact that—with the exceptions of India, Australia, Singapore, and perhaps South Africa—none of the states of the Indian Ocean littoral have the capability and capacity to address transnational security threats in the region's wider maritime domain in any meaningful way without assistance from outside powers. Absent concerted assistance efforts, this is unlikely to change in the next decade. The third is the ongoing, and in some cases increasing, maritime military involvement of the great powers from outside the Indian Ocean in the region's security issues. This involvement ranges from participation in formal and informal multilateral coalitions addressing transnational issues to bilateral military exercises with allies and partners. The last element is the increasing, and often novel, interaction among the maritime powers from outside the region in the Indian Ocean and with states of the Indian Ocean littoral.

Given the relative paucity of capacity in the region to address transnational issues, a US strategy that focuses on those issues—particularly one that is undertaken in a cooperative manner and emphasizes local and regional capacity building—will likely be welcomed by the majority of the region's states, particularly if such a strategy is accompanied by assistance and training programs. Such a strategy outwardly downplays power politics and couches ongoing bilateral security assistance programs in a less threatening way than if they were focused on increasing war-fighting capabilities that may stir security dilemmas. Capacity building, even if framed as increasing a state's ability to counter transnational threats, does also have some parallel benefits in addressing other local security concerns.

Current US military and diplomatic programs carried out by the State and Defense departments have, as part of their goals, addressing the range of transnational issues in the Indian Ocean. However, they are not first in priority in many cases, and rather than being based on a regionwide plan that looks across the Indian Ocean, the programs are developed either based on bilateral considerations or within the context of the objectives of the individual US Department of State regional bureau or Defense Department regional combatant command (COCOM).

MEETING US NATIONAL AND REGIONAL SECURITY OBJECTIVES

The focus on transnational issues in the Indian Ocean region connects directly to and supports US interests as enumerated in the 2010 US *National Security Strategy* and the January 2012 defense guidance document.[6] Specifically, the security of the United States, its citizens, and US allies and partners is threatened both by transnational terrorist groups and also by the proliferation of WMD. Since the end of the Cold War, the intersection of these two transnational issues—terrorism and WMD proliferation—has been viewed by every US administration as one of the most serious threats to US national security.

Although there are threats to the elements of the international economic system that reside in the Indian Ocean region from both states and from internal instability in key economic actors, these concerns are best addressed by bilateral or existing regional strategies. For instance, an Indian Ocean strategy is unlikely to bolster the internal political stability of the oil-producing Arab states in the Persian Gulf region against the ongoing effects of the "Arab Spring." Conversely, transnational threats to Indian Ocean–based elements of the international economic system in the form of piracy and terrorist attacks on economic infrastructure are recognized both as real and as a legitimate focus of national and multilateral efforts.

Though, so far, neither piracy attacks in the Gulf of Aden/Somali Basin nor the piracy/maritime crime efforts in and around the Strait of Malacca have been significant enough to have a serious global-level macroeconomic effect, they have prompted political/military reactions on the part of a number of regional and extraregional states and institutions.[7] The piracy attacks off the coast of Somalia certainly constitute a hindrance to international access to markets, strategic resources, and sea lines of communication, although it is unclear whether this hindrance can or will become serious enough for regional or extraregional states to attempt to address the land-based causes using large-scale military intervention, at least in the case of Somalia. In fact, despite a 2008 United Nations Security Council (UNSC) authorization for states to pursue pirates ashore in Somalia, the states both in and outside the Indian Ocean region have chosen to largely remain at sea or act through the very limited Somali government or other local proxies to get at the situation on the ground.[8] At a national level, then, piracy in the Indian Ocean region at its current levels is a nuisance issue in terms of its impact—directly or indirectly—on US prosperity.

Piracy off of Somalia, however, has created a demand signal for a response from the maritime communities in various states. It also provides an opening for organizations and states outside the Indian Ocean region to undertake maritime operations there. Many of the states and organizations involved in counterpiracy efforts off Somalia are taking part for a mix of domestic, economic, and strategic motives that are only partially based on the actual threat of piracy to global, or nationally flagged or crewed, commerce.[9] If a more strategic approach were taken, the United States could help leverage the issue to more efficiently and effectively enhance maritime governance capabilities for littoral states rather than relying primarily on states and organizations outside the Indian Ocean region.

Although the Combined Task Force–150 (CTF-150), which was established in the wake of the September 11, 2001, terrorist attacks, and the United States–led Operation Enduring Freedom in Afghanistan have been the primary vehicles for counterterrorism efforts in the maritime domain, it may be time to address this ten-year-old mission within the context of a broader, Indian Ocean–wide maritime campaign against terrorist groups. Again, the strategic concept presented in this chapter is to focus on transnational threats such as terrorist groups, to organize US strategy, other external suppliers of capabilities and capacity, and regional efforts. Bringing an Indian Ocean–wide focus may help to transform CTF-150 into something broader, or it may bring lessons learned from CTF-150 and the entire coalition maritime force experience to the broader Indian Ocean. This may be particularly timely in the wake of the US operation that killed Osama bin Laden and the upcoming change in US military posture in Afghanistan in 2014. In particular, it may help change the focus from one that was primarily about stopping core al-Qaeda members and leaders from using the maritime domain to transit from Pakistan to East Africa to one that addresses a wide range of Indian Ocean–based and active terrorist organizations, such as al-Shabaab and Lashkar-e-Taiba.[10]

The Indian Ocean is likely to remain one of the primary routes for the transit of WMD and associated materials and ballistic missile components.[11] It is also a region with a relative paucity of states committed to robust nuclear nonproliferation and counterproliferation policies. One example is the wide geographic swath of states that have not endorsed the Proliferation Security Initiative's (PSI's) Statement of Interdiction principles.[12] Since the advent of the PSI, a number of UNSC resolutions have authorized states to interdict ships and aircraft carrying WMD-related material to and from Iran and North Korea. This type of post hoc and relatively ad hoc norm creation and capability improvement could become more regularized and proactive in a region so critical to global maritime commerce, such as the Indian Ocean. An effort to produce a more focused implementation of counter-WMD activities within this region would support both US regional and global interests.

This strategy may, at first blush, appear to not address a long-standing US interest in preventing destabilizing shifts in regional balances of power. Borrowing from an early statement about the purpose of NATO, an Indian Ocean strategic approach that focused on state power balancing could be thought of as one that kept the United States in, China out, and India down.[13] This type of approach, in variants, is posited in chapters 7 and 8 by Michael Auslin and Teresita Schaffer, respectively, and to a much lesser degree in chapter 3 by William Martel. However, as a long-term proposition, a US Indian Ocean strategy that focuses on Washington's role in helping the region's states prepare for, combat, and respond to transnational threats will be more sustainable than one that places the emphasis on balance-of-power considerations. If one assumes that the US presence in the region helps to dampen potential destabilizing shifts in the regional balance of power, then an Indian Ocean regional strategy should help create a sustainable rationale for a long-term US presence and engagement. A transnational, threat-focused strategy for the Indian Ocean region, plus any subregional commitments of the United States to its allies and partners, should suffice to keep the United States in the region despite the rebalance and budget cuts.[14]

A strategy focused on combating transnational threats will not help keep China "out" of the Indian Ocean region, and such a goal is largely unworkable regardless of the US strategic approach to the region. As Martel argues in chapter 3, a traditional containment strategy applied to China in the region is not feasible. Rather, the strategic concept advanced here would seek to shape China's increasing maritime presence in the region. Specifically, it would provide China with opportunities for engagement and participation in activities, and potentially in institutions and organizations, that are focused on countering transnational threats in the region. In this way, China's maritime activities in the region would be channeled to providing collective security rather than looking solely after China's narrowly defined national interests. Such engagement would provide opportunities for greater transparency about China's military activities in the region and would therefore mitigate potential for suspicion. If China consistently chooses to demur from Indian Ocean activities that contribute to collective security and instead focuses on its own unilateral agenda, this in and of itself may be useful in terms of making a clear distinction to littoral countries between the US and Chinese approaches to the region.

Finally, an approach focused on transnational issues would provide India with a chance to join the United States and the Indian Ocean region's other great powers in providing a collective good. India's politicians are beginning to make policy pronouncements about India providing security in its neighborhood, which is a promising opening to a strategy of this type.[15] The United States is counting on India to play a larger, and stabilizing, role in the region.[16] Again, like China, India could be drawn into activities, and possibly institutions, in a way that it has not been heretofore. India has been historically wary of many multilateral institutions and activities (ranging from PSI to the CTF). It has also historically sought to minimize extraregional presence and influence in the region. This latter view has changed over the past decade, and India now generally welcomes the presence of the United States and most other extraregional navies in the region. China's increasing presence is an exception to this recent shift in policy. What has not yet changed is India's willingness to engage in activities that provide public goods within the context of multilateral efforts. India is still pursuing its fledgling attempt to establish the Indian Ocean Naval Symposium, but India has not thus far provided significant impetus to the initiative other than founding it. India's continuing unilateral approach to maritime military operations might worry some other Indian Ocean littoral states (Pakistan in particular). Weaving India into more multilateral efforts—whether formal or informal—may alleviate concerns about Indian hegemony in what it sees as its maritime sphere of influence.

APPLYING THE STRATEGY TO THE INDIAN OCEAN

The successful application of this strategic approach to the Indian Ocean region will require close cooperation between the American military and its regional partners on a wide range of operational issues, but especially those necessary to meet transnational challenges. It will also require deep engagement among the US military, intelligence agencies, and civilian departments and agencies because meeting transnational threats, by definition, demands whole-of-government responses.

Military Mission Areas / Defense Activities

Humanitarian assistance, and particularly disaster relief, will be missions with growing demand in the Indian Ocean region.[17] The United States currently prepares for these missions on a unilateral basis, and it trains and exercises for these missions in bilateral and multilateral formats with allies and partners. However, US efforts in the Indian Ocean are trifurcated among the three regional COCOMs—the Pacific Command, the Central Command, and the Africa Command. Although combatant commands have learned lessons and have adopted approaches from their counterparts (e.g., the Pacific Partnership, leading to the Africa Partnership Station), it is not clear that this is the most efficient and effective way to either build partner capacity or indeed to improve regional preparations, planning, prepositioning, prediction and analysis capabilities, or response capabilities. Something more is needed at the national strategic level to bring about more regular links and supporting efforts among these three regional commands.

In the area of counterproliferation, the global policy basis for enhancing regional implementation exists in the form of UNSC Resolution 1540, the various UNSC resolutions that apply to North Korea and Iran, the Global Initiative to Combat Nuclear Terrorism, and the PSI. The United States conducts a range of PSI field and tabletop exercises through a chairman of the Joint Chiefs' exercise program that is managed by the individual COCOMs. However, there is no comprehensive campaign plan associated with this set of exercises; nor has significant thought been given to enhancing particular regional implementation of interdiction or other counterproliferation, policy-related activities. As is discussed below, military forces will mostly play a supporting role in actual counterproliferation operations, but military organizational, planning, exercising, and lessons-learned cultures will help improve the capacity of interested and involved states across their own interministerial teams.

Under this strategic concept, counterterrorism activities in the Indian Ocean would consist of building national capacity to monitor activities in territorial waters and exclusive economic zones, tracking and sharing information about vessels of interest, and—in rare cases—taking action against vessels suspected of transporting terrorists or illicit supplies. Much of the military activity in this area would be preparing for either unilateral, or variable-geometry bilateral or multilateral, activities against terrorist organizations. This effort would require significant coordination across military, intelligence, and law enforcement agencies and organizations throughout the region. The primary thrust of counterterrorism activities in the Indian Ocean maritime realm would be to make the maritime environment as transparent, and therefore as hostile to terrorist use, as possible. Another element of counterterrorism would be working to improve the protection of critical, and growing, maritime infrastructure—such as offshore oil platforms and undersea cables—from a terrorist attack.

Enabling Capabilities and Concepts

One major enabling concept for this strategy is improved information sharing about maritime activities in the Indian Ocean. This may sound synonymous with maritime domain awareness (MDA), which is a navy and coast guard program to develop and share information about large ships at sea, but the exact types of information necessary for combating or responding to transnational threats and issues should be examined to see whether current MDA initiatives, either global or regional, are sufficient for any Indian Ocean strategic concept. An Indian Ocean strategy focused in part on transparency can leverage many existing initiatives related to maritime transportation and information sharing: regional MDA initiatives that are already under way, the Shared Awareness and De-Confliction Meetings (known as SHADE) that take place monthly in Bahrain in support of counterpiracy efforts both off the Somali coast as well as at centers such as the information fusion center at Changi in Singapore, as well as bilateral discussions that the United States has had with India concerning its securing its maritime approaches against possible future terrorist infiltrations.

Regional and Subregional Implementation

The implementation of the strategy outlined above will vary by subregion of the Indian Ocean based on a mix of the salience of the particular transnational issue, the political will and maritime capacities and capabilities of the states in the region, and US access and resource availability in that subregion. A key element, however, will be working to break out of subregional implementation approaches that rely on implementation by a single COCOM. US COCOMs should work across their area of responsibility seams and boundaries to collaborate on exercises, tabletops, and security assistance. In short, the United States should work to ensure that its own bureaucratic boundaries do not become additional artificial impediments to the implementation of an Indian Ocean–wide strategy.

Relations among US National Security Institutions

As with the strategic concept outlined by Teresita Schaffer in chapter 8, the strategy presented in this chapter would rely as heavily on diplomacy and law enforcement as it would on military capabilities or military cooperation narrowly drawn. The implementation of a US strategy of this sort would require significant support, and integrated assistance, from the Department of Defense, the Department of State, the intelligence community, and the range of law enforcement agencies and organizations in the US government. In particular, counterterrorism and counterproliferation have critical diplomatic and law enforcement aspects. Many states in the Indian Ocean region approach both counterproliferation and counterterrorism as primarily questions of law enforcement because of policy preferences. In addition, in the maritime realm, many states in the region place their maritime capabilities institutionally under law enforcement rather than military ministries. Some states in the Indian Ocean region do not have navies in the traditional sense but rather rely mostly on maritime law enforcement agencies and forces. For this strategy to be successful, the United States will need to meet these states where they are—which will require the US Coast Guard as well as US Customs and Border Protection to be an integral part of the development and implementation of the strategy for the Indian Ocean region. Fortunately, the US Coast Guard has had increasing experience with both international collaboration and deployments to the Indian Ocean region in the past decade.

Relations with Key Regional Players and International/Regional Organizations

Key allies and partners of the United States that are Indian Ocean region states can play a significant role in this strategy—providing resources, taking leads in various initiatives, and making the construct of an Indian Ocean transnational security issue–focused grouping not an entirely United States–led and –paid-for effort. However, the number of allies and partners with both capacity and will in the region is sparse—at least in terms of taking on an Indian Ocean–wide strategic approach. Australia would be the easiest to engage because of its long-standing and close alliance relationship with the United States. The new US–Australian defense relationship, which hinges on increased US access to Australian bases on the Indian Ocean rim, provides a solid base on which to build. However, Australia itself has limited resources and is only beginning to look anew at the Indian Ocean as a region for which it has to formulate a more complete set of policies and strategic approaches.[18] Growing attention in Australia to the Indian Ocean, however, may make for an opportunity to develop a US approach in concert with a close and highly capable ally. Although India has the most interest of any state in the security of the Indian Ocean region writ large, involving India in US initiatives, or getting it to take the lead in anything in the region that has a multilateral flavor, may be difficult and require significant time to work through India's bureaucracy and its slowly developing sense of its strategic place in the world.

This strategy, however, should not rely too much on a few US allies or partner states in the Indian Ocean region. Washington should be looking to encourage engagement and participation from all states in the region, and it should be seeking to get states, both large and small, to not only participate but also take leadership roles and responsibility for specific elements of addressing transnational issues that are either most important for that state or for which the state has a comparative advantage due to geography, history, unique capacity, or experience. Because there are no advanced multilateral security organizations in the Indian Ocean region, the United States should look for ways to get its regional partners to bolster those that do exist or encourage those organizations to take up particular issues. One small step in the right direction was the late 2012 addition of the United States as a dialogue partner to the Indian Ocean Rim Association for Regional Cooperation.[19] Equally encouraging were the reports that India played a major diplomatic role in securing for the United States that new, if limited, status. The Indian-founded Indian Ocean Naval Symposium (IONS) is another organization through which the United States could work to bolster this strategy based on transnational issues. Although Washington is neither a member nor an observer at IONS at this point, high-level US military officers have been invited to participate in some of the deliberations. One opportunity for the United States and IONS arises because Australia takes over the rotating two-year chairmanship in 2014. US strategy can also work without formal organizations, relying on an activities-based approach such as PSI and the Global Initiative to Combat Nuclear Terrorism.

RISKS AND UNCERTAINTIES

One significant risk in a strategy of this sort is that the United States will not achieve buy-in. Not all states, and certainly not many in the Indian Ocean region, see transnational security issues in the maritime realm as either pressing or as their primary security threat. Many Indian Ocean littoral states rarely focus on the maritime at all as a source of their security threats. In part this is historic for many states, and in part—particularly for states with weak capacity in the maritime realm—this is a natural policy adaptation to their inability to affect much in the maritime domain beyond, perhaps, their territorial waters.

A related risk is that of collective action. Once the United States announces, and indeed begins to take steps toward, increased attention to transnational security issues in the Indian Ocean region, there is a good chance that numerous states in the region will choose to free-ride, focusing on their own local security needs without contributing to addressing Indian Ocean–wide security issues. In addition, any strategy addressing transnational issues requires preventive action, something that is particularly difficult in gathering and sustaining international support over time. Finally, a related risk is that the United States simply will not have the capacity to conduct such a strategy in a time of constrained defense and foreign affairs budgets. The United States' pivot, or rebalance, to Asia (meaning primarily East Asia) and secondary focus on the Persian Gulf may consume all its available monetary and intellectual resources, leaving little time for the relatively methodical and long-term approach to the Indian Ocean outlined in this chapter.

Finally, many of the salient transnational issues in the Indian Ocean region are being addressed through various global initiatives, such as the international organization–based UNSC Resolution 1540 Committee or the looser, less formal PSI. In order not to be seen as duplicative, any US strategy for the Indian Ocean region that focuses on transnational security issues will need to link with these global efforts and not be seen as stealing the diplomatic lead from global efforts in which other states are already invested, either diplomatically or economically.

NOTES

The views expressed here are those of the author and do not necessarily reflect the views of the US Naval War College, the US Navy, or the US Department of Defense.

1. US Department of Defense, "Sustaining US Global Leadership: Priorities for 21st Century Defense," January 2012, www.defense.gov/news/defense_strategic_guidance.pdf.
2. United Press International, "Iran Will 'Block' Strait of Hormuz If Pressed," July 8, 2012, www.aljazeera.com/news/middleeast/2012/07/2012789645779519.html.
3. Andrew S. Erickson, Walter C. Ladwig III, and Justin Mikolay, "Diego Garcia and the United States' Emerging Indian Ocean Strategy," *Asian Security* 6, no. 3 (2010): 214–37.
4. US Department of State, ed., "Document 77: Study Prepared in Response to National Security Study Memorandum 199, 'Indian Ocean Strategy,' Washington, undated," in *Foreign Relations of the United States*, vol. E-8 (Washington, DC: US Government Printing Office).
5. James R. Holmes and Toshi Yoshihara, "China's Naval Ambitions in the Indian Ocean," *Journal of Strategic Studies* 31, no. 3 (2008): 367–94.
6. White House, *National Security Strategy*, 2010, www.whitehouse.gov/sites/default/files/rss_viewer/national_security_strategy.pdf.
7. In fact, cooperative efforts by regional states have significantly decreased the instances of piracy and armed robbery at sea in and around the Strait of Malacca. See Catherine Zara Raymond, "Piracy and Armed Robbery in the Malacca Strait: A Problem Solved?" *Naval War College Review* 62, no. 3 (Summer 2009): 31–42.
8. David McKeeby, "International Struggle against Piracy Comes Ashore in Somalia," US Africa Command, December 8, 2008, www.africom.mil/Newsroom/Article/6397/international-struggle-against-piracy-comes-ashore.
9. Andrew C. Winner, "Coalitions and Counterpiracy Operations: Something Old, Something New," paper presented at International Studies Association Convention, Montreal, March 2011.
10. Statement of Admiral Robert F. Willard, US Navy Command and US Pacific Command, before the Senate Armed Services Committee on the US Pacific Command Posture, February 28, 2012. He notes that Lashkar-e-Taiba is an increasing threat in the Indian Ocean area.
11. Hugh Griffiths and Michael Jenks, *Maritime Transport and Destabilizing Commodity Flows*, SIPRI Policy Paper 32 (Stockholm: Stockholm International Peace Research Institute, 2012).
12. Though the number of PSI endorsees has grown from 11 states at its inception in 2003 to 102 in early 2013, key states along the Indian Ocean littoral—such as Bangladesh, Burma, India, Indonesia, Malaysia, and Pakistan—have so far chosen not to endorse the initiative. For a list of the participating states, see US

Department of State, "Proliferation Security Initiative Participants," www.state
.gov/t/isn/c27732.htm.

13. David Wroe notes that "NATO's first secretary-general, Lord Ismay, famously
said the purpose of the alliance was to 'keep the Russians out, the Americans in
and the Germans down.'" David Wroe, "NATO: Trying to Keep the Americans
In," Globalpost, November 19, 2010.

14. In fact, the head of the US Pacific Command, Admiral Locklear, has begun to
use the phrase "Indo-Pacific" or "Indo Asia-Pacific" to refer to the region that is
the focus of the US rebalance. See, e.g., Statement of Admiral Samuel J. Locklear, US Navy, Command, US Pacific Command before the House Armed Service Committee on US Pacific Command Posture, March 5, 2013.

15. "Defence Minister Antony Underlines Indian Navy's Role in Providing Security
in the Region," October 11, 2011, http://maritimesecurity.asia/free-2/piracy-2/
defence-minister-antony-underlines-indian-navys-role-in-providing-security-
in-the-region/.

16. US Department of Defense, "Sustaining US Global Leadership," January 2012.

17. David Michael, "Environmental Pressures in the Indian Ocean," in *Indian Ocean
Rising: Maritime Security and Policy Challenges*, ed. David Michael and Russel
Sticklor (Washington, DC: Stimson Center, 2012), 113–29.

18. Stephen Smith, minister for defence, "Address to the Asia-Pacific Chiefs of
Defence Conference," Australian Department of Defence, November 7, 2012,
www.minister.defence.gov.au/2012/11/07/minister-for-defence-address-to-
the-asia-pacific-chiefs-of-defence-force-conference/.

19. "We Welcome Our Inclusion as Dialogue Partner in IOR-ARC: US," *Economic
Times*, November 3, 2012, http://articles.economictimes.indiatimes.com/2012-
11-03/news/34892149_1_ior-arc-indian-ocean-rim-association-dialogue-
partner.

PART III

CONCLUSION

CHAPTER 10

ENSURING ACCESS AND PROMOTING SECURITY IN THE INDIAN OCEAN

PETER DOMBROWSKI AND ANDREW C. WINNER

The premise of this book is that the Indian Ocean is becoming a distinct and increasingly important maritime region and that the United States therefore needs to consider, and potentially develop, a strategy for how it is going to pursue and protect its interests in this region. The chapter authors were asked to accept these premises and to develop possible strategies for the United States. Some authors used traditional US grand strategies as a point of departure, as they developed specific Indian Ocean strategies. Others eschewed existing models and built their strategy from their own view of the proper prioritization of US interests in the region, layered against an understanding of the current and future geostrategic environment in the Indian Ocean region. All the authors considered resource constraints in the development of their strategies. The chapters, considered both individually and as a whole, provide insights on the two major questions posed at the outset of this volume.

The first major question is whether a US strategy is even necessary for the Indian Ocean region. This question has two parts. The first is whether the Indian Ocean region—currently, or in the future—is important enough for the United States, or cohesive enough as a geographic region, to warrant its own strategy. And the second part is whether Washington could meet its objectives with current strategies or with minor adjustments to its current mix of policies and organizations. The second major question is whether grand strategy frameworks—for example, containment or cooperative security—can be adapted to fit US interests and objectives in the Indian Ocean or whether the new approaches developed by the chapter authors provide greater insight. What issues about the Indian Ocean did each strategy raise for consideration? How were these issues analyzed, prioritized, and dealt with by the individual strategic approaches? Did each of the strategies reach the same or similar conclusions? Did they raise the same issues, or were some better at uncovering issue areas or providing more insightful analysis? And finally, which strategy or strategies appear more cohesive and feasible?

KEEPING THE STATUS QUO

The chapter authors were asked to develop strategies based on the premise that the Indian Ocean is of increasing importance and that some sort of strategy should be considered. However, they were also given the freedom to challenge this assumption if their own research and analysis led them to a different conclusion. This is particularly true of those authors who do not begin their analysis with a particular grand strategic framework. None of the authors argues that a strategy is unnecessary or that the current approach is sufficient. Christopher Preble comes the closest to advocating this view by framing US strategy in the Indian Ocean within the broader context of an offshore balancing approach. He does not argue that the Indian Ocean is not a geostrategic region worthy of consideration.

Instead, Preble argues that the Indian Ocean is a relatively less important region for the United States in the coming decades compared with other regions such as East Asia, given shifts in the global balance of power and constraints on US resources. Therefore, he argues that US strategy toward the Indian Ocean region should cede primary responsibility for security issues to those whose interests are greater—whether the littoral states or other countries that see their own interests in the region as vital. And Preble thus does not argue for a continuation of the status quo; nor does he argue that current strategies and policies will suffice. In fact, he argues that current policies fail to make strategic choices because they often amount to laundry lists. In the Indian Ocean region, current approaches fail to adequately prioritize the use of US resources, and thus policy adjustments are necessary.

In chapter 7 Michael Auslin argues for looking beyond the Indian Ocean and addressing the broader Indo-Pacific region. Although some US policy officials have begun to speak in terms of the Indo-Pacific region, US government strategic documents and bureaucratic structures are not organized in those terms.[1] From Auslin's perspective, at least in terms of geographic scope, the existing approach to the Indian Ocean is inadequate and needs to be reconsidered. Chapter 2, Walter Ladwig's modern take on the Nixon doctrine, also makes clear that the current US approach is insufficient to meet American interests in the region. Ladwig frames his argument in terms of the scarcity of resources relative to announced commitments. He fears that US military, diplomatic, and political attention to the region is inadequate given the growing importance of the Indian Ocean. At the same time, he argues that the January 2012 "pivot" to the Asia-Pacific region was an announcement that was not, and will not be, backed by adequate resources. Indeed, a number of reports during the budget crisis of 2013 related to sequestration, funding defense operations using a continuing resolution, and potentially cutting defense spending even more beyond fiscal year 2013 call into question whether the Obama administration will be able to execute the Asia rebalance under austerity.[2] Ladwig attempts to avoid the trap of underresourcing the region by developing an alternative that has the United States more actively backing a set of the region's states whose interests largely correspond with those of Washington and that collectively may have adequate resources and proximity to address security in the region. His approach calls for policies of support that cross the current US military lines of responsibility, meaning that even tweaks of current bureaucracies—such as increasing coordination between the State Department's bureaus and the Department of Defense's regional commands responsible for the Indian Ocean—are likely to be inadequate.

In chapter 3 William Martel argues that the Indian Ocean does require a strategy beyond current thinking, but he makes a persuasive case that the issues in the region will not respond to the policy of containment, as traditionally understood.[3] In chapter 8 Teresita Schaffer bases her strategic analysis on the centrality of Asia in global geopolitics and the rise of China and India as a key component of that premise. Her approach requires rethinking diplomatic, economic, and military policies toward the Indian Ocean. For Schaffer, current thinking and structures are inadequate, as is relying primarily on the military instrument of national power. In chapter 6 Rodger Payne is relatively sanguine about the current US approach to the region, but he does argue for some significant adjustments. He suggests that the Obama administration's Asian pivot contains elements that foreshadow a cooperative security approach to the broader Asia-Pacific region. His recommendations for the Indian Ocean region consist largely of shifts and advances on current policies and relations. One area where he does advocate a substantially different approach is in thinking more seriously about arms control and confidence-building measures as a method of reducing great power rivalry in the Indian Ocean region. At the moment there is little mention of great power rivalry in the Indian Ocean in official US statements and documents, and there are no official initiatives promoting regional arms control or confidence-building measures. In chapter 9 Andrew Winner argues that transnational threats in the Indian Ocean call for strengthening both bilateral and multilateral arrangements. Given the relative weakness of multilateral institutions in the Indian Ocean region, increasing their authorities and capabilities to a level sufficient to meet the transnational threats in the region will require something more from the United States than simply tinkering on the margins of current policy. This is particularly so because the United States is not a formal member of most of the Indian Ocean–focused security and security-related institutions.

Finally, in chapter 5 James Holmes and Toshi Yoshihara develop a detailed critique of offshore balancing as a grand strategic approach for the United States and its potential application to the Indian Ocean region. They argue instead in favor of enhancing US maritime forward presence in the region.

Our introductory chapter raised two potential risks for the United States if it does not develop and implement a new, more formal, and more explicit strategy for the Indian Ocean. One was the risk of the suboptimization of the protection of US interests because of the lack of an overarching strategy coupled with the bureaucratic lines of authority that subdivide the Indian Ocean region. The various strategy chapters support the notion that American policies toward the Indian Ocean are suboptimal. Almost all the chapter authors identify issues and interests that are not adequately addressed and propose means to address these interests that could only occur with some substantial reorganization of the US national security implementation system.

A second risk identified in chapter 1 of this volume is that the United States' drawdown in Iraq and Afghanistan may be interpreted by its allies and partners as a broader withdrawal from the greater Indian Ocean region. This, in turn, could lead to China, India, or even nonstate actors filling the perceived power vacuum in ways that damage US security objectives. This could include the possibility that the region's states would bandwagon with China as it increased its presence in the Indian Ocean. Another consequence might be that the region's states could more aggressively pursue their own security needs. A perception that the United States is pulling back beyond merely winding down the Iraq and Afghanistan ground wars could increase the chances of destabilizing competition between India and China. This risk is addressed in detail in the pair of chapters by Christopher Preble and by James Holmes and Toshi Yoshihara. In chapter 4 Preble argues that the likely outcome of a real (and, in his view, recommended) drawdown of the US presence in the region would be a natural balance that would likely keep the peace or at least adequately address US interests. He also argues that the United States could surge forces back into the region if and when a crisis arises that is not mitigated by other states in the region. In chapter 5 Holmes and Yoshihara argue that such a withdrawal, and even the perception of one, is much riskier than proponents of offshore balancing concepts acknowledge, considering both the diplomatic practicalities of access and basing and also the changes in antiaccess capabilities that could keep extraregional US forces from reentering the Indian Ocean region when needed.

THE VALUE OF GRAND STRATEGIC FRAMEWORKS

Barry Posen and Andrew Ross's well-known article on competing visions for a US grand strategy posited four visions: neo-isolationism, selective engagement, cooperative security, and primacy.[4] Those four visions made sense, both as one looked to the past and in the context of the mid-1990s, when that article was published. As we developed this volume and considered which possible grand strategic frameworks might be useful in the Indian Ocean region, we considered an updated and modified version of the Posen-Ross visions. The chapter authors were not asked or required to stick rigidly to frameworks developed by other academics and analysts. Instead, some were asked to grapple with the question of a US strategy for the Indian Ocean from the general perspective of well-known and understood grand strategies. Neo-isolationism was examined—in the guise of its newer variant, offshore balancing—by Preble and by Holmes and Yoshihara. Ladwig's neo-Nixonian strategy can be seen as a form of selective engagement. Payne conducted a straightforward review of cooperative security and its application to the Indian Ocean region. Although containment was not mentioned as a grand strategic framework in the Posen-Ross article, because at that point there was not a great power, or peer competitor, to contain, by 2012 it was clear that some examination of the question of containing China had to be part of the discussion, at least in policy circles. Finally, given fiscal constraints and political realities after eight and one-half years of war in Iraq and more than a decade of war in Afghanistan, the grand strategic vision of primacy was likely well outside the bounds of reality. Auslin's chapter might be described as something between a coalition form of primacy and selective engagement.

One argument for using a familiar grand strategic framework to help in developing a strategy for the Indian Ocean region is simply that doing so opens up a wider range of initial possibilities than if one simply began consideration based on a given set of objectives and an understanding of the geostrategic environment. Without the range of grand strategic frameworks, the development of options could remain stuck within a narrow band—for example, minor variations on selective engagement. Asking an analyst to take an existing grand strategy and apply it to a particular region or problem may stimulate thinking and cause some assumptions to be usefully questioned.

INSIGHTS ON INDIAN OCEAN STRATEGY

Regardless of whether the proposed strategy is derived from an existing grand strategic framework or from an updated variant, four issue areas are apparent: geographic scope, the role of China, the role of India, and great power conflict in the Indian Ocean region. Some of the chapter authors' strategies explicitly grapple with these areas because they are central to the construction of their concept. Other strategic concepts deal with them in a more cursory fashion, but they still matter when considering which strategy might best advance and protect US interests in the Indian Ocean region.

Geographic Scope

Is the Indian Ocean a useful geographic space for the purposes of thinking about strategy generally, and more specifically, for the purposes of developing a US strategy to guide current and future deployments of power and resources? This volume is predicated on the assumption that the Indian Ocean region is important in geographic and strategic terms and is likely to become more so over time for economic and security reasons. However, this does not necessarily mean that the region should best be considered as a whole for strategic purposes. It may be that though the Indian Ocean is more important for achieving US national interests than in previous periods, it remains a lower-priority region than others such as the Persian Gulf (which can be thought of as a particularly important subregion of the Indian Ocean region) or Northeast Asia. In a time of strategic adjustment forced on US policymakers by domestic fiscal difficulties, the United States may need to consider strategic triage by accepting risk in the Indian Ocean in order to conserve resources for those areas more likely to threaten critical American interests in the short- to intermediate-terms.

After looking at US objectives, the geostrategic environment, and existing policies and governing structures (both US and international), it is also possible to conclude that the best way to approach the region is as a series of subregions, each with its own economic, political, and security dynamics. A strategy of subregions might allow the United States to devote more attention to the most pressing challenges in the Indian Ocean while not elevating the entire region to a higher priority than it deserves.

In his book *Monsoon*, Robert Kaplan goes to considerable lengths to paint the Indian Ocean as a region interconnected by history, economics, and close-knit ethnic diasporas.[5] As outlined in chapter 1 of this book, however, economic connections within the region are still in the process of being built—or rebuilt, if one accepts Kaplan's reading of the history of trade in the region.[6] Much of the maritime economic traffic is either across the ocean or from the region's countries or across the Indian Ocean to countries outside the Indian Ocean region. As is pointed out by Winner in chapter 9, on transnational threats, even the security threats in the Indian Ocean are dissimilar across the various seas, littorals, bays, and straits that make up the entire ocean. Piracy occurring in the Gulf of Aden and the Somali Basin has significant differences from the similarly named phenomenon in the Strait of Malacca.[7] These differences across regions may be sufficient to warrant a subregional approach rather than an Indian Ocean–wide strategy. A strategy of Indian Ocean subregions might take advantage of existing American commitments, including bases and diplomatic arrangements, while delegating some security responsibilities to Indian Ocean countries that are locally powerful but are not capable or politically ready to play a wider role in partnership with the United States across the Indian Ocean. Thus, for example, Australia might assume more security roles in the southeastern corner of the Indian Ocean and extend its activity northward toward Indonesia, Malaysia, and Papua New Guinea (whether this would sit well with the Australians, much less the Indonesians and Malaysians, is a separate issue). Despite this theoretical possibility, none of the chapter authors thought that a subregional approach makes sense; each developed a strategy that covers the whole Indian Ocean.

In chapter 7 Auslin takes his analysis in the opposite direction, arguing that the Indian Ocean is not necessarily the correct unit and that the scope of strategy should be expanded to encompass an Indo-Pacific region that connects the Indian and Pacific oceans. Questions about the correct geographic scope for a strategy have a number of components. One is whether there is a difference when one is considering a land region or a maritime region. Given the fact that the world's oceans have no boundaries and that maritime traffic, including military vessels, has and regularly exercises the right to innocent passage, it is difficult to argue that there is a logical boundary for any maritime domain, even at well-known straits or maritime chokepoints. Other than cases such as the Suez and Panama canals, where a sovereign state can choose to disallow passage, it is very difficult to actually choke off maritime commerce absent a significant military effort that brings with it risks of a military response. In the case of the Indian and Pacific oceans, Auslin makes a persuasive case that there are significant links between them, and in fact those linkages are what makes the entire region important to the United States. He argues that it is the linkage between Persian Gulf energy resources and the growing markets of East Asia and the maritime traffic between them that makes it necessary for the United States to see the region as a strategic whole.

Another element to consider in deciding about the geographic scope of any regional strategy is the span of control of the bureaucratic units of the US government that must execute that strategy. In the case of the United States, as noted at the outset of this volume, significant divisions exist within both the Defense and State departments regarding the Indian Ocean region. If one comes to the conclusion that an Indian Ocean–wide strategy is necessary, then the question arises of whether the existing set of bureaucratic structures and processes is sufficient to implement it. If one adopts an even larger geographic scope for a strategy, as proposed by Auslin, the question of bureaucratic divisions arises, as does the question of whether the geographic area of application is simply too large for any single entity to implement. At what point does a regional strategy become so large that it is, in essence, a global strategy?

The Role of China

This question of regional versus global scope is also related to another issue that is raised in most chapters: the question of the role of China in the Indian Ocean region. China's economic growth and its economic activism the world over raise the valid question of whether it is so significant that any Indian Ocean strategy must be a subset of a US strategy toward China and its rise. None of the analyses in this volume goes that far—to argue that China's significance is such that it should be looked at in the same way that the United States considered the Soviet Union during the Cold War. Although Martel's contribution to this volume discusses a Cold War–era strategy, containment, he notes that China's economic position in the world, and indeed the current global structure, make containment unsuitable. But he also recognizes the size and importance of China in any regional or global strategic calculation. In any case, at least exploring the possibility of containment makes some sense, given that over the last decade or so, several prominent American strategists have increasingly identified China as the greatest challenge to America's continuing its global supremacy for the remainder of the twenty-first century.[8]

The question of China and its role in the Indian Ocean remains an open one after one considers all the strategic options posited in this volume. Although it is important to consider China when thinking about an Indian Ocean strategy, there is currently no consensual view of China's role in this region. The discussion in a number of the analyses echoes that which took place when the United States last considered the question of an Indian Ocean strategy, during the Nixon and Ford administrations. In those deliberations, agencies were sharply divided over both the capabilities and intentions of the Soviet Union in the Indian Ocean.[9] A number of US government studies in the 1970s had concluded that the Indian Ocean was not a high priority for Washington, but there was concern that if Soviet activity increased, it might become an area of superpower dispute.[10] Recent scholarship argues that in the immediate aftermath of the Cold War, American strategists, "net assessors," and intelligence officials were already analyzing the potential impact on the US global position if China, India, or both managed to emerge as peer or "near" peer competitors.[11] In either case or both, the Indian Ocean would become a venue for competition.

In the broader literature cited by some of the chapter authors, the concern is expressed that China is now working to become a more significant strategic actor in the Indian Ocean region.[12] This increased presence and significance are often referred to as China's "string of pearls" strategy—shorthand for Beijing wanting to establish a series of military bases and access points along the Indian Ocean littoral from which it can more easily project military power in the region.[13] As of the writing of this volume, China has no bases or formal access arrangements in the region. In fact, most of the "pearls" so far seem to be commercial ventures, and some—like Gwadar in Pakistan—are not very successful commercial ventures at that.

The most significant Chinese military activity to date in the Indian Ocean region is its counterpiracy patrols in the Gulf of Aden, which take place under the legal and diplomatic umbrella of numerous United Nations Security Council resolutions concerning Somalia. Although China has not joined any of the formal organizations (NATO, the European Union) and informal task forces (Combined Task Force–151) conducting counterpiracy operations in the region, they are coordinating their activities at the tactical level and through monthly meetings with other countries and groups. This activity highlights a question that is central to any US consideration of Chinese activities in the Indian Ocean: How can Washington distinguish between Beijing's military activities that contribute to common security and those that might be threatening to US interests?

Only the offshore balancing concept allows a straightforward answer to this question. In the short- to medium-terms, other states in the region will balance Chinese activities if they become threatening. If they are of such a scope that a US return in force to the region is necessary, then presumably it would be obvious. Other approaches to US strategy, including Auslin's and Ladwig's approaches that advocate coalitions based on shared liberal values, have a hedging quality to them with regard to China. Schaffer is even stronger in her recommendations on hedging against China, arguing that both the United States and India have a shared interest in preventing both a future Chinese bid for primacy in the Indian Ocean and also any Chinese military or diplomatic activities that could impede US access to the region. Other strategic concepts, including those discussed by Winner and Payne, focus on building coalitions and institutions to combat transnational threats and leave the question of China relatively open—arguing that a strategy should allow for China to become part of the solution and positing that it is not yet part of any significant threat or problem for the United States in the Indian Ocean region.

The Role of India

Even more than China's role, the question of the role of India is central in every consideration of US strategy in the Indian Ocean. Although China's intentions and future capabilities in the Indian Ocean region are certainly debatable, India's intentions and current capabilities—in large part predicated by its central geographic location—are beyond debate. Although India does not publish a formal national security strategy, documents by key government constituencies, such as the Indian Navy, make it clear that India considers the Indian Ocean as an area of core vital interests.[14] The questions for the developers of a US strategy in the Indian Ocean, then, are four. First, what exactly are India's interests in the Indian Ocean region? Second, does India currently have, or will it have in the future, the diplomatic, economic, and military capabilities to be a significant force in Indian Ocean security—securing its own interests and possibly contributing to the security of others in the region? Third, what roles does it want to play in this maritime region—hegemonic, cooperative, or a mix? Fourth, and finally, what relationship does it want to have with the United States overall, and particularly within this region, which it considers as within its core zone of national interests?

Most of the chapter authors seem to assume that the United States and India have a significant overlap of interests in the Indian Ocean region. The 2012 US defense strategic guidance document that outlined the "pivot" to the Asia-Pacific region infers that commonality of interests as well.[15] Again, though official India is fairly circumspect about stating full-up alignment with any state, at least in the maritime realm the long standing suspicion of the maritime activities of all others—with the notable exception of China—in the Indian Ocean has changed.[16] Meanwhile, as in China, a growing community of strategists, who are either independent or are only loosely affiliated with the government in New Delhi through foundations and think tanks, are busily prodding elite opinion and calling attention to the national security challenges found from the Bay of Bengal to the Arabian Sea.[17]

India's extraordinary economic growth since the mid-1990s has provided it with the wherewithal to significantly upgrade its maritime military and power projection capabilities in the Indian Ocean region.[18] The Indian Navy's participation in humanitarian assistance and disaster relief missions and in counterpiracy patrols in the Indian Ocean demonstrate that there are both significant modern capabilities and a political will to utilize them in the region. Other improvements in maritime capabilities, such as the growth of India's coast guard, are in part a response to security threats such as the seaborne infiltration of terrorists who carried out the attack in Mumbai in November 2008.

Despite this growth in capabilities and willingness to project power to support national goals in the Indian Ocean, there are limits to how much India will be able to do in the near term to midterm, absent some significant shifts in its own policies. Although India has significantly modernized and improved its maritime military capabilities, the Indian government has policies in place—such as requirements for technology transfer and the indigenization of defense production capabilities as a long-term goal—that will continue to significantly slow, and at times possibly derail, the country's drive to obtain key capabilities.[19] In addition to limitations on the expansion of its capabilities, India faces significant challenges in deciding how to employ its new capabilities and influence. India is only beginning to adapt its national security institutions to its new, more significant, Asian and global role. More broadly still, well-informed observers express doubt that Indian foreign policy institutions are up to the challenge of asserting greater diplomatic influence.[20] Without a "software" upgrade, New Delhi will see limits in translating its capabilities into influence in the region.[21]

Even if India's capabilities were to continue growing at a significant rate and if India was able to improve its decision-making capabilities for foreign and national security policy, it is not clear that there is a consensus within India as to what role it would play in any US strategy toward the Indian Ocean. India has publicly stated that it is a "strategic partner" of the United States. From Washington's perspective, this implies a very close relationship, with overtones of the long-standing "special relationship" that the United States has had with London in the post–World War II world. From New Delhi's perspective, however, strategic partnership implies normalized relationships between states. India, therefore, has a large number of strategic partnerships, including with states with which the United States has less than cordial relationships.[22] The debate over the broad contours of India's future foreign and security policy, including how close a relationship to have with the United States, is far from over.[23]

Even with a significant growth of Indian capabilities and a recognized convergence of interests, there are limits to how closely India is willing to become involved in any US strategy for the Indian Ocean. The current US strategy for India seems to assume both an identity of interests and that US support for India in an Indian Ocean role will be welcomed and produce uniformly agreed-upon results. The 2012 US defense guidance document's one sentence on India reads as follows: "The United States is also investing in a long-term strategic partnership with India to support its ability to serve as a regional economic anchor and provider of security in the broader Indian Ocean region." Attempts in the recent past to align the two nations' interests in security fields—such as New Delhi's decision on purchasing a multirole combat aircraft—have not always turned out the way they were expected in Washington.[24] India has deployed its navy in counterpiracy patrols in the Gulf of Aden, but it has not joined the United States–led Combined Task Force–151, instead preferring to call for all counterpiracy efforts to be put under a "blue helmet" United Nations peacekeeping command—something not appealing in Washington.[25] The degree to which India is willing to play the kind of role that any US Indian Ocean strategy would envision will be limited by the factors outlined above.

India may be willing to become even more closely aligned with the United States if there is significant friction in the Indian Ocean that it believes that it cannot counter on its own. At the moment the only possibility of this sort would involve a significant and aggressive expansion of access and influence by China. It would also likely require patience on the part of American politicians and strategists, not to mention a willingness to acknowledge Indian regional equities, even when they conflict with American preferences.

Great Power Conflict in the Indian Ocean Region

This leads to the last common issue that weaves its way through the various strategy options in this volume: the question of whether the Indian Ocean is indeed going to become, as outlined in Robert Kaplan's book, the true nexus for conflict—particularly involving great powers—in the twenty-first century. At least some of the strategies outlined in this book indicate that any serious great power conflict in the Indian Ocean is a long way off, if it could happen at all. In fact, one objective of a US strategy should be to shape both activity in the Indian Ocean region and the behavior of the great powers that either are in or have interests in the region, in a manner that decreases the chance that any competition escalates to open conflict. Ideally, a successful strategy would involve the region's great powers in cooperative efforts that not only reduce the chances for conflict among them but also utilize their capabilities to address the security interests of the region's smaller states and provide a coordinated contribution to the security of the maritime domain.

How the United States approaches the Indian Ocean region remains an open question. As Michael Green and Andrew Shearer explained in early 2012, the United States has recently undertaken an interagency review of the region, at the initiative of the Office of the Secretary of Defense.[26] Several high-profile American delegations have visited India, Australia, and other regional players. Yet progress has been slow. Beyond the obvious overarching rebalance toward Asia announced by the Obama administration in January 2012, the press has not reported new policy initiatives involving the Indian Ocean specifically, much less the organization of US regional military commands or State Department bureaus to recognize the Indian Ocean in ways any different from the past decade. Even top-end bilateral initiatives in the region seem stuck. India–United States relations, though cordial, have not moved much beyond general agreements on civilian nuclear cooperation and talks on reducing impediments to defense sales and particularly defense technology transfer. Of course, to expect more given the other domestic and foreign challenges facing the Obama administration may be too ambitious, especially considering the constraints on potential regional partners and the long-term, tectonic shifts in the Indian Ocean's geostrategic environment.

In all likelihood the US approach to the Indian Ocean region will be another example of "muddling through."[27] As Steven Metz has pointed out, a unique set of cultural, organizational, and historical factors have long hindered the development of a coherent US grand strategy.[28] The pluralistic American political system extends even to the military and executive branch, which thus undermines the country's willingness and ability to think strategically. Muddling through is thus a "default" strategy with which many Americans are quite comfortable.[29]

As the chapters in this volume have demonstrated, accepting that the output of the policy process is unlikely to result in a consistent, fully coherent, executable, and executed strategy for the Indian Ocean region, or any other geographic region, does not mean that scholars and analysts should not use the "tool" of grand strategies to identify the issues facing the nation as it pursues its interests in an uncertain geostrategic environment. Even if the likely future of US policy in the Indian Ocean is closely related to the immediate past, including decisions like the invasion of Afghanistan (and all its subsequent consequences) made in the heat of crisis, both policymakers and military leaders should be self-conscious about the implication of their activities. Demonstrating the possibilities inherent to particular ideal types of grand strategies or hybrid approaches like the focus on transnational threats provides the intellectual framing that is necessary for clear thought, self-conscious policy choices, and serious debates not just within the global strategic policy communities but also within the government itself. In the case of the Indian Ocean region, this is critical because the rise of China and the possibility of great power conflict in such a commercially central region as the Indian Ocean will not go away anytime soon.

POLICY IMPLICATIONS FOR THE UNITED STATES

Given the considerations summarized above, in general, American policies in the Indian Ocean region and toward its littoral states are likely to remain quite similar to those pursued since the end of the Cold War, especially as American and coalition forces draw down from Afghanistan. If neither US national interests nor US security institutions as they are currently configured are likely to force the elevation of the Indian Ocean to an area of major concern (as implied by several, if not most, of the chapter authors) and thus result in major changes to US policies in the region, it is worthwhile asking what scenarios might change this assessment. How might the Indian Ocean become a critical area demanding both a coherent US regional strategy and a realignment of US security and foreign policies?

First, and foremost, China's future capabilities and actions in the Indian Ocean represent the most obvious potential source of policy change. If China's naval rise sufficiently threatens the potential security of the Indian Ocean as the locus of the key sea lines of communication underpinning the global economy, the United States may feel compelled, either on its own or in combination with other regional and perhaps extraregional powers, to elevate the Indian Ocean to strategic prominence. A continuation of the relatively limited engagement of the Chinese navy in the Indian Ocean documented over the past several years is unlikely to provoke serious changes. Rather, it would require one or more significant developments, such as a closer naval alliance between China and Pakistan, the development of a major Chinese naval base complete with forward-deployed forces, or perhaps regular patrols by Chinese naval flotillas including major combatants. Although none of these appear likely in the short term, they remain within the realm of the possible. Even if China does take such steps, much depends on how the United States and its regional partners interpret them. From one perspective, the rise of China's navy is both inevitable and not necessarily troubling. After all, China might become a net contributor to global and regional security even as it deploys more often and with greater capabilities in the Indian Ocean region. China's willingness to deploy to the Gulf of Aden to support its own economic interests and international antipiracy coalition objectives at least hints at this possibility.[30] From the opposite perspective, no matter how innocuous China's growing naval presence in the Indian Ocean may appear, the important strategic questions involve both trust and actual military capabilities. Prudent planners should consider what China could or might do rather than what it says it is doing and even actually does in operational terms.

Unsurprisingly, this book's chapter authors, as well as other academic experts on China and international relations more generally, are greatly divided on the question of China's intentions and capabilities, and on how the United States and the entire international community should interpret them. The longtime China specialist David Shambaugh concludes his analysis of the People's Liberation Army Navy (PLAN) forces by arguing that "although the PLAN may have such aspirations [to conduct "out-of-area operations" beyond its own littoral], at present it is only the missile, space, and cyber forces that are capable of projecting power globally."[31] In contrast, international relations specialists, especially those in the Realist tradition like Aaron Friedberg, are skeptical that China would be willing to cede command of the seas, including the Indian Ocean, to the United States as its military capabilities have grown commensurate with its economic power. Friedberg even suggests that the PLAN has several potential advantages in the contest for supremacy of the seas—China is using its continental position to free itself from vulnerability to blockades and interdiction (e.g., by building pipelines in Central Asia) while increasing its capacity to hold at risk the flow of energy and other commerce to important American allies, including South Korea and Japan.[32] Military analysts will continue to engage in contentious and unresolvable debates over the efficacy of blockades and counterblockades by the US Navy and the PLAN.[33]

Given the current and assumed trajectory of America's defense spending and force structure, the possibility of a long-term threat from China in the Indian Ocean region would cause severe stress in American defense planning. Most analysts are already projecting that the numbers of ships, aircraft, and other military assets available to the US Navy and its sister services will decline substantially during the next several decades.

Two potentially prudent policies in the face of uncertainty about Chinese capabilities in the Indian Ocean region are to focus on intelligence, surveillance, and reconnaissance and on cultivating long-term relations with the region's powers. The US Navy and various American intelligence agencies would lead enhanced intelligence-gathering activities, but it is unlikely that this would require greater forward presence than is currently maintained. Greater knowledge about Chinese activities in the region will allow for early warning and a better net assessment of the direction and strength of overall threats to American interests. In a similar fashion, warm relations with India, Australia, and other like-minded states will provide the United States with buffers and more knowledge of China's activities, both regionally and bilaterally. In short, these policies fit both Schaeffer's preference for hedging and the aspects of the cooperative approaches presented by Winner and Payne.

However, focusing solely on China as the only variable that could shift the importance of the Indian Ocean in the United States' strategic calculus is both narrow and risky. In the past, unforeseen circumstances have turned formerly insignificant countries and regions into centers of strategic importance for the United States, and this could happen again in the Indian Ocean region. The nuclear rivals India and Pakistan remain at loggerheads and the future could see crises between the two spill into the ocean. Potentially nuclear-armed midlevel powers such as Iran and Israel could clash in ways that could permanently change the security dynamic in the northwestern part of the Indian Ocean region. A new failed state in a crucial location along shipping lines could make Somali piracy seem insignificant by comparison. For all these reasons, the Indian Ocean region will at the very least need to be a watching brief for US policymakers, who will be regularly gauging whether this distant ocean (from Washington's perspective) has grown significant enough to warrant its own strategic approach.

NOTES

The views expressed here are those of the authors and do not necessarily reflect the views of the US Naval War College, the US Navy, or the Department of Defense.

1. It is worth noting that Admiral Samuel Locklear, commander, US Pacific Command, uses the regional designation "Indo-Pacific," given his responsibilities for US forces in the Indian and Pacific oceans. Donna Mile, "Locklear: Budget Uncertainty Threatens Asia-Pacific Rebalance," American Forces Press Service, www.defense.gov/news/newsarticle.aspx?id=119447.

2. Matthew Pennington, "Cuts Could Endanger US 'Rebalancing' toward Asia," Associated Press, March 1, 2013.

3. Since China began its economic and military rise nearly two decades ago, debates over American policy toward the entire Indo-Pacific region have often been framed, sometimes inappropriately, in terms of "containment." See David Shambaugh, "Containment or Engagement of China? Calculating Beijing's Responses," *International Security* 21, no. 2 (Autumn 1996): 180–209.

4. Barry R. Posen and Andrew L. Ross, "Competing Visions for US Grand Strategy," *International Security* 21, no. 3 (Winter 1996–97): 5–53.

5. Robert D. Kaplan, *Monsoon: The Indian Ocean and the Future of American Power* (New York: Random House, 2010).

6. Sugata Bose, *A Hundred Horizons: The Indian Ocean in the Age of Global Empire* (Cambridge, MA: Harvard University Press, 2006); Michael Pearson, *The Indian Ocean* (New York: Routledge, 2003).

7. Martin N. Murphy, "The Abundant Sea: Prospects for Maritime Non-State Violence in the Indian Ocean," *Journal of the Indian Ocean Region* 8, no. 2 (December 2012): 173–87.

8. Jeffrey A. Bader, *Obama and China's Rise: An Insider's Account of America's Asia Strategy* (Washington, DC: Brookings Institution Press, 2012); Aaron L. Friedberg, *A Contest for Supremacy: China, America, and the Struggle for Mastery in Asia* (New York: W. W. Norton, 2012); Michael D. Swaine, *America's Challenge: Engaging a Rising China in the Twenty-First Century* (Washington, DC: Carnegie Endowment for International Peace, 2011).

9. US Department of State, ed., "Document 77: Study Prepared in Response to National Security Study Memorandum 199, 'Indian Ocean Strategy,' Washington, undated," in *Foreign Relations of the United States*, vol. E-8 (Washington, DC: US Government Printing Office).

10. See sections on the Indian Ocean Region in *Foreign Relations of the United States*, ed. US Department of State (Washington, DC: US Government Printing Office), vols. 24, E-6, E-8.

11. Kai Liao, "The Pentagon and the Pivot," *Survival* 55 no. 3 (June–July 2013): 95–114.

12. Ashley J. Tellis, "Indian Ocean and US Grand Strategy," speech delivered for the National Maritime Foundation at India International Centre, January 2012.

13. For a careful analysis of China's activities in the Indian Ocean, see Daniel J. Kostecka, "Places and Bases: The Chinese Navy's Emerging Support Network in the Indian Ocean," *Naval War College Review* 61, no. 1 (Winter 2011): 59–78.

14. Integrated Headquarters, Ministry of Defence–Navy, *Freedom to Use the Seas: India's Maritime Military Strategy* (New Delhi: Ministry of Defense, 2007).

15. US Department of Defense, "Sustaining US Global Leadership: Priorities for 21st Century Defense," January 2012, www.defense.gov/news/defense_ strategic_guidance.pdf.

16. In *Freedom to Use the Seas* the Integrated Headquarters of the Ministry of Defence–Navy notes that the activities of Western navies in the Indian Ocean

are largely congruent with Indian interests. Its statements about China's maritime activities are much more ambiguous.

17. See, e.g., the works of C. Raja Mohan, including most recently, C. Raja Mohan, *Samudra Manthan: Sino-Indian Rivalry in the Indo-Pacific* (Washington, DC: Carnegie Endowment for International Peace, 2012). David Brewster analyzes changes in Indian strategic thought in "Indian Strategic Thinking about East Asia," *Journal of Strategic Studies* 34, no. 6 (December 2011): 825–52.

18. James R. Holmes, Andrew C. Winner, and Toshi Yoshihara, *Indian Naval Strategy in the Twenty-First Century* (New York: Routledge, 2009).

19. Nicholas Lombardo, "India's Defense Spending and Military Modernization," Current Issues 24 (Washington, DC: Center for Strategic and International Studies, 2011), http://csis.org/files/publication/110329_DIIG_Current_Issues_24_Indian_Defense_Spending.pdf.

20. Manjari Chatterjee Miller, "India's Feeble Foreign Policy: A Would-Be Great Power Resists Its Own Rise," *Foreign Affairs*, May–June 2013.

21. Daniel Markey, "Developing India's Foreign Policy 'Software,'" *Asian Policy* 8 (July 2009): 73–96.

22. Brahma Chellaney, "India's Strategic Partners, A System of Asian Partnerships," January 12, 2010, Stagecraft and Statecraft, http://chellaney.net/2010/01/12/indias-strategic-partners/.

23. Sunil Khilnani, Rajiv Kumar, Pratap Bhanu Mehta, Prakash Menon, Nandan Nilekani, Srinath Raghavan, Shyam Saran, and Siddharth Varadarajan, "Nonalignment 2.0: A Foreign and Strategic Policy for India in the Twenty-First Century," 2012, www.cprindia.org/sites/default/files/NonAlignment%202.0_1.pdf.

24. Ashley J. Tellis, "Decoding India's MMRCA Decision," *Force*, June 2011, 9–17, http://carnegieendowment.org/files/Force_June_2011-Ashley_J._Tellis.pdf.

25. Admiral Nirmal Verma, "CNS's Address at the 20th International Seapower Symposium," October 19, 2011, Newport, RI, http://pib.nic.in/newsite/erelease.aspx?relid=76798.

26. Michael J. Green and Andrew Shearer, "Defining US Indian Ocean Strategy," *Washington Quarterly* 35, no. 2 (Spring 2012): 175, 189.

27. The concept of "muddling through," as applied to policy issues, is an old-one dating back at least to Charles Edward Lindblom, "The Science of Muddling Through," *Public Administration Review* (Spring 1959): 74–88.

28. Steven Metz, "Why Aren't Americans Better at Strategy?" *Military Review* 77, no. 1 (January–February 1997): 187–90.

29. Scholars who have examined the tendency to muddle through in foreign policy and grand strategy include Robert Jervis, "US Grand Strategy: Mission Impossible," *Naval War College Review* 51, no. 3 (Summer 1998): 22–36; and John Lewis Gaddis, "Foreign Policy by Autopilot," *Hoover Digest*, no. 3 (2000); John Lewis Gaddis, "Muddling Through: A Strategic Checklist for the Post–Cold War World," in *Strategic Transformation and Naval Power in the 21st Century*, ed. Pelham G. Boyer and Robert S. Wood (Newport, RI: Naval War College Press,

1998): 123–35; and Edward N. Luttwak, "Why We Need an Incoherent Foreign Policy," *Washington Quarterly* 21, no. 1 (Winter 1998): 21–31.

30. Andrew S. Erickson and Austin M. Strange, *No Substitute for Experience: Chinese Antipiracy Operations in the Gulf of Aden*, Naval War College CMSI China Maritime Study 10 (Newport, RI: Naval War College Press, 2013), www.usnwc.edu/Research---Gaming/China-Maritime-Studies-Institute.aspx.

31. David Shambaugh, *China Goes Global: The Partial Power* (New York: Oxford University Press 2013), 294.

32. Aaron L. Friedberg, *A Contest for Supremacy: China, American and the Struggle for Supremacy in Asia* (New York: W. W. Norton, 2011), 228–32.

33. See, e.g., Sean Mirski, "Stranglehold: The Context, Conduct and Consequences of an American Naval Blockade of China," *Journal of Strategic Studies* 36, no. 3 (2013): 385–421; and a response by Evan Braden Montgomery, "Reconsidering a Naval Blockade of China: A Response to Mirski," *Journal of Strategic Studies* 36, no. 4 (2013): 615–62.

CONTRIBUTORS

Michael Auslin is a resident scholar and the director of Japan studies at the American Enterprise Institute (AEI) and is also a columnist for the *Wall Street Journal*. He is currently completing a book titled *Ocean of Risk: The Looming Threats to Asia's Future*, and is the author of *Pacific Cosmopolitans: A Cultural History of US–Japan Relations* (Harvard University Press, 2011), the report *Security in the Indo-Pacific Commons: Toward a Regional Strategy* (AEI Press, 2010), and the book *Negotiating with Imperialism: The Unequal Treaties and the Culture of Japanese Diplomacy* (Harvard University Press, 2004), as well as numerous magazine and newspaper articles. He has been named a Young Global Leader by the World Economic Forum, a Marshall Memorial Fellow by the German Marshall Fund, a Fulbright Scholar, and a Japan Foundation Scholar. Before his appointment to AEI, he was an associate and assistant professor in the Department of History at Yale University from 2000 to 2007. During that time he was also a senior research fellow at the MacMillan Center for International and Area Studies and the founding director of the Project on Japan–US Relations. He has also been a visiting professor at the University of Tokyo. He received a PhD from the University of Illinois at Urbana-Champaign, an MA from Indiana University at Bloomington, and a BSc in Foreign Service from Georgetown University.

Peter Dombrowski is a professor of strategy in the Strategic Research Department at the Naval War College. His previous positions include chair of the Strategic Research Department, director of the Naval War College Press, editor of the *Naval War College Review*, coeditor of *International Studies Quarterly*, associate professor of political science at Iowa State University, and defense analyst at ANSER, Inc. He has also been affiliated with research institutions, including the East-West Center, the Brookings Institution, the Friedrich Ebert Foundation, and the Watson Institute for International Studies at Brown University. He is the author of more than fifty books, monographs, articles, book chapters, and government reports. His awards include a Chancellor's Scholarship for Prospective

Leaders from the Alexander von Humboldt Foundation, the Navy Meritorious Civilian Service Medal, and the Navy Superior Civilian Service Medal. He received his BA from Williams College and an MA and a PhD from the University of Maryland.

James R. Holmes is a professor in the Strategy and Policy Department at the Naval War College. He is a Phi Beta Kappa graduate of Vanderbilt University and earned graduate degrees at Salve Regina University, Providence College, and the Fletcher School of Law and Diplomacy at Tufts University, where he was awarded a PhD in 2003. He graduated from the Naval War College with highest distinction in 1994 and was the recipient of the Naval War College Foundation Award, signifying the top graduate in his class. Before joining the Naval War College faculty in 2007, he was a senior research associate at the University of Georgia's Center for International Trade and Security; a research associate at the Institute for Foreign Policy Analysis; and a US Navy surface warfare officer, serving in the engineering and weapons departments on board the battleship *Wisconsin*, directing an engineering course at the Surface Warfare Officers School Command, and teaching strategy and policy at the Naval War College's College of Distance Education. He is the author of *Theodore Roosevelt and World Order: Police Power in International Relations* (Potomac Books, 2006); and coauthor of *Indian Naval Strategy in the Twenty-First Century* (with Andrew C. Winner and Toshi Yoshihara; Routledge, 2009); *Chinese Naval Strategy in the 21st Century: The Turn to Mahan* (with Toshi Yoshihara; Routledge, 2008); and *Red Star over the Pacific: China's Rise and the Challenge to US Maritime Strategy* (with Toshi Yoshihara; Naval Institute Press, 2010). He was coeditor of *Asia Looks Seaward: Power and Maritime Strategy* (with Toshi Yoshihara; Greenwood Press, 2008); and *Strategy in the Second Nuclear Age: Power, Ambition, and the Ultimate Weapon* (with Toshi Yoshihara; Georgetown University Press, 2012).

Walter C. Ladwig III is an assistant professor in the Department of Politics and International Relations at the University of Oxford. He is also a visiting fellow at the Royal United Services Institution. Previously, he was the America's Scholar at Merton College, Oxford, and a predoctoral fellow at the Miller Center of Public Affairs at the University of Virginia. His work has been published in *International Security*, *Asian Survey*, *Comparative Strategy*, *Small Wars & Insurgencies*, *Asian Security*, and *War in History*, in addition to several chapters in edited volumes. He has also commented on international affairs for the BBC, Reuters, and the Associated Press, and his commentaries have appeared in the *New York Times*, the *Wall Street Journal*, the *San Diego Union-Tribune*, the *Baltimore Sun*, the *Indian Express*, and the *Japan Times*. He received a BA from the University of Southern California, an MPA from Princeton University, and a PhD from the University of Oxford.

William Martel is associate professor of international security studies at the Fletcher School of Law and Diplomacy at Tufts University, and has research and teaching interests in foreign policy, international security, and public policy. His books include *Victory In War: Foundations of Modern Strategy* (Cambridge University Press, 2011), and the forthcoming *Grand Strategy in Theory and Practice* (Cambridge University Press, 2015). He has published articles in the *Cambridge Review of International Affairs, The National Interest, Washington Quarterly, The Diplomat, Orbis,* and the *Wall Street Journal.* He teaches seminars on ballistic missile defense, cyber, and space with the Massachusetts Institute of Technology's Lincoln Laboratory at the Naval War College, serves on the editorial board of the *Naval War College Review,* and is the principal investigator in joint Fletcher School–MIT Lincoln Laboratory studies on formulating codes of conduct for cyber and space. He was formerly a professor of national security affairs at the Naval War College, and he served on the professional staff of the RAND Corporation in Washington. He was an adviser to the National Security Council, and a consultant to the Defense Advanced Research Projects Agency and the US Air Force Scientific Advisory Board. He received his AB from Saint Anselm College, a doctorate from the University of Massachusetts–Amherst, and was a postdoctoral research fellow at the Center for Science and International Affairs at the John F. Kennedy School of Government of Harvard University.

Rodger A. Payne is department chair and professor of political science at the University of Louisville and a faculty affiliate of its Center for Asian Democracy. He is coauthor of *Democratizing Global Politics* (State University of New York Press, 2004) and *The Power of Ideas II* (Butler, 2008) and has written more than forty journal articles and book chapters in edited volumes. He previously taught at Northwestern University and was a visiting research fellow at Harvard University's Belfer Center for Science and International Affairs, Stanford University's Center for International Security and Cooperation, and the Program on International Politics, Economics, and Security at the University of Chicago. He received a dissertation fellowship from the International Peace and Security Studies Program, which was cosponsored by the Social Science Research Council and the MacArthur Foundation. He graduated from the University of Kansas and was a member of its two-person National Debate Tournament championship team. He completed an MA and PhD at the University of Maryland–College Park.

Christopher A. Preble is the vice president for defense and foreign policy studies at the Cato Institute. He is the author of several books, including *The Power Problem: How American Military Dominance Makes Us Less Safe, Less Prosperous, and Less Free* (Cornell University Press, 2009), which documents the enormous costs of America's military power and proposes a new grand strategy to advance

US security; and *John F. Kennedy and the Missile Gap* (Northern Illinois University Press, 2004), which explores the political economy of military spending during the 1950s and early 1960s. He was also the lead author of *Exiting Iraq: How the US Must End the Occupation and Renew the War against Al Qaeda* (Cato Institute, 2004); and he coedited *Terrorizing Ourselves: Why US Counterterrorism Policy Is Failing and How to Fix It* (with Jim Harper and Benjamin Friedman; Cato Institute, 2010). In addition to his books, he has published more than 150 articles in major publications, including *USA Today*, the *Los Angeles Times*, the *Financial Times, National Review, The National Interest, Harvard International Review*, and *Foreign Policy*. He is a frequent guest on television and radio programs. Before joining Cato in 2003, he taught history at Saint Cloud State University and at Temple University. He was a commissioned officer in the US Navy, and served onboard the USS *Ticonderoga* from 1990 to 1993. He received a PhD in history from Temple University.

Teresita C. Schaffer is an expert on economic, political, security, and risk management trends in India and Pakistan, as well as on the region that extends from Afghanistan through Bangladesh. She also serves as a senior adviser to McLarty Associates, a Washington-based international strategic advisory firm. In her thirty-year career in the US Foreign Service, she was recognized as one of the State Department's leading experts on South Asia, where she spent a total of eleven years. Her other career focus was international economic issues. She served in US embassies in Pakistan, India, and Bangladesh, and from 1992 to 1995 as US ambassador in Sri Lanka. During her assignments at the State Department in Washington, she was director of the Office of International Trade and later deputy assistant secretary of state for the Near East and South Asia, at that time the department's senior South Asia policy position. She created a South Asia program at the Center for Strategic and International Studies and directed it from 1998 to 2010. She is the coauthor of *How Pakistan Negotiates with the United States: Riding the Roller Coaster* (with Howard B. Schaffer; US Institute of Peace Press, 2011). She is also the author of *India and the US in the 21st Century: Reinventing Partnership* (Center for Strategic and International Studies, 2009), which is widely recognized as the leading work on the post-2000 United States–India relationship and its future prospects. Her earlier writings include *Pakistan's Future and US Policy Options* (2004); *India at the Crossroads: Confronting the Challenge of HIV/AIDS* (2004); a series of other studies on HIV and public health issues in India; and two studies on women in development in Bangladesh (1985). She is a trustee of the Asia Foundation and serves on the Board of Directors of the American Academy of Diplomacy. She received a BA from Bryn Mawr College and studied at the Institut d'Etudes Politiques in Paris. She did graduate work in economics at

Georgetown University. She speaks Hindi, Urdu, French, Swedish, German, and Italian, and she has studied Bangla and Sinhala.

Andrew C. Winner is a professor of strategic studies and chair of the Strategic Research Department at the Naval War College. His areas of focus are South Asia, nonproliferation, US Maritime Strategy, the Middle East, and US national security. He is director of the Indian Ocean Regional Studies Group at the Naval War College. In June 2007 he was awarded the US Navy's Meritorious Civilian Service Award for his work on the US Navy's new Maritime Strategy. Before his current appointment, he was a senior staff member at the Institute for Foreign Policy Analysis. And before joining the institute, he held various positions at the US Department of State on the staff of the undersecretary of state for arms control and international security affairs and in the bureau of political-military affairs, where he worked on nonproliferation, security in the Persian Gulf, arms transfer policy, bilateral security dialogues, NATO enlargement, and security assistance. He is the coauthor of *Indian Naval Strategy in the 21st Century* (with James R. Holmes and Toshi Yoshihara; Routledge, 2009), and he has written numerous journal articles and book chapters on issues ranging from energy security to counterproliferation. He received a PhD from the University of Maryland–College Park, an MA from Johns Hopkins University's Paul H. Nitze School of Advanced International Studies, and an AB from Hamilton College.

Toshi Yoshihara is a professor in the Strategy and Policy Department at the Naval War College, where he also holds the John A. van Beuren Chair of Asia-Pacific Studies. Previously, he served as a visiting professor in the Strategy Department at the Air War College. He has also served as a senior research fellow at the Institute for Foreign Policy Analysis. He is the coauthor of journal articles on Chinese maritime strategy that have appeared in *Comparative Strategy*, the *Naval War College Review*, *Defense and Security Analysis*, *Issues and Studies*, *Orbis*, and *Proceedings*. He is also coauthor of *Red Star over the Pacific: China's Rise and the Challenge to US Maritime Strategy* (with James R. Holmes; Naval Institute Press, 2010); *Indian Naval Strategy in the Twenty-First Century* (with James R. Holmes and Andrew C. Winner; Routledge, 2009); and *Chinese Naval Strategy in the Twenty-First Century: The Turn to Mahan* (with James R. Holmes; Routledge, 2008). He received a PhD in international relations from the Fletcher School of Law and Diplomacy at Tufts University, an MA in international relations from the Paul H. Nitze School of Advanced International Studies at Johns Hopkins University, and a BSFS in international relations from the School of Foreign Service at Georgetown University.

INDEX